Antitrust: The Person-centred Approach

Abayomi Al-Ameen

Antitrust: The Person-centred Approach

Springer

Abayomi Al-Ameen
Visiting Research Fellow
British Institute of International
and Comparative Law
London
United Kingdom

ISBN 978-3-319-34732-5 ISBN 978-3-319-01724-2 (eBook)
DOI 10.1007/978-3-319-01724-2
Springer Cham Heidelberg New York Dordrecht London

Printed on acid-free paper

Springer is part of Springer Science+Business Media (www.springer.com)

Preface

Antitrust laws and policies have developed through high level theories that seek to designate goal(s) and specify procedures for antitrust institutions. Within each theoretical construct and also through fresh insights, the goals and specifications of antitrust undergo constant refinement: new grounds are discovered, old assumptions are replaced and exigencies dictate the activities of relevant institutions. Thus, by its nature, change is a constant in antitrust. This interesting "evolutionary" process is greased through a flowing stream of empirical analysis, argumentations, counterarguments, assertions, rhetoric, polemics and iconoclasms. However, even as antitrust continues to evolve, one thing remains constant — the single constant is simply the manner of theorising antitrust. Most antitrust theories seek to establish the tasks of antitrust institutions. For instance, they propose the goals that antitrust institutions should champion. They argue on the veracity of a procedure. They debate on the necessity of a measure. They argue top-down.

The postulations within and between these top-down schools of thought come in different shapes, most of which are undeniably relevant to antitrust as they give to the field both content and meaning. Notwithstanding, the problem is that if we isolate the reasoning within a particular theory and forge an antitrust regime on such reasoning, our framework will likely fail to give due consideration to the interests of persons. This is because the chosen theory is likely to eliminate any other form of antitrust analysis. The consequence is that antitrust is diminished as a result of its incompleteness and attendant exclusion of interests.

However, there is yet to be a single acceptable principled approach to antitrust analysis as authorities, courts, practitioners and scholars often fail to reach a convergence on simple terms because they understand those terms through different ideologies.

As a result of the problems associated with the present way in which we analyse antitrust, there is a temptation to propose an account of antitrust that avoids or corrects the present problems. However, before such step is taken, it is important to ascertain why a new paradigm is really needed. This is what brings us to the crux of this thesis. Where a particular antitrust issue is decided based on a mistaken assumption that the theory applied in any instance is complete, a possible consequence is that the reasoning in such a case might unduly disparage those persons whose interests might very well have been protected if a broader foundation was adopted. Another likely effect is that we might end up protecting interests which, if the chosen theory was not mistaken in some way, would not have been protected. It is thus proposed as an idea of justice that we take a bottom-up, non-normative perspective to antitrust analysis. In an attempt to accomplish this goal, the person-centred approach to antitrust is developed and evaluated. Generally, this approach seeks to introduce a perspective to antitrust analysis whereby issues are conceptually addressed from the position of antitrust subjects. In any given case, antitrust subjects are those: consumers, businesses, individuals and societies that have interests in specific antitrust issues, be it market-related, fairness or on public policy grounds.

The thesis develops the conceptual basis for the pursuit of "justice as inclusiveness". To achieve this, it recognises the need to deemphasise the normative content of antitrust theories and practices. The thesis recognises that to achieve the inclusiveness sought, antitrust analysis must adhere to the principles of pure procedural justice whilst also remaining intelligible and functional for policy-making, adjudication and enforcement. To achieve this, the person-centred approach identifies the requirement of broadness as an essential condition. However, in order to avoid conceptual absurdities, the scope of the person-centred account of broadness is clearly delineated.

It must be noted that rather than seeking to build a conclusive theory of antitrust (which might fall short as being incomplete and mistaken), the person-centred approach simply states a perspective which gives a broader outlook on antitrust in order to accommodate a variety of interests held or that can be held by different persons.

To reiterate, my motivation for this research stems from the perceived need for justice (as inclusiveness). This germane requirement of justice is unlikely to be noticed if antitrust is addressed strictly through a top-down paradigm.

The main theme and specific arguments in this thesis are generally the result of queries, some of which are stated below:

On Substantive Antitrust

- Should antitrust be based on a single/limited value(s) or should it be left open to the vagaries of what antitrust subjects may consider to be of interest in antitrust?
- What are the practical disadvantages of a single/limited value approach and how does a broad scope solve them?
- What form should the broader scope take?
- What are the practical challenges that a plural valued system attract? For example uncertainty, unpredictability, practicality? Are they real concerns and, if so, how can they be remedied?

On Antitrust Enforcement

- What is the proper mode of enforcing antitrust?
- On what criteria do we determine if the system is broad enough at the enforcement level?

- Can institutions seek conflicting goals in their enforcement?
- What should be the scope of our enforcement effort and what does this mean to the task of accommodating the interests of different antitrust subjects?
- The thesis makes due reference to seasoned scholarly materials and also draws on established legal and economic theories. To drive my points, I analogise with EU law and US antitrust law. There is, however, a stronger emphasis on the former.

London, UK Abayomi Al-Ameen

Can institutions seek conflicting goals in their enforcement?

4. What should be the scope of our enforcement? In turn, what does this mean for the task of accommodating the interests of different antitrust subjects?

The thesis makes due reference to seasoned scholarly materials and also draws on established legal and economic theories. To drive my point, I deal both with EU law and US antitrust law. There is, however, a stronger emphasis on the former.

London, UK Al-Ameen Al-Ameen

Acknowledgements

This book is largely a product of my Ph.D. which I undertook at the School of Law Swansea University. I am grateful to God for guarding my path through the most trying times of my research. A lot of thanks also goes to Professor Jukka Snell for critiquing my ideas and guiding me through the turbid stage of velocity. I also thank Dr. Bebhinn Donnelly-Lazarov for her exemplary support. Thanks also goes to Dr. Christopher Townley for his remarkable scrutiny.

I undertook my research with the kind financial assistance of Swansea Law School. I truly did find the environment at the Law School encouraging as the staff members had a positive disposition towards me. I also thank the British Institute of International and Comparative Law (BIICL) as it gave me the enabling environment to reflect on my work and fine-tune it for publication as a monograph.

Finally, I thank my family for their continued support and forbearance.

London, UK Abayomi Al-Ameen

Contents

Chapter 1
Antitrust: The "Other" Mode of Analysis

1.1 Introduction

The prevailing theories and practices in antitrust are important as they, in fact, serve as the spine of antitrust laws and policies. It would, as such, not be far-fetched to say that without theories antitrust law will make no sense.[1] Theories set out conditions that guide our analysis and application of the law. Notwithstanding their value, it does appear that if one looks at antitrust from a different perspective, the prevailing antitrust theories have their downsides—the divergence in the manner in which the field is understood and applied sometimes give the impression that the field is convoluted, confusing or confused.

Proponents of specific antitrust theories explain, explore and evaluate the field through the primary values inherent in their theories. They interpret issues in light of their theories. In sum, they take their peculiar antitrust theory as the back-bone of antitrust which sometimes require the elimination of values which are alien to the theory under consideration. It is however noticeable from an outsider's point of view that in eliminating non-compatible values, such a proponent is prone to denouncing all together, other theories that recognise such non-compatible value. The variety of values that could be sought through antitrust should be preserved and celebrated as they potentially increase the interests that can be served when tackling issues.[2] Thus, any claim that a theory of antitrust contains all that is to be known about antitrust must be addressed with a lot of circumspection because antitrust itself is ever-evolving and transient.

A good way to highlight the inherent incompleteness and transient nature of antitrust analysis is by applying postmodern philosophical thought. Generally,

---

[1] Drexl et al. (2009), vii.

[2] As Schuab notes, these debates lie between contentions that competition rules should be instruments to serve pluralism and democracy, as against claims that antitrust provisions should be limited to protecting the efficient functioning of the markets or extended to controlling economic power. See Schaub (1998), p. 121.

A. Al-Ameen, *Antitrust: The Person-centred Approach*,
DOI 10.1007/978-3-319-01724-2_1, © Springer International Publishing Switzerland 2014

postmodernism has been described as a set of critical, strategic, and rhetorical practices employing concepts such as difference, repetition, the trace, the simulacrum, and hyperreality to destabilise other concepts such as presence, identity, historical progress, epistemic certainty, and the univocity of meaning.[3] In other words, postmodernists seek to challenge pre-existing notions, beliefs, interpretations and assumption by identifying alternative meanings. This is an established school of thought and its underlying principles have been applied in different contexts and have developed along different sub-schools in different fields. Notable scholars that have explored this school of thought include Lyotard with his Postmodern Conditions,[4] Nietzsche[5] and Foucault[6] on genealogy and subjectivity, Deleuze's productive difference, and Derrida's deconstruction.[7]

Being a legal (interdisciplinary) thesis, the postmodern thought is channelled through critical legal theory with specific reference to Derrida's *deconstruction*. Thus, from the postmodern point of view, the fallibility of theories, principles, and laws will be assessed in light of the idea of justice with the ultimate aim of identifying the justice deficit that is inherent in any single account of antitrust.[8]

To state briefly, deconstruction challenges any position of "truth" or "knowledge" by elucidating a "counter-truth" or "counter-knowledge" which Derrida refers to as the position of the "Other". Thus proceeding from the premise that every position can be deconstructed, the idea of justice that will be sought in this thesis takes into account all these different interpretations and positions. As it would be thoroughly explained below, the basis for seeking justice by accommodating different interpretations of antitrust is partly because each account, whilst strengthening the interest of one party, has the potential of harming the interest of the "Other". Hence, in order to maintain the possibility of protecting such interests, we have to build an inclusive account.

To build such inclusive account, we cannot possibly rely on deconstruction because it does not provide any transcendental idea of justice.[9] As such, we would have to follow a constructionist/reconstructionist path by building an account which is based on inclusiveness.

[3] Stanford Encyclopaedia of Philosophy, *Postmodernism* (30 September 2005). http://plato.stanford.edu/entries/postmodernism/.

[4] Lyotard (1984).

[5] Nietzsche (1967).

[6] Foucault (1975).

[7] Jacques (1973, 1974, 1978).

[8] To put the underlying postmodern ideology firmly into legal context and ultimately into antitrust context, due reference will be made to the works of Cornell, Balkin, and Peritz.

[9] This assertion is explained in Sect. 1.2 below.

1.2 Deconstruction, Justice, and Antitrust

Postmodern analysis is not new to antitrust as it has been recognised over a decade ago that "[a]ntitrust is the perfect vehicle for illustrating postmodernism's fundamental tenet that texts do not have a single determinate meaning reflecting the author's intention."[10] However, its application to antitrust has been in an historical context. For instance, Peritz sought to challenge the belief that the framers of the Sherman Act were motivated by specific ideals. He argues that there is no single or true meaning for US antitrust law as it is merely an open-ended text that is quite porous to the prevailing norms of political economy[11] such that, any discourse about the true meaning and interpretation of the law "is a rhetorical exercise in favour of a particular normative vision and not meaningful dialogue about the original intent and legislative purpose."[12] Peritz established this claim by painstakingly detailing how from generation to generation the supposed "intent" had been interpreted and exploited in accordance with the exigencies of such times. He believes his postmodern account showcases the "forgotten voices, rejected dissenting opinions, declined positions, and disparaged theories"[13] that were part of early debate. He sought to "throw open an archive of counterpolicies and counterarguments, to recall the conflicts engaged in and the alternative views so fiercely held, views whose appeal continue to inspire debates about political economy".[14] His aim is to situate competition policy as a social, economic, and political construct that takes on different legal understandings in different contexts and at different historical moments.[15]

The postmodern scepticism underlying this thesis is similar to that of the likes of Peritz given that it seeks to establish the values in alternative modes of normative analyses. However, this thesis differs significantly from such accounts for a number of reasons. First, this thesis addresses antitrust from the deconstructive point of view as against the genealogy and subjectivity (historical) position. Secondly and more importantly, postmodern thought is only relied on to the extent that it helps to situate and illuminate the fallibility of laws and also to identify the essential criterion for achieving justice in antitrust. Central to this thesis is the fact that the impossibility of finding correct normative answers to substantive legal issues implicitly mean that subjective interpretation of substantive laws would certainly be "unjust" to some. Thus, what is sought here is to identify the implicit unjustness in the different ways of interpreting antitrust whilst also seeking to establish an idea of justice that will bridge the gap between antitrust laws/theories and justice.

[10] Waller (1997), pp. 435, 436.

[11] Peritz (1996), p. 5.

[12] Waller (1997), p. 438.

[13] Peritz (1996), p. 5.

[14] Peritz (1996), p. 5.

[15] Peritz (1996), p. 5.

In the most basic form, Derrida's deconstruction seeks to question underlying assumptions about how something is constructed by constructing an alternative which is outside the limit of the initial construction. It is therefore more or less about building new ways of viewing and interpreting things that are seemingly established as opposed to "deconstructing" such seemingly established order. Though Derrida's account and postmodernism in general have been criticised as meaningless and nihilistic,[16] it is, without doubt, valuable as it helps to unbind our scope and moves us closer to creativity through the possibility of questioning.

Applied to the question of law and justice, Derrida stated that law is essentially deconstructible either because the history of law often changes with time or because law's ultimate foundation is by definition unfounded. He however argued that the fact that law is deconstructible is not bad news. Rather, it could be good for politics and historical progress. He thereafter made some seemingly self-contradictory statements which illuminates how complicated it is to seek justice through law. He stated that it is the deconstructible structure of law that makes deconstruction possible as justice itself is not deconstructible. He emphasised that the deconstructability of law (for example, of legality, legitimacy or legitimation) makes deconstruction possible. Also, the undeconstructability of justice makes deconstruction possible. The result therefore is that deconstruction takes place in the interval that separates the undeconstructability of justice from the deconstructability of law. He stated further that "[i]t is possible as an experience of the impossible, there where, even if it does not exist (or does not yet exist, or never does exist), there is justice. Whether one can replace, translate, or determine the *x* of justice, one should say: deconstruction is possible, as impossible, to the extent (there) where there is (the undeconstructible)."[17]

Balkin puts the deconstructionist argument about the relationship between law and justice into perspective by situating the reason for deconstruction in the first place. He stated that we might engage in deconstruction in order to demonstrate that the law or some part of the law is unjust. The aim could also be to show that the law or part of it conceals aspects to social life that we believe to be important, and that its failure to adequately deal with such aspect leads to injustice. We might also engage in deconstruction simply to showcase the ambiguity, uncertainty, and impenetrability of legal texts. Further, we might engage in deconstruction simply to show the tensions and contradictions within legal doctrines. Pretty much all these motivation for deconstructing will come into play in this thesis. I start first by deconstructing traditional antitrust theories/laws for the sole purpose of showcasing the tensions and contradictions inherent in them. My contention is that the deconstructability of individual antitrust theories renders any claim that any one theory covers the whole of antitrust to be mistaken, and therefore ultimately unjust. Afterwards, I will assess whether the injustice inherent in these traditional theories justifies the introduction of an alternative approach, not only for the purpose of

[16] For example Habermas (1987).

[17] Derrida (1990), pp. 919, 945.

deconstructing the traditional approach but also to cure the justice deficit. The two issues will be treated in turn.

1.2.1 Injustice in Traditional Antitrust

Generally, it could be argued that the proponents of the prevailing theories in antitrust would be convinced about the "justness" of their theory even where such theory does not directly countenance any form of justice. For instance, we could relate the consumer welfare concern about wealth distribution to some form of distributive justice. Also, the economic freedom thought has its basis in distributive justice.[18] Even the efficiency theories can be linked to some form of utilitarian justice.[19] It is thus ideal to assess all the accounts through the notion of justice.

The basic application of deconstruction will reveal that every account of justice is in real fact a statement of law which is intrinsically deconstructible and is thus unable to meet the "undeconstructible" idea of justice which it seeks to attain. Also, the inherent conflict between each of the account of justice also shows the deconstructability of justice itself. The exercise here is primarily to deconstruct the idea of justice underlying some of the mainstream antitrust theories. This naturally leads us to raise questions about the true content of the term "justice" in the context of antitrust. The task here however is to show the gap that exists between the ideas of justice upon which antitrust could be based. This analysis will very much bring to light Kolm's statement that

> [i]ndeed, any theory [that claims] to answer *all* questions of justice by application of the same specific principles or set of principles is easily proven to be **mistaken**, by counterexamples, and to be **insufficient** for practical application. Simplistic and reductionist universal claims are unwarranted and impossible dogmatism.[20]

The mainstream theories on antitrust seek to address antitrust strictly through the application of their specific principles. Some of these theories will be briefly explained and thereafter deconstructed through their shortcomings as identified by other theories. For example, illustrating with the price theory, where agreements are assessed through the strict principles of price theory, competition is strictly seen as consisting of: "[c]onstant technological rivalry between autonomous firms, unconstrained by so-called nonstandard contracts; that is, agreements that constrain the discretion of purchasers and competitors. This rivalry, it is said, result in an

---

[18] Their root in distributive justice stems from the inspiration they derived from Schmoller's *sociopolitik*. See John (2007).

[19] It has been argued that even though they claim to be value neutral, efficiency theories are inherently normative and as such based on some form of value judgment. See Stucke (2009), in Marsden and Waller (2009), p. 21.

[20] Kolm (1996), p. 10. (Emphasis mine, italics in original.)

equilibrium of competitive prices, output, and other terms of trade, an equilibrium that maximizes social welfare. Within this paradigm, any contractual arrangement that produces output, prices, or other terms of trade that depart from the competitive baseline is prima facie anticompetitive and properly subject to condemnation absent concrete proof of some justification that outweighs the harm."[21] This perception of competition, for instance, informs the US Rule of Reason. It also informs the goal competition law is set to achieve which in this case would be the enhancement of (total or consumer) welfare. In practice, this theory will require that a party alleging the anti-competitive effect of an agreement establishes a prima facie case by proving "actual detrimental effects". This requirement, in line with price theory, rests upon a presumption that any departure from the prices or other terms of trade produced by technological rivalry reflects an anti-competitive exercise of market power.[22] Similarly, the requirement that pro-competitive benefits offset or outweigh anti-competitive effects by reducing prices or preventing their increase rests upon price theory's partial equilibrium trade-off model and its assumption that any benefits resulting from a contract or transaction coexist with anticompetitive effects reflected in a prima facie case.[23]

Basic deconstruction of this assumption undertaken below will show that, just like any other claim which seeks to address agreement strictly through its principles, this price theory-based account is bound to be mistaken and insufficient as it does not fully describe how antitrust can be analysed. It would thus be revealed that antitrust law is not based on a single value. Rather, it is undergirded by an array of irreducible independent values which are plural and diverse. As such, all relevant antitrust theories must discard all theoretical claims to completeness since such claims in general run "afoul of the plurality of values and the phenomenon of value incommensurability."[24]

It must be acknowledged at this point that the prevailing theories on antitrust policy are rich in foundation. They describe the institution of antitrust through their theory in such a lucid manner that even staunch sceptics might be convinced. For example, ordoliberals understand competition within the constitutional framework which, they argue, is designed to clarify the relationship between government and individuals. To them, the guarantee of individual freedom and economic progress are the mainstay of competition policy[25] and, as such, should form the basis of all its statutory interpretations.[26] On the other hand, there are those who explain that

[21] Meese (2003), p. 80.

[22] Meese (2003), p. 80.

[23] Meese (2003), p. 124.

[24] Borrowed from Sunstein (1996), pp. 98–99.

[25] Gerber (1998); Sauter (1997). See also van Miert (1998). He stated that Articles 101 and 102 TFEU are not replicas of ordoliberal thought, but their structure bears the imprint of ordoliberal political philosophy.

[26] Wolf for instance says that neither economic nor social policy goals should play a part in competition analysis. See Wolf (2007), p. 131.

competition law and policy should be solely concerned with the need to attain market efficiency. Also, there are those who argue for a wealth transfer standard for antitrust and so on.

The claim is that these theories are all mistaken in some sense which makes it imperative that we apply a different approach that will correct their mistakes. This is because these theories expound on antitrust strictly within the confines of their doctrines.

To show the mistakes inherent in these theories, reference could be made to the views of practitioners and theorists who are often locked into their school of thought and as a result are normally convinced about the merit of their positions and the failings of others. The outcome of such banter between theoretical positions reflect that when it comes to real life decisions, one is faced with differing plausible theories, each of which is claiming to govern not merely a part but all of antitrust. As such, one of the mistakes inherent in these theories is noticeable from their manner of argumentation—they seek to justify normative claims and discredit other normative claims by referring to their own normative claims which themselves need to be justified. The process of argumentation is mistaken because it simply leads to an infinite regress.[27] For instance, some scholars explain all antitrust issues through the idea of allocative efficiency because they believe that allocative efficiency is the bedrock of all or certain aspects of antitrust.[28] Those who hold this view often disregard the fact that their normative claim to allocative efficiency in itself needs further justification considering that it fails to explain some issues which others consider to be antitrust concerns. Another instance stems from the fact that efficiency theorists normally build antitrust into efficiency and vice versa when arguing against other theories. For example, they contend that economic freedom is not a good proxy for antitrust analysis where it produces fundamentally different results from those which would be achieved where efficiency standards are applied.[29] Argumentations of this nature breed *petito principiis*.

The tension between these principles of antitrust are evident when one considers the often fierce criticism and counter-criticisms between the various scholars and practitioners. For example, Bork, an advocate of the efficiency theory, was of the opinion that outside the idea of efficiency, "'[c]ompetition' . . . meant the preservation or comfort of small businesses . . . the preservation of political democracy, the preservation of local ownership, and so *ad infinitum*." He noted that though these cornucopias have their attraction, "when it comes to finding and applying a policy to guide adjudication, horns of plenty make anything resembling a rule of law impossible."[30] He also criticised theories based on fairness and freedom as being based on "uncritical sentimentality".[31] In the same light, doctrines that seek to

[27] Gorman (2007), p. 207.

[28] See e.g. Odudu (2005).

[29] See e.g. Hawk (1995), p. 978.

[30] Bork (1978), p. 427.

[31] See McKenzie (2000).

protect small businesses from the stranglehold of big businesses have also been characterised as nothing more than a "jumble of half-digested notions and mythologies".[32] Also, the consumer welfare school argue that efficiency "does not reflect the interest of consumers in preventing monopolists from extracting monopoly profits. It ignores various other interests that may be expected to flow from a competitive economy, including diversity of sources, variety of product and innovation."[33] One of the mistakes inherent in the efficiency school, as shown by the economic freedom proponents is that ideas based on efficiency are undemocratic and totalitarian.[34]

Further, ordoliberal ideology seeks to limit the understanding of antitrust to fundamental right/fairness while economic welfare-based accounts prefer to limit antitrust to rational choice. These claims are to be disregarded to the extent that they claim completeness since they fail to evince the whole of antitrust: with regards to efficiency, some commentators have rightly challenged the use of efficiency as the ultimate proxy and aim of antitrust. They argue that it cannot be right that antitrust requires us "to squeeze the greatest possible efficiency out of business".[35] Its incompleteness is also reflected by the fact that efficiency-based antitrust policies do not always have positive effect as they may very well exacerbate issues.[36] Lande for instance, cautions against the use of efficiency approach as the sole assessment criterion. He is of the opinion that, rather than focusing on total welfare, wealth transfer or "price to consumer" should also be considered. He shows that total surplus is an insufficient criterion for antitrust by arguing that any increase in total surplus be matched by an increase in consumer surplus as that would show that efficiency benefits were passed or would be passed to consumers.[37] The incompleteness of economic freedom ideology is showcased by the fact that restriction of competition may arise without a restriction of freedom to compete. For example, such restriction of competition may be the inherent effect of cooperation between competitors which cannot be characterised as a restriction of freedom. For example, joint selling or buying without exclusivity, information exchange, and inherent effects of joint ventures/minority shareholdings between competitors.[38]

These kinds of fierce criticisms can also come from within a particular theory. For example proponents of market efficiency are uniform in their pursuit of social welfare effect. However, either because they differ about the standard of welfare or about the definition of efficiency itself, theorists seem to take time to show the weakness in other accounts. For instance, regarding the Rule of Reason, Stucke

[32] Bork (1978), p. 54.

[33] Fox (1981), pp. 1140, 1161.

[34] See e.g. Watrin (1999), pp. 91–95. Economic freedom theorists claim to prefer a state of inefficiency as long as there is freedom as against *totalitarian* but efficient state of affair.

[35] Fox and Sullivan (1987), pp. 956–959.

[36] ICN (2007), pp. 21–22.

[37] Lande (1988), p. 429.

[38] See Schaub (1998), p. 124.

argues that neo-classical economic theories which are often premised on rational profit maximising behaviour might falter and thus be shown to be mistaken under the searching scrutiny of the "burgeoning behavioural economic literature" on the grounds that they fail to reflect marketplace realities.[39] Regarding the definition of efficiency, Fox criticises the Chicago school on the ground that they define efficiency only in terms of artificial output limitation which is inefficient by definition because it blocks the flow of resources to the production of goods that people need.[40]

Also, some of the value-based arguments between scholars have revealed that none of the individual theories can effectively describe all the issues that can reasonably be attributed to antitrust. For instance, we can argue that though price theory can explain some aspects of antitrust, it does not go well enough to effectively explain all issues in the present day. The price theory which has been shown to underlie the US position on efficiency in antitrust is premised on a number of assumptions. With regard to the application of the Rule of Reason to restrictive agreements, the Transaction Cost Economics (TCE) theory challenges the underlying assumptions by showing that some of the principles under the price theory are not in consonance with modern day realities and as such should be substituted with a more reflective description under the TCE.[41]

As shown above concerning the Rule of Reason,[42] Meese establishes that it is the price theory's definition of competition that drives each of the three requirements. He however argues that each of the price-theoretic assumptions animating the current structure of Rule of Reason analysis in the US is inconsistent with recent advances in economic theory in particular, transaction cost economics. He shows the mistake inherent in the Price theory by stating further that:

> [a]ccording to [transaction cost economics], technological rivalry unconstrained by non-standard contracts can produce suboptimal results, as firms and consumers struggle to overcome various costs of transacting in an atomistic market. As a result, the transaction cost paradigm assumes that nonstandard contracts are presumptively efforts to overcome these costs, thus better serving consumers and society at large. On the other hand, price-theoretic competition—technological rivalry unconstrained by nonstandard contracts—will often result in a market failure, that is, output, price, and other terms of trade different from those desired by consumers and society at large.[43]

This goes to show that there are plural justifiable positions even within the narrow economic welfare model of antitrust which all add up to give us a fuller understanding of antitrust. In effect, any claim that one of the economic welfare theories fully explains antitrust to the exclusion of the others is bound to be mistaken.

---

[39] Stucke (2009), p. 21.

[40] Fox (1985–1986), p. 1714.

[41] Meese (2003), p. 80.

[42] See text accompanying n 22–25 above.

[43] Meese (2003), p. 81.

The contention that no single theory can make claim to the whole of antitrust can be extended to the enforcement part of antitrust. Some efficiency theorists would argue that enforcement should strictly be based on cost efficiencies.[44] It is also possible to advocate a corrective justice basis for antitrust enforcement[45] perhaps because it vindicates the normative equality between parties.[46] The point here is simply that none of these accounts can solely explain how best to fashion an enforcement regime as each can be deconstructed from the position of the "Other".

Those who oppose the idea of a multi-goaled antitrust regime might think that antitrust should be set up to achieve limited goal(s) such as efficiency while, for example, human right law protects freedom. Such suggestions are not only theoretically and practically inappropriate, they also unwisely peg antitrust into an isolated field as though it is not influenced or does not influence other areas of law. The practical concern is that it suggests that when handling a single case, one is meant to exhaust competition issues (on the basis of, for instance efficiency) before an antitrust focused court. Then the same case can be taken to a different forum where the court is to address issues firmly in light of some other laws.

1.2.2 The Way Forward

The problem of justice as it relates to antitrust has been identified, to wit, that the present theories on antitrust are individually deconstructible such that they raise questions as to their justness. The task here therefore is to forge an account of justice that seeks inclusiveness as it is believed that we can get closer to achieving justice by recognising the principles set by the different antitrust accounts.

This task should not be seen as seeking to build a substantive (undeconstructible) account of justice for antitrust. Rather, it should be seen as an attempt to protect the interests of different parties (within practical limits) through a procedural framework. I will therefore assess the alternative procedural accounts of justice that could form the basis of justice as inclusiveness—Habermas' communicative ethics and person-centred approach. After thorough analysis, preference is given to the person-centred approach.

To start with, even though the idea of *justice as inclusiveness* is independent of the theory of deconstruction, it is still important to show that the account of justice that is eventually chosen does not contradict the deconstruction ideology which, without equivocation, forms the basis for denouncing the present modes of antitrust analyses. One cannot overlook the possibility that Derrida's deconstruction presupposes that all accounts of law and justice are deconstructible coupled with

[44] See e.g. *Associated Gen. Contractors v CSCC* 459 US 519 (1983); *Florida Seed Company and Anor v Monsanto* 915 F.Supp. 1167 (1995).

[45] Robertson (2000), p. 741.

[46] Weinrib (1996).

the fact that majority of deconstructionists think that justice is an impassable difficulty or paradox for any legal system rather than a transcendent ideal.[47] If this is truly the case, the idea of *justice as inclusiveness* will itself be deconstructible especially in light of the laws that would seek such inclusiveness. Hence, even if there is an improvement to the law and its application because of the adherence to the idea of *justice as inclusiveness*, such improvement would likely lie somewhere between small and inconsequential. On the other hand, if a transcendental idea of justice (such as justice as inclusiveness) can practically exist within the remit of deconstructionist philosophy, it means in effect that such account of justice can substantially move the law closer to achieving justice.

Even though most deconstructionists including Derrida do not approve of transcendental justice, there is scope for believing that an overarching idea of justice can be in line with deconstructionist ideology. For instance, Balkin thinks differently as regards the question whether and (if possible) how an ideal account of justice should be formulated. He believes that human practice of deconstructive argument is rhetorical as the arguments are always limited encounters with the many potentially deconstructible features of law, language and culture. In other words, deconstruction does not generally involve a scientific or algorithmic process but is rather informed by the values and commitments of the individual deconstructor and the direction he chooses to investigate. As such, while the practice of deconstruction is infinite, we respond to our pre-existing moral and political commitment which tells us when to stop. Balkin contends that we are only able to engage in this rhetorical practice because of the deconstructability of human law, convention, and culture. He however queries what makes such critical deconstruction possible in the first place. Quite contrary to other deconstructive disciples, Balkin contends that for human law, convention, and culture to be deconstructed for normative purpose (which is implicit in rhetorical deconstruction), the practice "must rest on the assumption of transcendental human values—and, in particular, a transcendental value of justice."[48]

One should however not be confused as to the oxymoronic nature of the phrase "transcendental deconstruction" as Balkin agrees that since human legal creations are always to some degree unjust, justice cannot be fully determined by any positive norm of human law, culture or convention. As such, positive norms must fall short of our value of justice. Hence, this means that Balkin's reference to "transcendence" merely means that we must postulate a human value of justice which transcends each and every example of justice in human law, culture and convention even though we realise that such value of justice is insatiable and can never be fulfilled by human law. He stated that "the normative use of deconstruction becomes . . . 'transcendental' deconstruction, because it must presume the existence

[47] See e.g. Cornell's redefinition of deconstruction in Cornell (1992). Also Cohen (1935), pp. 809, 812.

[48] Balkin (1994).

of transcendental human values articulated in culture but never adequately captured by culture."[49]

Balkin states further that "transcendence", which he refers to should not be seen as concerned with "an ideal of determinate content that exists separate and apart from human law, culture and convention." He contends that it should rather be seen as "the insatiable yearning or longing for justice lodged in human heart" which, to him, is an urge that can never be fully appreciated by the positive norms of human culture.

This thesis proceeds on the basis of Balkin's perspective on deconstruction and justice. It is imperative at this juncture to ascertain an idea of justice which people in a civilised society will undoubtedly yearn for. It is argued that "justice as inclusiveness" fits quite well with such transcendental idea of justice as it does not sound beyond reason that each and every one would yearn for a right to a voice in decisions that affect them even though such yearning is insatiable.[50] The peoples' yearning for justice will be pursued through a procedural framework.[51]

However, even though Balkin helps us to appreciate the possibility of forging an account of transcendental justice which is not necessarily opposed to the deconstruction ideology, he does not go as far as detailing how we can best tailor the law to strive at such transcendental value. How can we make sense of antitrust with the deconstructed principles of antitrust whilst also striving towards inclusiveness as the ultimate criterion of justice? Considering the decontructability of transcendental moral values, can we really build up an account of justice on the basis of inclusiveness? Can we really solve the problem of incompleteness militating against traditional antitrust? Can we really construct a solution? Would such construction be compatible with the theory of deconstruction?

It is the position in this thesis that it is possible in principle to construct a theory aimed at justice as inclusiveness. Deconstruction is not only about criticism. In fact, Bankovsky contends that deconstruction is not opposed to the constructive and reconstructive approaches to justice.[52] If this is the case, can we therefore formulate an idea of justice for antitrust while still respecting the tenets of deconstruction? If yes, what will be the philosophical premise of such account?

With regards to the first question, it is contended that regardless of pessimism expressed by the likes of Cornell, the pursuit of an idea of justice is still a relevant exercise within deconstructive thoughts. This response is justified by the fact that Derrida stimulates debate by constructing the position of the *Other*.

---

[49] Balkin (1994).

[50] See Cohen (1971), pp. 63–79.

[51] See generally Thibaut and Walker (1975).

[52] Miriam Bankovsky, *Social Justice after Kant: Between Constructivism and Deconstruction (Rawls, Habermas, Levinas, Derrida)* Thesis submitted to the School of History and Philosophy at the University of New South Wales in fulfilment of the requirements of a PhD in Philosophy, September 2008.

The critical issue therefore lies in the second question; how should such account of justice be formulated? It has been stated above that the "yearnings of the people" could be the desire of individuals to influence decisions that affect them. This, they will normally seek to achieve through a fair procedure. To put the question differently therefore, we need to ascertain how procedural justice can be achieved in antitrust issues. As stated above, Habermas' communicative ethics and the person-centred approach will be assessed. However, before these alternatives are detailed, the values of procedural justice will be briefly identified.

Procedural justice helps to legitimise judicial and political decisions. As stated by Young, decisions should be considered legitimate "only if all those affected by it are included in the process of discussion and decision-making."[53] The requirement of inclusiveness should not be taken too literally to mean that everyone affected by a decision in any trivial way ought to be directly involved in the decision-making. Young notes that "affected" here means "at least that decisions and policies significantly condition a person's options for action."[54] Also, this idea of procedural justice embodies a norm of moral respect as opposed to being treated as means. People are treated as means "if they are expected to abide by rules or adjust their actions according to decisions from where determination their voice and interests have been excluded."[55]

Specifically linking the issues of procedural justice and legitimacy to the judicial setting, Tyler identifies two primary goals of the judicial system which are first, to provide people with a forum in which they can obtain justice as it is defined by the framework of the law, and secondly, that the court should be able to handle problems in a way that leads the public to accept and be willing to abide by the decisions made by the court.[56] With regards to this second goal, it has thus been shown that the manner in which disputes are handled by the courts have an important influence upon people's evaluations of their experiences in the court system. Hence, participants would accept "losing" more willingly if the court procedures used to handle their case are fair.[57] Procedural justice has thus been identified as the key to the development of stable and lasting solutions to disagreements.[58]

---

[53] Young (2002), p. 23.

[54] Young (2002), p. 23.

[55] Young (2002), p. 23.

[56] Tyler (2007), p. 26.

[57] Lind and Tyler (1988); Tyler (2000), p. 117.

[58] Tyler (2007), p. 27.

1.3 Constructing the Procedure for Justice as Inclusiveness

Bankovsky is of the opinion that deconstruction theory is not opposed to constructionist theories of justice. Balkin also attempts to create an account of "transcendental deconstruction". It is on the basis of these two deconstructionist assertions that this thesis finds the impetus for the construction of a procedure that meets the justice requirement of inclusiveness. In order to fully appreciate the essential ingredient for inclusiveness in antitrust, Rawls' delineation of procedural justice will be helpful. Rawls recognises that justice has commonly been associated with outcomes or state of affairs rather than procedures when in real fact, substantive justice and procedural justice should go hand in hand.[59] He identified four instances in which these two concepts of justice can be linked.[60] The first, is where we know what justice requires and we also have in place a procedure that could be relied upon to yield the sought after outcome. Such instance will be characterised as perfect procedural justice. Secondly, we might know the outcome that is required as a matter of justice but our best procedure for reliably generating the sought after outcome is imperfect. This can be characterised as imperfect procedural justice.

Another category relates to those instances where we do not know what the just outcome entails in substantive terms but we can rely on the procedure. In such instance, we may say that so long as there are fair procedures in place to determine winners and losers, the outcome or state of affair it produces is just. This is what Rawls refers to as pure procedural justice. The use of such procedure to arrive at a determinate and substantive judgment of justice is considered ideal where we have no clear, determinate noncontroversial independent standard of what justice demands. A fourth category is where procedural fairness is used to arrive at a determinate and substantive judgment of justice even though the procedure is insufficient to establish the justice of the results, as long as it is sufficient to establish a less demanding normative standard. This is termed quasi-pure procedural justice.

Pure or quasi-pure procedural justice is premised on giving people their due. As it can be inferred from the deconstruction of the prevailing antitrust theories, it appears there is no clear, determinate, noncontroversial method for picking a person's due as a matter of justice. As such, *justice as inclusiveness* will have to be constructed on the basis of (quasi) pure procedural justice.

Considering that the there are no clear, determinate, and noncontroversial method of picking a person's due, it is inevitable that the procedure adopted for achieving inclusiveness contains at least two core elements—it must accommodate plural interests and it must facilitate objectivity in decision making. Hence, in light of the underlying deconstructionist philosophy, the construction of an alternative means of understanding and addressing antitrust issues will only be worth the while

---

[59] Rawls (1972), p. 85.

[60] Rawls (1972), p. 85.

if it fulfils these two requirements. First, Habermas' Communicative Ethics will be assessed[61] and afterwards, the person-centred approach will be introduced.

1.3.1 Habermas' Communicative/Discourse Ethics

The task here is to evaluate Habermas' discourse ethics in light of the requirement of broadness and objectivity with the ultimate attempt of formulating an account of antitrust that is premised on the idea of justice as inclusiveness.

To state in basic terms, discourse ethics is premised on the assumption that moral problems can be solved in a rational and cognitive way as long as its procedure follows the principle of impartiality (principle of universalisation). It also recognises the plurality of values and therefore accommodates the different conceptions and interpretations of the "good life" as may be discerned from different norms.[62]

Discourse ethics allows for different positions to be expressed, the consequence of which is that the better argument prevails. It should be understood that the normative positions expressed by participants are not to be treated as proposition or assertive sentences. As such, they are not to be assessed on the basis of "truthfulness" but rather on the "weaker assumption of validity claim that is analogous to the validity claim of truth". For instance, the normative claim that margin squeeze ought not to be considered anticompetitive cannot be assessed on its "truthfulness" but rather on its validity in the particular context. This can be compared with an assertion that Article 101 TFEU covers restrictive agreements which can be assessed on its truthfulness or otherwise.

With regards to the principle of universalisation, Habermas states that a norm is valid only if "all affected can accept the consequences and the side effects its general observance can be anticipated to have for the satisfaction of everyone's interests." This condition could be fulfilled where: there is equal participation of all those who are affected, the postulate of *unlimitedness*, and the postulate of seriousness and authenticity.

Prominent legal scholars, such as Alexy, have transposed Habermas' discourse ethics into legal jurisprudence. Alexy argues that discourse is a necessary requirement for reaching correct judicial outcomes. This dialectical approach, he says, forges coherence, clarity, empirical truth, consideration of consequences, weighing of reasons, the analysis of the genesis of normative convictions, everyone's right to

[61] Dworkin's idea of inclusiveness is not considered as he address the issue from both substantive and procedural standpoint. See Dworkin (2000). It is my contention that substantive account of inclusiveness is fraught insurmountable challenges which undermines the very purpose of justice (at least in the antitrust context). This thereby necessitates our focus on procedural justice.

[62] See generally Habermas (1998).

participate and freedom and equality in discourse.[63] He also asserts that objectivity and correctness are components of rationality as "the law is an idea that is intrinsically connected with the idea of objectivity."[64] He states further that "[o]bjectivity is an essential feature of law, a feature that is not compatible with complete subjectivity of the purposes at issue. . ."[65]

So far, it appears that the discourse ethics sits well as the basis of the idea of *justice as inclusiveness* particularly when one considers that it addresses the core requirements stated above. It is however contended that Habermas' communicative/discourse ethics should not be relied on as an instrument for attaining (quasi) pure procedural justice because the account cannot guarantee objectivity/impartiality. The basis for this scepticism can be observed from a more in-depth analysis of Alexy's work and also Andriychuk's application of dialectical reasoning to antitrust.

With regards to the application of the discourse theory, Alexy concedes to the weakness of the theory. He stated that a correct solution to a conflict of interest can only be achieved by considering the relative weight of the conflicting interests. He argues further that "[t]here exists . . . no absolute and . . . objective-scale that makes it possible to measure and compare the conflicting interests made by those who have them."[66] He also concedes to Heidemann[67] that dialectics is not synonymous with correctness as there could be a divergence between what is correct or objectively valid and what is achieved as a result of a real discourse.[68] Alexy states that "[t]he relationship between correctness and discourse is indeed, one of the most serious problems of the discourse theory".[69] He however tries to defend the focus on normative convictions by contending that the final answer reached at the end of the dialectal exercise is not entirely subjective because argumentations from different interests will have to be balanced by arguments that meet the claim of correctness as far as possible.

Notwithstanding the attempt to salvage the discourse theory as an impartial account, one would have to agree with Heidemann who argues that the discourse theory must fail on the ground that it cannot establish "a constitutive relations between the performance of a real discourse and the objective validity of the result."[70] Moreover, dialectical reasoning presupposes the weighing of values. The problem here is that we cannot claim to have an objective procedure where

63 The Discourse theory is a procedural theory of practical correctness or truth. See generally Alexy (1989).

64 Alexy (2007a), p. 360.

65 Alexy (2007b), p. 49.

66 Alexy (2007a), p. 362.

67 Heidemann (2007).

68 Alexy (1988), pp. 61–64.

69 Alexy (1988), pp. 61–64.

70 Heidemann (2007), p. 312.

we make judgments about competing values based on their intrinsic qualities as we would be drawn in the fallacy of merging mutually incompatible ideals.[71]

In order to illustrate the practical difficulty and the potential for inherent subjectivity especially when applied in legal context, Andriychuk's dialectic antitrust is hereby analysed. Andriychuk advocates for dialectical antitrust which would help in forging a systemic understanding of competing competition policy values. He states that dialectical antitrust explains the necessity of the "competitory process". The discretion given to antitrust enforcers should be substantial as they should be empowered to set up the most effective format of competition which should not be predetermined by other values.[72] As such, competition should be protected and promoted as a thing in itself, as an independent public virtue.[73] Dialectical antitrust however allows that competition as an independent economic value "competes" with other public values such as consumer welfare. Thus, the fine-tuning required of the regulator should be such that it reflects the basic expectations and priorities of society. For instance, where there is a tension between different schools, dialectical antitrust reassesses each of the theories and test their applicability to different economic contexts. This is to be done by applying a *parenthesis theory* "which presupposes to undertake an analytical inclusion of different public goals in separate 'boxes'".[74] As such, when one is faced with complex antitrust issues, we are to for instance, assess those issue in light of economic freedom in its own unique box. This is to be carried out for other competing theories as well. He argues that dialectical antitrust tries to understand and explain competition rather than provide prescriptions.

The difficulty of maintaining impartiality when the discourse ethics is applied in the legal context is evident in Andriychuk's work. For instance, he gives clear preference to economic freedom by seeking to protect competition even as he acknowledges "other legitimate societal values". The tendency to categorise these goals *ex ante* as less important than economic freedom is evident as Andriychuk argues that competition, being a thing in itself and populated by independent public virtue deserves protection and promotion.[75]

Based on the foregoing therefore, it is thought that even though Habermas' discourse ethics is interesting as a constructionist account of the idea of justice, the particular dialectical procedure cannot in practice achieve the germane requirement of *justice as inclusiveness* in antitrust.

[71] The problem is equally present in Andriychuk's dialectical antitrust. He stated that "[i]nasmuch as none of the mainstream doctrines is capable of solving all existing internal conflicts of antitrust policy, there is a possibility of applying the elements of different schools depending on the context." See Andriychuk (2009), p. 93.

[72] Andriychuk (2009), p. 155.

[73] Andriychuk (2009), p. 155.

[74] Andriychuk (2009), p. 155.

[75] Andriychuk (2009), p.155.

1.3.2 Person-Centred Approach

Considering that Habermas' discourse ethics (which is arguably the foremost account of (quasi) pure procedural justice) has been found wanting and thus unable to attain justice (as inclusiveness) in antitrust issues, I hereby attempt to construct an alternative procedure called the person-centred approach. The thesis will substantiate this approach and then critically assess (in both theoretical and practical context) whether: (i) it escapes the narrowness and consequent deconstructability of the prevailing antitrust theories; (ii) it is theoretically well grounded; (iii) it is capable of practical application.

At this juncture, a brief summary of the approach is given. The person-centred approach to antitrust seeks broadness in antitrust analysis by focusing on the persons interested in or affected by antitrust issues. The logic behind assessing antitrust through the eyes of persons is that it ensures that adequate consideration is given to the possible interests that could arise from any single antitrust issue. A clear advantage with this model of antitrust analysis is that it serves as a good avenue to assess whether antitrust policies and practices do in fact take into account the interests of antitrust subjects. Also, this approach effectively provokes a different way of thinking about antitrust issues—it seeks to trigger debates on issues such as whether it may be better to expound and rationalise antitrust through the interests that antitrust subjects really have in antitrust disputes. When applied, this approach requires that the individual interests are to be scrutinised on a case-by-case basis in order to reach a reasoned conclusion as to whether to accommodate a particular reasoning. To be able to engage in such elaborate and broad analytical exercise, it therefore behoves that the person-centred approach places "persons" as the focal point of antitrust theorisation, exposition, evaluation, practice and implementation.

The approach holds dearly the positions of different antitrust subjects; antitrust subjects include all persons (both natural and artificial) that could be implicated in antitrust related issues. As such, included among the mix are; the consumers, competitors, alleged infringers and those persons who could not be categorised as consumers but are primarily victims of deadweight loss and so on.

It must be noted that the person-centred approach does not have any technical meaning. It simply requires that the interests of antitrust subjects should be taken seriously. As such, it is not to be applied like a theory but rather as a philosophical stance. Thus, it simply requires that antitrust terms are addressed from a broader perspective as the approach considers the traditional theories to be narrow and mistaken. Further, it should be noted that the person-centred approach should not be understood as an outright attack on the veracity of traditional theories.

In an attempt to avoid the narrowness of contemporary antitrust theories, the person-centred approach requires a broad platform. However, the requirement of broadness is not an end in itself. The approach is sought primarily because of the need to take seriously the various interests that may be affected in antitrust related issues. There are a number of arguments that could be made to support this approach. First, the person-centred approach makes us see clearly that our society is truly many-centred and is thus characterised by networks of interlocking interests. Also, from a strictly conceptual angle, it is a less demanding way of ideating both substantive and procedural antitrust—it is less demanding because it helps to avoid the temptation to shoe-horn pre-determined theories into antitrust. Rather, it in fact aligns with the practical reality which is that there are varied interests which might legitimately seek protection in antitrust cases. In some sense, it could also be seen as a better approach because it embraces the complexity of antitrust interests and hence is a more realistic approach. It is more realistic in the sense that it helps to avoid abstracting in a mechanical way, the aims and objectives that antitrust institutions (should) pursue. In reality, institutions put various factors into consideration even in antitrust cases.

As a result of its open-textured nature, the person-centred approach guards against undue value judgments about the various accounts of antitrust. A major weakness of theories that are laden with value judgments is that they are excessively built on an internal point of view.[76] As it will be shown, the person-centred approach is built on tested theoretical accounts of Sen's Capability approach. At the centre of all this applied theory is the notion of the antitrust subject where the "subject" is either a single unit or an aggregation of persons.

1.4 Conclusion

It has been shown in this chapter that the present top-down approaches to antitrust analysis have the tendency to cause injustice through the exclusion of the interests of one/a section of antitrust subjects. We are able to draw this conclusion by using Derrida's deconstruction to showcase the incompleteness of traditional antitrust theories. To solve this potential problem, it was considered imperative to construct a different mode of antitrust analysis. It was noted in this chapter that a strictly procedural framework is required if we are to meet up with the requirement of *justice as inclusiveness*. Two alternatives were thus identified—Habermas' discourse ethics and the person-centred approach. The former has been jettisoned as it fails to meet the neutrality required from a pure procedural framework. Still proceeding with the task of constructing a compliant procedural framework, the remainder of this thesis will be dedicated to developing and evaluating the person-centred approach.

---

[76] As shown above in Chap. 2, this conclusion can be drawn from our finding that the theories are inherently incomplete.

References

Alexy R (1988) Problem of discourse theory. CRÍTICA 58:61–64

Alexy R (1989) A theory of legal argumentation (trans: Adler R, MacCormick N). Clarendon, Oxford

Alexy R (2007a) Thirteen replies. In: Pavlakos G (ed) Law, rights and discourse: the legal philosophy of Robert Alexy. Hart, Oxford, p 360

Alexy R (2007b) An answer to Joseph Raz. In: Pavlakos G (ed) Law, rights and discourse: the legal philosophy of Robert Alexy. Hart, Oxford, p 49

Andriychuk O (2009) How the theory of dialectical antitrust perceives the role of competition authorities. ICC Glob Antitrust Rev No. 2:93

Balkin J (1994) Being just with deconstruction. Yale Law School. Faculty Scholarship Series. Paper 271. http://www.yale.edu/lawweb/jbalkin/articles/beingjust1.htm

Bork R (1978) The antitrust paradox. Free Press, New York, p 427

Cohen C (1935) Transcendental nonsense and the functional approach. Columbia Law Rev 25 (809):812

Cohen C (1971) Have I a right to a voice in decisions that affect my life? Nous 5:63–79

Cornell D (1992) Philosophy of the limit. Routledge, London

Derrida J (1990) Force of law: the mystical foundation of authority. Cardozo Law Rev 11 (919):945

Drexl J, Idot L, Monéger J (eds) (2009) Economic theory and competition law. Edward Elgar, Cheltenham

Dworkin R (2000) Sovereign virtue – the theory and practice of equality. Harvard University Press, Cambridge

Foucault M (1975) Surveiller et Punir: Naissance de la Prison Gallimard, Paris. English edition: Sheridan A (1977) Discipline and punish: The Birth of the Prison (trans: Sheridan A). Pantheon, New York

Fox E (1981) The modernization of antitrust: a new equilibrium. Cornell Law Rev 66(1140):1161

Fox E (1985–1986) Consumer beware Chicago. Mich Law Rev 84:1714

Fox E, Sullivan L (1987) Antitrust—retrospective and prospective: where are we coming from? Where are we going? N Y Univ Law Rev 62:956–959

Gerber D (1998) Law and competition in twentieth-century Europe: protecting prometheus. Oxford University Press, Oxford

Gorman J (2007) Three-person justification. In: Pavlakos G (ed) Law, rights and discourse. Hart, Oxford, p 207

Habermas J (1987) The philosophical discourse of modernity (trans: Lawrence F). Cambridge University Press, Cambridge

Habermas J (1998) The inclusion of the other: studies in political theory. MIT, Cambridge (Chapter 1)

Hawk B (1995) System failure: vertical restraints and EC competition law. Common Mark Law Rev 32(4):978

Heidemann C (2007) The concept of validity in a theory of social action. In: Pavlakos G (ed) Law, rights and discourse. The legal philosophy of Robert Alexy. Hart, Oxford, p 301

ICN (2007) Report on the objective of unilateral conduct laws, pp 21–22

Jacques D (1973) Speech and phenomena and other essays on Husserl's theory of signs (trans: Allison DB). Northwestern University Press, Evanston

Jacques D (1974) Of grammatology (trans: Spivak GC). Johns Hopkins University Press, Baltimore

Jacques D (1978) Writing and difference (trans: Bass A). University of Chicago Press, Chicago

John KD (2007) The German social market economy – still) a model for the European Union? Theor Appl Econ 3(508):3

Kolm S-C (1996) Modern theories of justice. MIT, Cambridge, p 10

Lande R (1988) The rise and (coming) fall of efficiency as the ruler of antitrust. Antitrust Bull 33:429

Lind A, Tyler T (1988) The social psychology of procedural justice. Plenum, New York
Lyotard J-F (1984) The postmodern condition: a report on knowledge (trans: Bennington G, Massumi B). University of Minnesota Press, Minneapolis
Marsden P, Waller S (2009) Antitrust marathon: antitrust and the rule of law. Loyola Consum Law Rev 22:21
McKenzie R (2000) Trust on trial: how the microsoft case is reframing the rules of competition. Perseus, New York
Meese A (2003) Price theory, competition and the rule of reason. Univ Ill Law Rev 80
Nietzsche F (1967) On the genealogy of morals (trans: Kaufmann W). Random House, New York
Odudu O (2005) The boundaries of EC competition law. Oxford University Press, New York
Peritz R (1996) Competition policy in America. Oxford University Press, New York, p 5
Rawls J (1972) A theory of justice. Oxford University Press, Oxford, p 85
Robertson E (2000) A corrective justice theory of antitrust regulation. Cathol Univ Law Rev 49:741
Sauter W (1997) Competition law and industrial policy in the EU. Clarendon, Oxford
Schaub A (1998) Competition policy goals. In: Ehlermann CD, Laudati L (eds) European competition law annual 1997: the objectives of competition policy. Hart, Oxford, p 121
Stucke M (2009) Does the rule of reason violate the rule of law. UC Davis Law Rev 42:1375
Sunstein C (1996) Legal reasoning and political conflict. Oxford University Press, New York, pp 98–99
Thibaut J, Walker L (1975) Procedural justice. Lawrence Erlbaum Associates, Mahwah
Tyler T (2000) Social justice: outcome and procedure. Int J Psychol 35:117
Tyler T (2007) Procedural justice and the courts. Court Rev 44:26
van Miert K (1998) The future of European competition policy, 17 September. Available at: europa.eu.int/comm/-competition/speeches/
Waller S (1997) Market talk: competition policy in America. Law Soc Inq 22(435):436
Watrin C (1999) Germany's social market economy. In: Kilmarnock A (ed) The social market and the state. Social Market Foundation, London, pp 91–95
Weinrib E (1996) The idea of private law. Harvard University Press, Cambridge
Wolf D (2007) Competition policy objectives. In: Ehlermann CD, Atanasiu I (eds) European competition law annual: enforcement of prohibition of Cartels. Hart, Oxford, p 131
Young I (2002) Inclusion and democracy. Oxford University Press, New York, p 23

Chapter 2
Person-Centred Approach

2.1 Introduction

Having established the deconstructability of prevailing antitrust theories in the preceding chapter, the imminent need to construct an alternative mode of antitrust analysis was established. An alternative mode was considered essential in order to meet the requirement of justice as inclusiveness. As potential candidates, Habermas' discourse ethics and the person-centred approach, were identified. However, the discourse ethics proved inadequate as it fell under scrutiny. This left us to consider the other alternative—the person-centred approach. This approach is the primary contribution of this thesis. However, for it to be adopted as the ideal mode of analysing antitrust for the purpose of achieving the requirement of justice as inclusiveness, it has to withstand the thorough scrutiny which the discourse ethics has been put through. At this point though, there is not much to scrutinise. Thus, given that it is a whole new approach, it is imperative that the contours of the person-centred approach are established first and then consequently scrutinised. This chapter paves the way for the thorough elucidation of this approach by emphasising its core attributes with adequate reference to competition law and policy.

The remainder of this chapter is thus divided into six sections. Section 2.2 contains a summary of the person-centred approach. Section 2.3 identifies the values of this approach vis-à-vis the top-down approaches. Section 2.4 details the requirements of the proposed approach. Section 2.5 focuses on the requirement of broadness while Sect. 2.6 delimits the scope of broadness sought by addressing the term "competition". Section 2.7 contains the conclusion.

A. Al-Ameen, *Antitrust: The Person-centred Approach*,
DOI 10.1007/978-3-319-01724-2_2,

2.2 Person-Centred Summarised

The person-centred approach is built on tested theoretical accounts such as Coleman's idea of rights and Sen's Capability approach. At the centre of all these applied theories is the notion of the antitrust subject where the "subject" is either a single unit or an aggregation of persons.

Since we are addressing antitrust from the bottom, a conceptually sensible way of conducting the analysis would be to build an account of antitrust right. It makes sense that if we are arguing from the position of persons and for the advancement of antitrust subjects, we should be able to ascertain whether there could be antitrust right which might require advancement and also to confirm the persons who actually have rights which should be vindicated. This task is important, considering the fact that the notion of the antitrust subjects span through all possible actors and subjects of antitrust analysis. Another advantage of this right-based proxy is that it could simplify the task of policy makers, enforcers and the court as it allows us to address issues closely through the questions that our account of antitrust right raise.

At the moment, many a theory concerning both the substantive and procedural aspects of antitrust are modelled on "firm" theories such as rational choice, economic freedom, deterrence etc. These theories are not without their value. The contention however is that they cannot solely dictate the process and content of antitrust right. As such, it is imperative that our account of right accords with broadness. Though the reasons for these assertions are fleshed out in subsequent chapters, a brief exposition on what we expect of the person-centred approach is given below:

2.2.1 *Substantive Aspect*

The reason for substantiating an alternative approach to antitrust is because, as shown above, the traditional approaches run the risk of being incomplete and inherently mistaken with their narrow analyses of antitrust issues. However, in suggesting alternatives, it is imperative that a host of concerns which might impact on market behaviour should be considered. For instance, thorough theoretical exercise could help us make sense of the plural values which have been neglected or at best acknowledged in passing by antitrust scholars. In the substantive aspect, it helps us to de-bias antitrust law and policy by challenging the exclusivity of some of the prevailing axioms on antitrust and supplanting them with broader and much more inclusive conceptual foundations.

It should be reiterated that the person-centred approach is strictly a procedural mechanism aimed at justice as inclusiveness. Hence, based on this premise, it should go without saying that our reference to *antitrust right* is merely in the procedural context. As such, to say that a person has antitrust right is to say that such person is entitled to procedural justice by being included in issues that involve or affect them. Thus, as it would be shown, the term antitrust right does not countenance any particular normative usage of the term right as it merely means that we are bound to consider the interrelatedness of interests held by persons in any given instance. For example, the way we conceive their relationship and the specific interests and values would influence how competition and hence, anti-competition is defined. Interests that could be considered in any given antitrust issue could range from employment to environment, integration, economic freedom to efficiency and so on.

Our conception of how certain antitrust issues are to be addressed have a direct bearing on our definition of competition and restriction and so on. To avoid errors, we must apply a broad-enough concept. Broadness can be ensured at the analysis stage by simply recognising that no single way of analysing right can conveniently represent all interests. Thus, in order to determine what best represents the interest of different persons, the person-centred approach avoids holding a normative stance as is often the case when one applies traditional antitrust theories.

Though it is possible that our idea of right in individual cases is influenced by one of efficiency, economic freedom, integration, industrial policy theories and so on, the extent to which they influence our idea of what best represents the interests of individuals and as such the goal of antitrust in such instance depends on what we consider to be correct. The idea of correctness cannot be premised on subjective considerations. Thus, the proper way of analysing the right and thereby determining the case-specific "goal(s)" of antitrust should result from our objective analysis of competing interests. However, maintaining objectivity is not always as easy as it may sound. Antitrust institutions would often have to deal with multitude of claims; for instance, a self-interested *x* who finds that competition is defined strictly through efficiency may genuinely think that another theory—perhaps economic freedom—would have been better; a bystander may think that *x's* claim should not be rejected merely because some efficiency theories say so.

Recognising these difficulties, "correctness" is to be achieved in relation to the first two questions on antitrust right by applying realistic theoretical constructs. This substantive aspect is thus primarily modelled on the capability approach and a decisional framework termed "antitrust pluralism". The veracity and practicality of these frameworks would also be assessed.

2.2.2 Enforcement Aspect

In line with the person-centred approach, the aim at this point is to ascertain how antitrust should be enforced. The best way to enforce antitrust is to take note of the varied interests that could figure in antitrust enforcement. It is conceded that due to the nature of enforcement regimes, it is essential for institutions to set out well-defined prime enforcement objective(s). Nevertheless, antitrust institutions must be willing to balance such set priorities with alternative objectives. The argument is that if an antitrust body blindly insists on the pre-set enforcement objectives, it is bound to be in error at some point. The major task thus lies in maintaining a balance between the pre-set objectives and alternative objectives as individual cases may require. When such regime finds that an approach or methodology leaves certain antitrust subjects compromised, it must be willing to make the necessary improvement so as to protect the interest of such aggregate of antitrust subjects. The challenge that however arises is that since the person-centred approach to antitrust takes cognisance of all conceivable antitrust subjects, it must be certain that the proposed solution does not by itself create a unique deficit for some other (unit or aggregate of) antitrust subject(s). Thus, with equal measure, institutions would have to approach their antitrust enforcement task with a good dose of dynamism and caution.

Conclusively, it must be stated that the person-centred approach is not foolproof. In the substantive aspect, it raises concerns such as uncertainty which, if not properly managed, might complicate the field of antitrust even more than traditional theories—if a regime forges an account of antitrust that dwells on some or all interests that individuals could truly value, it might be faced with an herculean task in finding the appropriate interest which should eventually be vindicated. At the enforcement aspect, even with our best effort at incremental enforcement, we might still be unable to explain the extent to which a core enforcement priority (either in public or private antitrust) should accommodate other factors. This could generate its unique form of uncertainty as well.

2.3 Value of the Person-Centred Approach Vis-à-Vis Top-Down Perspectives

Arguing from a bottom-up point of view, it is not too far-fetched to contend that the person-centred approach, being a bottom-up, broad and open account, could in principle increase the tendency of achieving inclusiveness. Also, based on the fact that different possibilities are to be considered, the bottom-up perspective could potentially increase the demand for greater thoroughness. As such we might be able to spot some often overlooked advantages and ills that result from the top-down accounts. For example, we can observe not merely that specific antitrust theories confine the reach of antitrust authorities and courts, but also that such confinement invariably impacts on the interests of persons. In effect, we can conclude that such narrow top-down accounts do not give adequate attention to antitrust interests.

Top-down antitrust accounts are akin to Sunstein's top level theories[1] as they require firmly pre-set premises for the application of the law. Thus, just in the same way that top level theories can be criticised, one could say that top-down theories are equally "ill-suited to the extent of social heterogeneity and to the plurality of

[1] See generally Sunstein (1996).

relevant values at stake."[2] More specifically, as it is herein shown, theories based on the top-down approach to antitrust fail primarily because they do not: (1) fully reflect antitrust practice and, as such, do not totally reflect what courts could truly consider; (2) explain scenarios that fall outside their narrow construct; (3) reflect the array of interests that could arise from a single antitrust issue.

2.4 The Person-Centred Requirements

It would be foolhardy to build an entirely new concept of antitrust. This means in effect that any concept or perspective on antitrust must draw on the foundational core and established theories of antitrust in one way or another. Hence, it is imperative that the person-centred approach herein developed takes account of the present top-down theories regardless of their ills and shortcomings. The extent of their relevance to the bottom-up account however need be clearly stated—for instance, they will be of value only to the extent that they accord with the primary conditions for the person-centred analysis which are that: antitrust analyses must be flexible, there must be adequate information, and that it must allow the incorporation of broad range of factors and interests. These conditions are addressed and substantiated through an evaluative exercise that showcases the ills of the top-down approaches while at the same time, drives home the value of the person-centred approach.

This sub-section is divided into two parts. Section 2.4.1 emphasises the significance of the requirement of flexibility to the person-centred approach. In order to establish an acceptable reason for developing the person-centred analysis as a possible alternative to the traditional top-down approaches, rule-based accounts of competition law will be shown to be prone to the peculiar problem of inflexibility. It will then be shown that the potential problem(s) does not arise where the person-centred approach is applied. Further, in an attempt to solidify its basis, the person-centred approach is linked to certain laudable legal requirements such as the need to obtain adequate information for the purpose decision-making as well as the need for broadmindedness in legal discourse, analysis, decision-making, implementation and enforcement.

2.4.1 A Flexible Framework

A basic requirement of the person-centred approach under consideration is that antitrust analysis should be based on a flexible framework. It thus goes without saying that from a person-centred perspective, any account of antitrust modelled on

---

[2] Sunstein (1996), p. 99.

rigid rules would not be ideal.[3] This requirement should apply to every antitrust issue. It has unequivocally been stated that rigid rules must be avoided. One must however not lose sight of the fact that this assertion is not against rules per se but against rules that are inflexible and prone to blind dogmatic application. Person-centred analysis recognises the value of rules—by their making, rules are aimed at specifying outcomes before particular cases arise and, as Sunstein states, rule-making is often thought to be the signal virtue of a regime of law as one might legitimately argue that the rule of law requires a system of rules.[4] Moreover, rules could be desirable in the sense that they limit permissible grounds for actions and arguments. Rules by their very nature can play an enormous role in a heterogeneous society as they help in containing people of limited time and capacities.[5] As acknowledged by Sunstein, rules "save effort, time and expenses." He states further that "[b]y truncating the sorts of value-disputes that can arise in law, [rules] also ensure[s] that disagreements will occur along a narrowly restricted range."[6] Rules thus have a tremendous advantage over other alternatives in this regard.

One particular characteristic of rules is that they generally say that considerations that are relevant in many settings are not relevant to the issue they address. "Rules will say what sorts of considerations bear on what issues, and what sorts of considerations do not. Rules decide questions of appropriate role, and they say what is relevant for people in different social roles."[7] This much is good about rules. The point at which we have to become wary of rules is when they interfere with interests. Even though it is inevitable to trade-off interests when concrete decisions are to be made, it would be inappropriate to engage in such trade-off solely on the grounds of external benefits such as administrative convenience.[8] Further, when one gets fanatical about rules, it becomes quite easy to be blinded to some of the imperfections that result from such rules. The danger of unwavering fondness for rules can be noted from Hayek's position. He was fanatical about rules so much that he was willing to perpetuate injustice in the name of rule-making. He stated that "[t]he important thing is that rule enables us to predict other people's behaviour correctly, and this requires that it should apply to all cases—even if in a particular case we feel it to be unjust."[9] The reasoning underscores the danger of adhering to rigid rules as it may make people too mechanical such that they may

[3] It should be noted that it is not the aim of this thesis to obliterate rule-making and to promote a regime totally devoid of rules. Rather, the criticisms of rules should be seen strictly in the light of "excessively rigid rules" while the promotion of flexibility should be such that even where a regime is rule-based, it allows for a discretional application of the law.

[4] Sunstein (1996), p. 102.

[5] Sunstein (1996), p. 106.

[6] Sunstein (1996), p. 106.

[7] Sunstein (1996), pp. 107–108.

[8] It is quite often said by some scholars that certain goals should not be pursued by antitrust authorities not because they are inappropriate but simply because it will increase the "workload" of staff and other related concerns.

[9] Hayek (1944), p. 114.

insist on applying "general principles to particular cases [even where] they lead to palpable absurdity."[10]

No matter how seemingly uncontroversial a rule might appear, it is not far-fetched to expect that substantive debates would arise at the stage of interpretation. We can thus wonder why we should be unduly fixated on rules especially where they may prejudice (some) antitrust interests.

Also, the general nature of rules and their blindness to particular instances is not always a virtue but rather a political vice, because a just system allows us to adapt the particular circumstances that shape individual cases. In effect, it may not be inappropriate in specific instances to say that rigid rules are obtuse since ideal justice is flexible and based on the situation at hand.[11]

In the context of the person-centred perspective, any theory that prescribes rigid antitrust rules will hardly be able to withstand scrutiny. It will struggle to show that its mode of analysing antitrust will fit in with the heterogeneous nature of society. As such, whatever the justifications are, we must keep in mind that "rules may misfire, precisely because they are too rigid and because they are laid down in advance; they go badly wrong when applied to concrete cases not anticipated when the rules are set down."[12]

Moreover, strictly from the antitrust context, sheepish application of rules may be a clear sign of incompetence and lack of rigour. For instance, we can infer from Posner's statement that strict adherence to rules is often the easy way out for the mediocre and incompetent. Posner stated that it was perhaps due to the lack of substantive economic knowledge that trial lawyers tended to be combative in antitrust cases rather than reflective. He stated further that government lawyers who were young or mediocre applied rules slavishly because of their incompetence. Posner asserted that they "fashioned a body of substantive doctrine and a system of sanctions and procedures that are poorly suited to carrying out the fundamental objectives of antitrust policy."[13]

Other germane reasons why we should be cautious of excessive rule-making in the context of antitrust is that they will most likely end up being over- or under-inclusive if assessed by reference to their purpose. This conclusion is strengthened by the fact that rules can be easily outrun by changing circumstances. Also, legal abstraction involved in rule-making may sometimes mask bias. Rules may also

[10] Sunstein (1996), p. 15. In fact, a closer look reveals that not all the values attributed to rules are true. Rules cannot always do what proponents of rule-making expect. This is because rules are not really what they appear to be—we would find out that rather than answering all questions in advance, the best rules might still provoke substantive disagreement at the moment of their application. As such, since even the best rules would inevitably require *ex post* interpretation, the aspiration of rule-bound justice is greatly undermined, Sunstein (1996), p. 121.

[11] Sunstein (1996), p. 15.

[12] Sunstein (1996), p. 15.

[13] Posner (1976), pp. 231–236.

drive discretion underground. Another likely downside of rules is that they may allow evasion by wrongdoers and can lead to procedural unfairness.[14]

The likelihood that we might be inflicted with the downsides of rule-making in market-related issues is pretty high. As Joskow observes, the relationship between the wide arrays of market structures, organisational arrangements, transactional attributes and contractual arrangements in a market economy and the market performance indicia of concern are imperfectly understood from both the theoretical and empirical perspectives. As such, there is always a tension between the specification of clear simple rules and their confrontation with situations where their rigid application can lead to type I or II errors.[15] It is even more pertinent that we desist from strict rule-making in antitrust because it is a dynamic field[16] that requires the complex interplay of law and economics.

It can be safely assumed that we should avoid rigid rules in most areas of law because the law has to be able to respond to changes in society. For example, courts have had to reinterpret their procedural rules on taking of evidence which was drafted prior to the computer age. If they are to keep up with the pace of the society, laws must be flexible enough to allow for a broader interpretation of relevant provisions in light of the technology in question. To this extent, the need to avoid rigidity is not unique to competition law. There is however a more peculiar reason why avoidance of rigidity is important for antitrust—there is good reason to avoid rigidity in fields that still struggle with very foundational issues of definition. It is contended that antitrust is one of such fields. For instance, we still struggle with foundational issues such as "what is competition?" The problem pertaining to the volatility of the definition of germane terms is not cosmetic as definitions and theories have a very strong influence on actual implementation and interpretation of competition rules.

To illustrate the peculiarity of the need to avoid rigid rules in antitrust, patent law is compared with antitrust law. In both areas of law, there are certain conditions and requirements which have to be interpreted in light of specific facts. For example, in most jurisdictions, patentability requirements include that an invention must: be of a patentable subject matter; novel; and involve an inventive step. In the same vein, there is often the need to identify the relevant market in antitrust cases. If one thus isolates the requirement of "novelty" under patent law and the question of "relevant market" under competition law and seek to interpret them in light of the changes in society, it is possible to give the same justification for requiring flexibility in the interpretation of both requirements. For instance, it could be observed that there might be need to avoid rigidity in the interpretation of the novelty requirement so as

---

[14] Sunstein (1996), pp. 129, 130–135.

[15] Joskow (2002), p. 100. For example, where we rigidly apply antitrust rules without taking into account our imperfect understanding of market structures, organisational arrangement, market performance indicia and so on, we run the risk of allowing anti-competitive practises (type I error) or punishing a pro-competitive behaviour (type II error).

[16] Femi Alese in Marsden and Waller (2009), p. 42.

not to deny a hitherto uncommon but legitimate claims such as "product by process" patent claims. Many would decry an irredeemably rigid system which is not willing to adapt to such scientific advancement.[17] In similar vein, provision regarding market definition must not be rigid and relevant authorities must not be numb to changing business environment which might impact on the scope of the market that is considered relevant. For example, regarding the requirement of demand substitutability in ascertaining the relevant market, it is imperative to remain flexible[18] and to adjust counterfactuals accordingly. For instance, it could be important to take due note of present conditions in ascertaining whether a consumer is likely to switch to another product in the event of a Small but Significant Non-transitory Increase in Price (SSNIP). Though it can be presumed that a product is not substitutable where there are transaction and information search cost involved in buyer switching to other suppliers, one must not disregard the peculiarities of individual issues and the societal trends. For instance, certain non-price factors or even brute consumerism might change the nature of an erstwhile inelastic market such that consumers would switch as a result of a SSNIP even where they will incur increased searching cost thereby making hitherto non-substitutable products interchangeable.

Having noted the similarity in the justification for flexibility under both patent law and competition law, it is imperative to identify the antitrust-specific concern against rigidity. In many areas of law, foundational issues of definition are relatively settled. Even where the boundaries of such laws are not well defined, it is often an academic or theoretical concern as to whether such field of law can be considered a coherent and distinctive subject of law. Thus, even if there are foundational issues of definition, they are hardly of intrinsic importance to the field per se.

It must be noted that antitrust does by all means form a distinct area of law. It should also be noted that there is grave uncertainty in terms of foundational definitions. Since there is no doubt as to the distinctiveness of antitrust laws, the issue of foundational definitions should be taken more seriously. It is important to identify the uniqueness of these definitional issues in antitrust by comparing antitrust law with patent law which is another fairly distinctive area of law. To a large extent, it is uncontroversial to assert that a patent consist of a set of exclusive

---

[17] See generally the following US cases: *In re Stephens*, 345 F.2d 1020, 145 USPQ 656 (CCPA 1965); *Scripps Clinic & Research Foundation v. Genentech Inc.*, 18 USPQ 2d 1001; *Atlantic Thermoplastics Co Inc. v. Faytex Corp*, 23 USPQ 2d 1481 (Fed. Cir. 1992) rehearing denied, 24 USPQ2d 1138; *Columbia University v. Roche Diagnostics GmbH*, 57 USPQ2d 1825 (D. Mass. 2000).

[18] See generally Willem Boshoff, "Antitrust Market Definition: Rationale, Challenges and Opportunities in South African Competition Policy" [http://www.compcom.co.za/assets/Uploads/events/Fourth-Competition-Law-Conferece/Session-4B/Boshoff-Market-Definition.pdf].

right which is granted to protect an invention.[19] On the other hand, the term "competition" cannot be so easily defined[20] which implies that there is a greater need to avoid rigidity in antitrust law.

Another important reason why some degree of flexibility is required in antitrust law stems from the fact that it is a dynamic field. In Europe for example, in the primordial days of competition enforcement, agreements that restrain competition were interpreted formally to cover any restraint on a trader's freedom which was likely to affect the market. Whether or not an agreement restrains competition was decided in the abstract without a market analysis. This formalistic approach resulted in type I and type II errors as restrictions that are not legally enforceable were permitted, even if they restricted competition substantially, while enforceable horizontal restrictions on conduct were voided even if they did not.[21] However, in the recent past, Europe has unequivocally denounced its previous mechanical approach to competition law analysis. In the *Article 81(3) Guidelines* for instance, the Commission stated that the standards in the "guidelines must be applied in light of the circumstances specific to each case. This excludes a mechanical application. Each case must be assessed on its own fact and the guidelines must be applied reasonably and flexibly."[22]

A degree of flexibility can be noticed in European competition law when one considers how the relevant European institutions assess provisions such as Article 101 of the Treaty for the Functioning of the European Union (TFEU). Arrangements prohibited by Article 101 include those where a supplier restricts its distributors from competing with each other, and as a result, the (potential) competition that could have existed between the distributors is extinguished. However, the European Union recognises that certain restraints may in certain cases not be caught by Article 101(1) when the restraint is objectively necessary for the existence of an agreement of that type or that nature.[23] For instance, territorial restraints in an agreement between a supplier and a distributor may for a certain period of time fall outside Article 101(1), if the restraints are objectively necessary in order for the distributor to penetrate a new market.[24] Similarly, a prohibition imposed on all distributors not to sell to certain categories of end-users may not be restrictive of competition if such restraint is objectively necessary for

[19] Note that the difficulty of defining the term "invention" in patent law is a secondary definitional issue just like the problem with defining "relevant market", "market share" "restriction" etc. under competition law.

[20] See Sect. 2.6 below.

[21] See Korah (1973), pp. 188–189.

[22] Commission—Guidelines on the application of Article 81(3) of the Treaty OJ No. C 101 of 27.04.2004. Para 6.

[23] See in this respect, the judgment in Case 56–65 *Société Technique Minière v Maschinenbau Ulm GmbH* [1966] ECR 235; Case 258/78 *L.C. Nungesser KG and Kurt Eisele v Commission* [1982] ECR 2015.

[24] See para 61–62 Guidelines on Vertical Restraints (2010/C 130/01)—OJ C 291 of 13.10.2000.

reasons of safety or health related to the dangerous nature of the product in question.[25]

Another example is the question of market power. The present position in Europe is that the prohibition of Article 101(1) only applies where, on the basis of proper market analysis, it can be concluded that the agreement has likely anti-competitive effects on the market unless the practice is considered to have an anti-competitive object.[26] In *European Night Services v Commission*,[27] the Court of Justice stated that in order to find an anti-competitive effect, it is necessary to show that the market shares of the parties exceed the thresholds set out in the Commission's *de minimis* notice.[28] Further, the Commission is of the opinion that the fact that an agreement falls outside the safe harbour of a block exemption is in itself an insufficient basis for finding that the agreement is caught by Article 101 (1) or that it does not fulfil the conditions of Article 101(3). Findings, it states, should be based on individual assessment of the likely effects produced by the agreement.[29]

Also, the flexibility of a regime can be assessed by the way it determines the restrictiveness or otherwise of an agreement. For example, should authorities and courts focus on per se analysis or should the effects of agreements be assessed as well? Does the classification into per se and rule of reason approaches require some flexibility? If we say that a particular type of agreement (such as resale price maintenance) is to be considered illegal per se, should we be able to alter this at a later stage where the circumstance requires us to look at the effect instead or are we to abide strictly by the rule which dictates the form by which we assess such agreements?[30] In line with the bottom-up perspective, we must be willing to consider fresh insights. For example, in the US case of *Continental T.V., Inc. v. GTE Sylvania Inc.*,[31] the Supreme Court abandoned its hostility towards vertical restraints. It recognised that certain contracts which were once deemed unlawful per se may in fact attenuate or overcome market failure with the result that courts should evaluate such agreements under the more forgiving Rule of Reason. According to Meese, such decisions implicitly recognise that contracts producing price, output, or other terms of trade different from the *status quo ante* can be

[25] Art 81(3) Guidelines, para 18.

[26] See in this respect Joined Cases T-374/94 and others, *European Night Services v Commission* [1998] ECR II-3141.

[27] See in this respect Joined Cases T-374/94 and others, *European Night Services v Commission* [1998] ECR II-3141.

[28] See in this respect Joined Cases T-374/94 and others, *European Night Services v Commission* [1998] ECR II-3141.

[29] 81(3) Guidelines para 24.

[30] See generally the Guidelines on Vertical Restraints.

[31] 433 U.S. 36, 38–39, 59 (1977).

beneficial, and there is no reason to confine this reasoning to decisions policing the boundaries of the per se rule.[32]

The EU example can be noted from the Research and Development (R&D) aspect. The previous Research and Development Block Exemption Regulation did forbid certain agreement which it categorised as hardcore violations. However, the new regulation reflects a systemic change as some agreements which were considered "hardcore" may now be placed under the category referred to as "excluded restrictions". Article 6 of new Regulation[33] now allows as "excluded restriction" things such as a prohibition to challenge the validity of intellectual property rights, protecting R&D after completion of the R&D and so on.

The dangers of an extreme rule-based culture in antitrust is also vivid in the enforcement aspect. The US has a long standing tradition of awarding treble damages in antitrust suits. Determining whether multiple damages are an effective means to reach institutional goals is truly a complex task. This complication arises as a result of the many different types of conduct that might require the award of multiple damages. It is also worsened by numerous circumstances under which such conduct could occur, be discovered, and prosecuted.[34] Notwithstanding this, those who argue for an automatic multiple damages regime base their arguments on three main reasons. They say that: (1) treble damages are necessary to deter potential antitrust wrongdoers; (2) treble damages provide necessary incentives for private plaintiffs to bring antitrust suits; and (3) treble damages fully compensate victims of anticompetitive conduct.[35]

Noting the advantages of treble damages, the question is not whether the award should be allowed or not. Rather, it is whether it should be applied blindly and uniformly. As queried by Greenfield et al, even if we rightly conclude that some conduct such as price-fixing and market allocation should attract harsh penalties, whether all antitrust wrongdoers should automatically face multiple damages is another matter, particularly given the other severe penalties that wrongdoers face.[36] The strictness of the rule on treble damages means there is a risk that the law will either be over-deterring or fail to deter.[37] As such, one would expect that the inherent difficulty in assessing the ideal state of damages suggests that the question of multiple damages may best be resolved on a case-by-case basis rather than through uniform rules.

---

[32] Meese (2003), p. 81.

[33] Commission Regulation (EU) No. 1217/2010 on the Application of Article 101(3) of the Treaty on the Functioning of the European Union to certain categories of Research and Development Agreements.

[34] Greenfield and Olsky (2007).

[35] See, e.g., ABA Antitrust Section, Monograph No. 13, Treble-Damages Remedy 16–21 (1986).

[36] Greenfield and Olsky (2007), p. 4.

[37] Greenfield and Olsky (2007), p. 4.

A major irony of the automatic treble damages rule is that the uncompromising nature of such rule could weaken the system such that infringing companies may go unpunished. If one of the primary reasons necessitating treble damages is to deter, it does then appear to be counter-intuitive that the regime is even worsened as a result of the rule-based nature of the treble damages. Greenfield et al state in this regard that:

> it is impossible to divorce the question of remedies from the procedural and substantive standards that govern antitrust litigation. Over the past decades, the U.S. courts have imposed heightened evidentiary, antitrust injury, and standing requirements on plaintiffs seeking to bring antitrust claims... Although it is very difficult to determine how much of this movement towards restricting private actions is attributable to the judicial concern about over-deterrence from treble damages awards, it seems likely that treble damages have played a role. Accordingly, the treble damages remedy in some instances may have the unintended consequence of *limiting* the circumstances under which plaintiffs can recover.[38]

There are advantages that can be derived from the application of specific rules. In particular, rules can play a huge role at both the procedural and substantive levels of antitrust as they may help to prevent uncritical ideas from creeping into the field. This value notwithstanding, we must not lose sight of the fact that because of its unique dynamics, antitrust is not well suited for strict rules. Antitrust issues are not only highly fact intensive. They also depend heavily on a mixture of the antitrust ideas, the circumstance surrounding a case, and specific characteristics of the market in which the issue has arisen. It will therefore be disingenuous to have an "ideal" type of antitrust which is to be sought through strict rules.

From the foregoing, it becomes clear that antitrust laws should be applied flexibly. From the person-centred perspective, this is even the more so considering the fact that some interests may be unduly jeopardised where we apply a rigid construct.

2.4.2 Adequate Information

Apart from having a flexible framework, the person-centred approach makes it imperative that decision-makers have and obtain adequate information. Though not exclusive to it, this condition is built into the person-centred account in order to be able to decide firmly between different interests. It is thus expected that as a result of the unavoidable conflict of interests, antitrust institutions must, as a preliminary condition, seek adequate information at both the investigation and the decision-making stages. These stages are explained in turn:

[38] Greenfield and Olsky (2007), p. 13.

2.4.2.i Investigation Stage

Antitrust institutions must actively source obvious and non-obvious information pertaining to various interests as identified through the person-centred perspective. It is thus expected that for an antitrust regime to prevent or at least limit errors, antitrust arbiters must have adequate knowledge of market structures, organisational arrangements, transactional attributes and contractual arrangements in a market economy and the market performance indicia of concern and so on. However, due to human imperfections, we cannot possibly guarantee the perfect market information in order to eliminate errors. We are however expected to strive and put in extra efforts (within reasonable cost) to ensure that the knowledge we have and the information we seek with regards to specific issues are actually the best we could possibly get. This is particularly essential for authorities who have to make firm decisions on antitrust issues. For instance, with regards to antitrust adjudication, it might mean that the courts and antitrust authorities should be willing to follow an inquisitorial approach as opposed to an adversarial approach[39] where the former generates more concrete and relevant information.

Over the years, there have been continuous debates as regard the trial procedure that helps most in obtaining the relevant information in a case.[40] When one extends this debate to antitrust, it does appear that the need to consider the inquisitorial approach is strengthened because parties who are meant to play the role of claimant may not be easy to identify. They might also be too large in number which would raise free-rider concerns. In such instance, information is best gathered through inquisitorial approach whereby the antitrust authority or court plays the role of an impartial or active judge.[41]

In the public sphere, it might be that institutions should make use of tools beyond their traditional investigative powers. They should be able to (if and when required) make use of other means that could help in information gathering. In Europe for instance, chapter V of the Regulation 1/2003[42] endows the Commission with various powers which include the power to request information[43] and power to

[39] Inquisitorial approach should be preferred as long as it avoids extremism. See generally Neven (2006), p. 741.

[40] See generally Tullock (1988), pp. 3–27. Posner (1988), p. 29. See also the empirical analysis of Froeb and Kobayashi (2001), pp. 267–72. Also, Shin (1998), pp. 378–405.

[41] See Neven (2006), p. 763. This could be with or without a prosecutorial bias. For a contrary view on the preferred approach, see Bruce Lyon "How should Decisions be made in a Competition Authority?" [http://competitionpolicy.wordpress.com/2011/06/02/how-should-decisions-be-made-in-acompetition-authority/#more-579].

[42] Council Regulation (EC) No. 1/2003 of 16 December 2002 on the implementation of the rules on competition laid down in Articles 81 and 82 of the Treaty *OJ L 1, 4.1.2003*.

[43] Council Regulation (EC) No. 1/2003 of 16 December 2002 on the implementation of the rules on competition laid down in Articles 81 and 82 of the Treaty *OJ L 1, 4.1.2003*, Art 18.

conduct inspections.[44] In the performance of its duties, Article 18 allows the Commission to request for "all necessary information"[45] vital to its duties. Article 18(2) states the conditions of the request which are that the Commission must state the legal basis and purpose of the request, with specific reference to: the information required; the time-line within which it is to be provided; and the penalties for non-compliance.[46] Article 19 empowers the Commission to interview natural and legal persons for the purpose of collecting information relating to the subject matter of an investigation. However this interview can only take place with the consent of the interviewee and there is no penalty for providing false or misleading information. Also, the possibility of a dawn raid also increases the chance of obtaining relevant information. Article 20 enables the Commission to conduct all necessary inspection on business premises.[47] If it finds it necessary, the Commission can inspect other premises and also individuals' homes.[48] The possibility of obtaining information is also enhanced as the fining guidelines provide that refusal to cooperate with or obstruction of the Commission's activities may be a basis for increasing the fine payable by the firm whose activity is under review.[49]

These administrative powers indicate that the European Commission is modelled to actively seek relevant information. However, the system is by no means foolproof as the information gathered might be inadequate or even misleading. Where the traditional investigative powers prove inadequate, institutions should be willing to do more in order to fill potential voids and consequently secure various interests that may be injured as a result of the gap. For instance, so as to increase the chance of obtaining relevant information, the institution could initiate a leniency programme. This scheme has been adopted with a substantial degree of success at both sides of the Atlantic. Another means of gathering relevant information is through the application of forensic economics. Information could also be sought through reward schemes.[50]

---

[44] Council Regulation (EC) No. 1/2003 of 16 December 2002 on the implementation of the rules on competition laid down in Articles 81 and 82 of the Treaty *OJ L 1, 4.1.2003*, Art 20 and 21.

[45] For the definition of "all necessary information", see case C-36/92 *PSEP v Commission* [1994] ECR 1-1911.

[46] See Reg 1/2003, Article 23. The Commission has a choice between making a simple request or a decision. Where the Commission opts for a simple request, the firm would not be obliged to answer although there would be penalties for providing wrongful or misleading information. The firm is however expected to respond to the Commission's request as failure to respond could lead to imposition of penalty under Article 23. The letter must also state that the firm has the right to seek judicial review, should any penalty be imposed.

[47] This inspection could either be by agreement or with an element of surprise.

[48] Council Regulation (EC) No. 1/2003 of 16 December 2002 on the implementation of the rules on competition laid down in Articles 81 and 82 of the Treaty *OJ L 1, 4.1.2003*, Art 21. This should however be done with judicial authorisation, see also Recital 26.

[49] Commission—Guidelines on the method of setting fines imposed pursuant to Article 23(2)(a) of Regulation No. 1/2003. OJ C 210 1.09.2006.

[50] These tools are addressed in Chap. 6.

Worthy of particular mention is the UK's market investigation whereby relevant authorities are inclined to actively assess markets over a period in order to ascertain the state of competition. Section 5 of the Enterprise Act 2002 provides, amongst other functions, that the UK Office of Fair Trading is to obtain, compile and keep under review information about matters relating to the carrying out of its functions. One way of achieving this function is to undertake market studies. Particularly, the Market and Policy Initiative Division of the OFT is responsible for examining how well markets are functioning and for considering when a market investigation reference would be appropriate.[51] For instance, the OFT may make market investigation reference to the Competition Commission when it has reasonable ground for suspecting that one or more of the features of the market prevent, restrict or distort competition.[52]

Also in line with the bottom-up perspective is the Commission's effort aimed at overcoming the structural information asymmetry in the private aspect of antitrust enforcement. For instance, the Commission suggests that a minimum level of disclosure *inter partes* for EU antitrust damages cases should be ensured across the EU. In particular, some of the Commission's suggestions are that: national courts should, under specific conditions, have the power to order parties to proceedings or third parties to disclose precise categories of relevant evidence. Disclosure is however not automatic as the claimant has to show to the satisfaction of the court that he is unable, applying all efforts that can reasonably be expected, otherwise to produce the requested evidence.[53]

2.4.2.ii Decision Stage

In line with the bottom-up perspective, it is important that antitrust enforcers and courts are awake to the complexity of interests and entitlements (for instance, interests of complainants, alleged infringers and the industry as a whole). As such, they are required to obtain adequate information about those interests and the different possible interpretations before they go about their decisional activities.

The problem with the top-down approaches is that issues are addressed by alluding only to information and opinions which are considered important by the respective theories. The danger here is that we could be in error (be it type I or type II)[54] as we are likely to jettison the necessary additional information because of our myopic inclination. To illustrate this point, Sen's *Fable of the Bamboo Flute* is

[51] See generally Whish (2008), pp. 439–468.

[52] Section 13 United Kingdom Enterprise Act 2002. Note generally that there is presently a proposition to merge the OFT and the Commission to form the Competition and Market Authority.

[53] European Commission, "White Paper on Damages Actions for Breach of the EC Antitrust Rules" *COM (2008) 165 final*. 4.

[54] Note that for the purpose of this thesis, type I and type II errors are not to be predetermined by reference to any theoretical metric. In other words, the terms are not to be understood as terms of art as, they are, for instance, understood by efficiency theorists.

instructive—How should an arbiter resolve a dispute between three individuals over ownership of a bamboo flute where the flute was made by A, B can play it best and C (unlike the others) has nothing else to play with? The resolution of such dispute which is quintessentially a dispute about ownership of a resource is contingent on the information available to the arbiter. Take it that the alternatives available to the arbiter are mutually exclusive and any choice made is conclusive and irreversible. If the information put before the arbiter is simply that the first individual "made the flute", and if the arbiter thinks strictly through Marxian–Nozickian rule of allocation, she would allocate the flute to the first individual. If the information is however that the second individual "can play the flute" and if the arbiter is persuaded by Benthamite–Utilitarian rule, she would allocate the flute to the second individual. Finally, if the information made available to the arbiter is about the "poorest" of the three and if she is persuaded by a Rawlsian rule, she would allocate the flute to the third individual.

As far as the person-centred approach is concerned, we cannot underestimate the need to ask the three questions prior to choosing—who made it, who plays it best and who is the most disadvantaged. It however does not end here. We should also endeavour not to be locked into any of the three rules of allocation.

However, from a neutral point of view, the alternative approach herein developed is not without its downsides. For instance, with regards to the condition for decision-making, an expected objection is that the process of seeking information might be too expensive. In fact, we cannot afford to engage in an uncontrolled information gathering exercise.[55] A more comprehensive evaluation of this alternative approach vis-à-vis the traditional approach will thus be conducted in subsequent chapters.

2.5 The Requirement of Broadness Expatiated

The ultimate requirement of the alternative herein developed is that antitrust analysis must be broad. This requirement invariably combines the requisite flexibility and adequacy of information. It could thus be stated that the precondition for the application of the person-centred approach is that antitrust analysis should be open-textured so as to ensure that plural interests are respected.

It is imperative that the very idea of broadness envisaged under the alternative approach is clarified; the idea of broadness here encapsulates notions beyond mere flexibility. While flexibility and broadness may intersect in a lot of ways, they are no synonyms. Take for example the general effect-based approaches to antitrust analysis. Many economists would passionately and convincingly argue for a case-by-case reasoned analysis of antitrust issues. In fact, those who call for a "more

[55] It would be disingenuous to aim at absolute information in antitrust. See generally McGowan (2005), p. 1185.

economic approach" in Europe are particularly critical of rigid and formalistic approaches which mean in effect that they are in favour of a flexible approach to antitrust analysis.

The US's Rule of Reason and Europe's Article 101(3) exemptions are illustrative of the flexibility that exists in antitrust even if we consider it from the top-down perspective. In order to determine whether a particular agreement violates antitrust laws, the US applies a three-step tests in their rule of reason analysis which is generally believed to help courts distinguish those contracts that harm or destroy competition by creating or exercising market power from those that promote it.[56] First, a plaintiff must establish a prima facie case by showing that the restraint produces tangible anticompetitive harm. Typically, the plaintiff would have to show "actual detrimental effects" such as increased price or reduced output.[57] Second, the defendants must prove that their agreement produces "pro-competitive" benefits that outweigh the harm implicit in plaintiff's prima facie case.[58] Third, even if the defendants can substantiate the claim, the plaintiff can still prevail by proving that the defendants can achieve the same benefits by means of a "less restrictive alternative."[59]

In assessing the pro or anti-competitive effect of agreements in Europe, Article 101(3) TFEU affords the flexibility required. The sub-article contains four cumulative conditions which, if satisfied, would not void a generally anti-competitive agreement. First, the agreement must contribute to improving the production or distribution of goods or contribute to promoting technical or economic progress, for instance, where such improvement leads to efficiency gains. Second, the restrictions must be indispensable to the attainment of the efficiency gains. Third, consumers must receive a fair share of the resulting benefits. To satisfy this condition, the efficiency gains attained by the indispensable restrictions must be sufficiently passed on to consumers. Hence, efficiencies only accruing to the parties to the agreement will not suffice. Finally, the agreement must not afford the parties the possibility of eliminating competition in respect of a substantial part of the products in question.

It can be observed that there are areas in both EU and US antitrust law and practice where flexibility is not only welcome but also promoted. However, this does not mean that they are broad, or at least, "broad" in the context of the alternative bottom-up perspective. The bottom-up perspective will consider the US rule of reason not to be broad enough for instance because it focuses on the concept of efficiency. The European equivalent is also not broad enough from a person-centred perspective despite the possibility of arguing that it allows for

---

[56] Meese (2003), p. 80.

[57] See, e.g., *Re/Max Int'l Inc.*, 173 F.3d at 1014–1015.

[58] See *NCAA v. Board of Regents of the University of Oklahoma*, 468 U.S. 85 (1984), at 113–120 where the court upheld the plaintiff's claim because the defendant failed to prove existence of pro-competitive benefits.

[59] See, e.g., *Law v. NCAA*, 134 F.3d 1010, 1019 (10th Cir. 1998).

notions beyond efficiency and economic welfare.[60] Moreover, it appears that even its relative broadness might be pegged in the wake of the call for a "more economic approach". In fact, a read through the recent Horizontal Guidelines[61] indicates that Article 101(3) is likely to be interpreted more narrowly thereby further distancing it from the broadness required when addressing antitrust from a bottom-up perspective as it appears that the Commission seeks to focus on efficiency.

To show that the flexibility achieved in Article 101(3) is unlikely to match the bottom-up idea of broadness, we can consider the debate whether environmental concerns in their own right are likely to be factored into the decision to grant exemptions. In its 2001 Guidelines, the Commission affirmed that improving the environment contributes to improving production or distribution or promotion of economic or technical progress.[62] It has even mentioned environmental protection in at least three decisions.[63] The Commission had explained how environmental protection is to be weighted in the Article 101(3) balancing exercise. In fact, its provision on the mode of assessing cost has led some scholars to argue that Article 101(3) might very well accommodate environmental protection as a matter of public policy. Monti had considered that the requirement that the "net benefit goes to consumers" in Article 101(3) actually refers to consumers as a whole. In other words, it would mean that we look at the benefit to the society at large rather than to consumers of the products in question.[64]

The fluid argumentations of scholars notwithstanding, just like in the US, the flexibility in Article 101(3) is likely to be considered narrow when antitrust issues are assessed from a bottom-up perspective. For example, all indications in the 2011 Horizontal Guidelines are that efficiency and nothing else should be the basis upon which flexibility is to be employed regarding horizontal agreements. Moreover, the aspect of the 2001 Guidelines which arguably left open the room for public policy has been narrowed. The Commission unequivocally states that "for the purposes of these guidelines, the concept of "*consumers*" encompasses the customers, potential and/or actual, of the parties to the agreement".[65] This removes the possibility of viewing the public in general as "consumers".

It is equally important that we assess the enforcement part in light of broadness. Concerning private antitrust for instance, while the US courts seek to ensure efficiency of the process, there has been an attempt in Europe to promote a damages regime.[66] The manner in which enforcement is undertaken in the US requires some

[60] Guidelines on the applicability of Article 81(3) of the EC Treaty to Horizontal Cooperation Agreements OJ C 3 06.01.2001.

[61] Guidelines on the applicability of Article 101 of the Treaty on the Functioning of the European Union to Horizontal Co-operation Agreements OJ C11 14.1.2011.

[62] Guidelines on the applicability of Article 81(3) of the EC Treaty to Horizontal Cooperation Agreements OJ C 3 06.01.2001. Para 193.

[63] Commission Decisions, *Assurpol*, OJ 1992 L37/16 para 38; *Ford/Volkswagen*, OJ 1993 L20/14 para 26; and *Exxon/Shell*, OJ 1994 L144/20 para 68.

[64] Monti (2002), p. 1065; Monti (2007), p. 92; López (2002).

[65] Horizontal Guidelines 2011, para 49.

[66] White Paper (2008).

flexibility. This is because decisions on procedures and entitlements depend on what is considered efficient in the case at hand. For instance, an efficient process of antitrust enforcement seeks deterrence if the enforcement cost is manageable. Thus, in looking for the "most efficient enforcer"[67] and efficient enforcement,[68] the regime would have to balance the need for deterrence with the transaction cost. Where the transaction cost is zero, everything can be thrown into achieving deterrence. However, such a regime might have to temper its deterrence drive if the transaction cost (either in terms of administrative cost or error cost) may be too high. In Europe as well, the willingness to adjust the procedures and practices so as to remove the unnecessary clog in private antitrust enforcement is also a sign that the regime is open to alternatives.

Their relative flexibility in enforcement notwithstanding, the important question is to see if these regimes' enforcement modus are in fact broad enough. There is no clear answer to this because what is broad enough within the context of a bottom-up analysis need to be balanced with what is feasible in implementation and enforcement. Thus, just as it has been emphasised in the preceding part, a thorough evaluative exercise will be conducted in assessing whether the very idea of broadness as promoted through the alternative bottom-up perspective is practicable. The answer to this query will ultimately lead us to determining whether the proposed alternative is truly worthy of trumping the traditional approach or whether antitrust is better off with the traditional approach despite its shortcomings.

2.5.1 Broadness Applied: The Example of Enforcement

By according with the broadness required by the bottom-up perspective, we can fully reflect on all possibilities that may impact on various interests. The task at this point however is for us to determine what a broad antitrust regime should be like. In the substantive aspect, it is pretty straightforward; we should consider the different meanings of terms and the different standards which can be applied. We should also ensure that it is not applied in a way that infringers are able to escape capture or that some actions or inactions are allowed or disallowed solely because a single theory recognises or does not recognise them as infringements. This concern is strengthened if we streamline our analysis strictly through individual theories. There is thus a great deal of assessing and balancing that has to be done to avoid this problem. Achieving broadness at the enforcement aspect could even be more daunting. This is because institutions often have set enforcement goals and procedures. If one thus puts the bottom-up perspective on broadness in context, it might appear that such set goals and procedures might be too narrow. However, it is argued that the

[67] In the US, the conditions were set in the case of *Associated Gen. Contractors of Cal., Inc. v. California State Council of Carpenters*, 459 U.S. 519 (1983).

[68] That is in terms of fines.

requirement of broadness can still be achieved despite the fact that enforcers have clear goals, objectives and procedures. It is for them to seek to achieve their goals through a broad mind-set. In a nutshell, the broadness required in antitrust enforcement is directed at the enforcers and the court. The level of their broadmindedness will be evident when one considers how much they are willing to modify their practices in order to reflect the peculiar factors that are unique to individual cases.

For illustrative purpose, a detailed exposition is given on how institutions could reason broadly while attempting to meet their institutional goals or objectives. Thus, for the sake of this analysis, an example of private action is given. Let us assume that an antitrust regime vindicates private claims based on their belief that injured victims should be compensated. In such regime, it is still for the court to consider whether compensation will truly vindicate antitrust interests. If in its remedial disposition, the arbiter strictly requires that in order to grant compensatory award, the claimant has to prove the correlativity of gains and losses. It might disregard the fact that there could be cases in which it is necessary to alter those conditions because of the unusual difficulty the claimant might face as a result of the conditions. In difficult cases, the inability of a corrective justice-based regime to conceive the problem might, in effect, frustrate certain interests. From the bottom-up perspective, it is for us to consider in individual cases whether any specific goal which might be sought by an antitrust regime does not contain loopholes that might eventually jeopardise the effort to protect the society at large. Hence, if a particular mechanism is likely to lead to absurdities in specific cases, the relevant institution should take time to fully reflect on alternatives.

I illustrate here how an institution which has a set procedure for remediation in private antitrust actions can be broadminded in its disposition especially in difficult instances. I continue with the example of compensation. In those difficult cases, it will be for the relevant institution to take a practical view on whether their *ex ante* procedure be applied strictly or whether it should be modified or substituted. Generally, since no goal is all encompassing and perfect, there are bound to be loopholes. Thus, where we align with compensatory justice in antitrust, we should readily appreciate other thoughts such as those based on economic reasoning (for example, game theory) which may play a vital role in determining what the form of action should be.

The institutions could follow a descriptive bottom-up model. For instance, the analysis could be centred on the (prospective) violator. Assuming a firm wants to decide whether to join a cartel, we could assume (beyond the idea of moral rightness or wrongness of such decision) that the firm weighs its decision on a cost/benefit basis—it may consider the possibility of being apprehended by the authorities and the likely penalty. In addition, this firm might have to consider the possibility of private actions by consumers.

Based on this brief scenario, antitrust institutions could (aside from establishing breach through the harm to consumers) test the effectiveness of compensatory remedy by factoring-in the (prospective) infringer's likely thought process. Thus, they could proceed on the assumption that within its rational decision making process, the firm will consider the worst possible effect of its breach and thereafter decide whether its unlawful conduct could go unpunished. Breach will be advantageous where the damages and the cost of litigation are below the possible gains from anti-competitive practice. A firm will thus go ahead with the planned breach if the likelihood of being apprehended is below the benefit it would derive from the cartel. It is for the institution to pre-empt the firm and juggle its conclusions on how compensations could be sought. If it considers that the procedural requirements for granting compensation might tilt the cost over the benefit in the (alleged) infringer's cost-benefit calculus, the authorities would have to find a way to streamline such procedural requirements.

In this instance, one could suppose that in order to ascertain the propriety of the procedure for the particular case in hand, the court could mirror the firm by considering the steps the firm might take in ascertaining the "efficiency" of its breach. For instance, we could assume that the firm might consider all the possible responses that might result from its decision to either engage in anti-competitive practice or abstain from it. Applying game theory idea, the court might find that a firm will be faced with at least four possibilities which are:

- The firm engages in price-fixing but consumers do not sue;
- The firm engages in price fixing and consumers institute court actions;
- The firm does not go ahead with the price-fixing arrangement so consumers do not have any reason to sue;
- The firm does not engage in price fixing but consumers sue anyway.

The firm will be more concerned about the first two possibilities since the last two are even farther beyond its control and they do not involve a breach on its part. The court might have to take into account that the firm might seek to take advantage of the loophole in the compensation regime. For instance, the firm could employ strategies that will indirectly influence consumers' decisions to sue or not to sue. Depending on how the relevant institution conceives the likelihood that infringing firms can exploit the regime, the institution (because of its broad thinking) could modify the goal or the means of achieving the goal in specific cases.

For the relevant institution to accord with the requisite broadness, it must think exhaustively on how such firm might take advantage of the system. For instance, the company could, together with the other participants in the cartel, increase prices slightly and gradually on a broad range of products over a long period of time. The concern here is not about the firms' evading capture. The purpose might be that even if their practice is found to be anti-competitive, they would have succeeded in de-motivating consumers from instituting private actions since the products might span various markets and, as such, different categories of consumers who will all suffer "negligible" losses compared to the transaction cost of litigation.

If the likelihood of such sinister calculation is high, an antitrust institution that addresses antitrust from the bottom-up perspective should assess the possible reaction of a rational consumer in order to determine whether the level of his motivation to sue will change as different procedures and remedies are applied.[69]

In sum, the broad factors that might deserve the attention of the relevant institution may include the following:

- Whether antitrust institutions should vindicate antitrust claims through a corrective justice mechanism in order to restore the injured to their pre-violation state. This in particular takes care of the interest of the victims;
- In the same vein, they have to consider whether the mechanism is effective enough to deter anti-competitive practice. This is imperative in order to protect an even wider set of interests which includes victims, potential victims and other firms;
- Thus, antitrust institutions should avoid a "too narrow and inflexible" enforcement strategy because;

  (i) There is always the risk that companies may outsmart the enforcement institution by plotting strategies to, for instance, frustrate consumer actions by making private action undesirable on a cost/benefit basis;
  (ii) Legal processes discourage certain potential claimants (direct purchasers) from instituting remedial actions since they have passed on the overcharge and have thus incurred no loss;
  (iii) For indirect purchasers, the expected value of trial is so low that a lawsuit will be an economically irrational decision;

Conclusive therefore, it is opined from a person-centred point of view that a much deeper thought is given to the idea of broadness.

2.5.2 Is Broadness Becoming the Norm in Antitrust Analysis?

Above, the ills of the theories based on the top-down approach have been identified. It has however been emphasised above that the argument proffered in favour of the person-centred approach should not be considered definitive but rather should be seen as a substantiation of a point of view which still need to be thoroughly evaluated. At this juncture however, the thesis moves from the "ought" and "ought not" by assessing some patterns of antitrust analysis in order to ascertain

[69] In general, private actions are often a function of the remedy sought. Ideally, the effect should be that the availability of a substantial pecuniary remedy (e.g. account of profit) will increase the filing of legal complaints since the remedy increases the value of trial. In the long run however, the potential defendant will become cautious of its acts in order to avoid the injuries that propel law suits. The logical consequence therefore is that anti-competition will become economically "unfashionable" and law suits will reduce accordingly. The institution should also reflect on how structural constraints will impact on antitrust interests.

whether (and if so) the extent to which the notion of broadness implied by the bottom-up perspective is discernible from the present practice.

Moving from abstraction to real practice, can it be said that institutions truly act within the straight-jackets of theoretical constructs such that their activities would hardly be broad enough? It is contended that at the moment, institutions do not in fact channel their thoughts too narrowly. As Hawk observes, there is a consensus among stakeholders from different enforcement regimes that there is a considerable gap between the rhetoric of competition law objectives and the reality of their actual implementation.[70]

To show that enforcers and courts might be inclined to address issues from a broader perspective than the prevailing theories suggest, some of the cases on Article 101 decisions of the Court of Justice are instructive.

Concerning the case of *GSK v. Commission*[71] which addressed Article 101 TFEU, the Court of Justice was primarily asked to assess Glaxo's differentiated pricing system for its products within the internal market. In general, Glaxo attempted (through sales conditions) to restrict parallel traders who sought to profit from arbitrage opportunities which arise from low prices imposed on medications in Spain. Deciding on the propriety of the practice, the Commission held that the sales condition which restricted parallel trade amounted to an infringement of competition rules. The General Court however did not agree with the Commission and rather assessed whether the clause resulted in a violation through a consumer interest analysis. In essence, the General Court opined that since the prices of medicines were shielded from the incidence of demand and supply, it could not be presumed that the clause would restrict competition to the detriment of the final consumer. As such, the Spanish intermediaries who take advantage of the arbitrage opportunities might as well keep the advantage.[72]

However, the Court of Justice reasoned differently. Regarding Article 101(1), it stated thus:

> First of all, there is nothing in that provision to indicate that only those agreements which deprive consumers of certain advantages may have an anti-competitive object. Second, it must be borne in mind that the Court has held that, like other competition rules laid down in the Treaty, Article [101 TFEU] aims to protect not only the interests of competitors or of consumers, but also of the market, and in so doing, competition as such.[73]

The Court of Justice disagreed with the General Court's position which was that consumers are restricted to the "final consumers". The Court of Justice's reasoning reflects a level of broadness as this shows that consumers could also include businesses. Some degree of broadness is also evident from the Court's statement

[70] See Hawk (1998), p. 353.
[71] Case C-501, 513, 515 and 519/06 *GlaxoSmithKline Services Unlimited v Commission* [2009] ECR I-9291. Hereinafter referred to as *Glaxo*.
[72] See Case T-168/01 *GlaxoSmithKline Services v. Commission* [2006] ECR II-2969.
[73] *Glaxo* [2009] 2, 63.

to the effect that not only consumers but also competition in its own right is worthy of attention in antitrust.

The observations made in this part could possibly give the impression that the law is already taking account of the requirement of broadness, thereby reducing the imperativeness of an alternative approach. Nevertheless, it would not be accurate to say that antitrust institutions and courts always apply in full the concept of broadness in their antitrust analysis. This means therefore that there is still a material difference between the traditional approach (whether theoretical or practical application) and the alternative person-centred approach. As such, despite the tendency for authorities to occasionally apply the concept of broadness in their antitrust analysis, it remains a worthy exercise to assess whether the traditional approach should be substituted with the person-centred account.

2.6 Delimiting the Scope of the Broadness Sought

So far, this thesis has continuously emphasised the primary aim of the person-centred approach which is to accommodate different interests in antitrust issues. This inevitably requires that the framework for antitrust analysis should be broad if one is to truly avoid the injustice that could result from excluding some interests. However, caution must be taken in applying a broad framework for antitrust in order not to blur the scope of antitrust claims such that any interest that claims to be "antitrust-related" is accepted within the person-centred framework. Even where we are intuitively aware of what really is an antitrust issue, there seem to be nothing yet in the above explanation of the person-centred approach that showcases a principled way of determining what falls within and outside of antitrust. If reliance is placed solely on intuition, there is a serious risk that on the watch of the person-centred approach, antitrust will degenerate into an unintelligible discipline which is itself a recipe for arbitrariness.

Thus, in order to avoid over-stretching the bounds of antitrust, I attempt here to delimit the scope of the broadness sought by analysing the term "competition". It should be noted that it is not the aim here to actually fashion a definition or to give a conclusive description of what competition entails. Rather, the aim is to keep the focus of the person-centred process on issues that truly matter to antitrust.

The term competition has been defined severally. For instance, competition is defined in the Oxford English Dictionary as "the action of endeavouring to gain what another endeavours to gain at the same time". Apart from the general idea of competition, there is a different idea of "competition" which is often used by economists. This idea of competition, it has been recognised, has a theoretical dimension absent from its everyday use and, as such, to the economists, it has become a term of art that has broken away from its ordinary usage.[74]

[74] Black (2005), p. 8.

To start with, it is taken as trite that the term competition as referred to in this thesis means "economic competition".[75] This leads us to the next query which is how to determine what amounts to economic competition. The answer to this query is far from straight-forward as even economists have not reached a consensus in defining the term. As Bork noted, there is yet to be "one satisfactory definition of 'competition'"[76] as the term "has taken a number of interpretations and meanings, many of them vague.[77]

To illustrate the absence of satisfactory definition for the term "competition", reference will be made to the analysis and counter-analysis of scholars on two specific interpretations of the term; the definition of competition as a state of perfect competition and as a process of rivalry. Each of these conceptions of competition has a unique effect on what is considered to constitute an antitrust concern. For instance, with regards to the former, competition is seen as constituting nothing other than a state of perfect competition which involves "no presumption of psychological competition, emulation, or rivalry".[78] Applying such a definition, a cooperative behaviour between competing firms would not necessarily be considered to be anti-competitive.[79] On the other hand, where competition is identified as implying rivalry between firms, we are invariably looking at the effect of competition by merging the concept of competition and the market which thus allows for the introduction of behavioural content in defining the term. In other words, "competition" is regarded as a phenomenon of exchange.[80] This definition relates systematically to the technique of production within, or to the organisational form of firms. In this regard, this concept of competition puts prime importance on economic goods (price and quality) and to the firm's external relationship in the market.[81] As a result, cooperative behaviours will be treated with circumspection.

The two distinct definitions identified above have been faulted as inadequate or inappropriate. For instance, definition of competition through the idea of perfect market is considered inappropriate because perfect competition is a state that is quite incompatible with the idea of any and all competition and even if it is compatible, it is incapable of actual realisation.[82] The idea of competition is also considered antithetical because despite the fact that perfect competition results from free entry of a large number of formerly competing firms, such a state of the market would lead to a situation where the relationship of firms have evolved and progressed to the point where "the effect of competition have reached their limit".[83]

---

[75] "Today it seems clear that the general goal of the antitrust law is to promote 'competition' as the economist understand that term" Areeda and Hovenkamp (2006) para 100a.

[76] Bork (1978), p. 61. See also Stigler (1957), p. 1.

[77] Vicker (1995), pp. 1, 3. See also Kobayashi (1970).

[78] Knight (1968), pp. 639–656.

[79] See e.g. TCE approach in Meese (2003).

[80] McNulty (1968), p. 645.

[81] McNulty (1968), p. 645.

[82] McNulty (1968), p. 643.

[83] McNulty (1968), p. 642.

This definition is also considered less than ideal because by viewing the term through the theory of monopolistic competition, it fails to take account of the concept of competitive market.[84]

The criticism for the definition of competition as a process of rivalry is that contrary to the assumption that rivalry and self-interest serves as the spine of competition which consequently implies efficiency as an integral definition of the term, there is no unblemished evidence (empirical or otherwise) linking firm rivalry and productive efficiency.[85] Also, it has been argued by Stigler that the fact that this definition merges the concepts of competition and the market is rather unfortunate as each deserved a full and separate treatment".[86]

There are also those who are of the opinion that the definition of competition is not restricted to either of these interpretations. For instance, Black sought to identify what constitutes a state of economic competition and what it mean when it is said that A competes with B.[87] He identified that the operation of competition between A and B could be expressed in more than one way—one may compete via rivalry or through cooperation etc.[88]

Based on these different views about the intrinsic meaning of competition, different ways of viewing a competitive state emerges. For instance, competition can be identified in normative terms. It could also be identified, as a matter of policy, through its effect.[89]

Though the specific inadequacies in the economic concept of competition have been said to impact on both analyses and policies,[90] it is hereby argued from the person-centred point of view that such inadequacies should be celebrated rather than condemned. Also, it is equally good, especially in order to delimit the scope of the person-centred analysis, that we clearly recognise competition as meaning "economic competition" even though the concept cannot be firmly defined. What this means in practice is that even within the broad framework of the person-centred approach, claims could only be instituted where they fall in line with one or more of the definitions of economic competition.

As a result of the diverging analysis of the term, scholars such as Bork attempted to streamline the various definitions of economic competition. For instance, Bork mentioned five conventional ways of discussing the meaning of competition. He states that competition has been seen as: a process of rivalry; the absence of restraint over one firm's economic activities by another firm; the state of the market in which the individual buyer or seller does not influence the price by his purchase or sale; the existence of fragmented industries and markets; and a state of affairs in

[84] Moore (1906), pp. 211–230.
[85] McNulty (1968), p. 656.
[86] Stigler (1957), p. 6.
[87] Black (2005), pp. 6–32.
[88] Black (2005), pp. 6–32.
[89] Stucke (2012), pp. 30–31.
[90] McNulty (1968), p. 639.

which consumer welfare cannot be increased by moving to an alternative state of affairs through judicial decree.[91]

It is contended that accounts that seek to define competition in one way to the exclusion of others will not fit with the person-centred approach. Thus, for example, competition should not be seen strictly in the Borkean sense whereby the term is intrinsically linked to consumer welfare. Rather, the alternative definitions should be accommodated within the definition of economic competition even though each definition of competition is individually deconstructible. It is important to accommodate the different conceptions of economic competition which one is only able to do if rigid interpretation of the term is avoided. Fuchs has thus rightly noted that:

> [T]he lack of a comprehensive definition of competition is not a relevant deficiency [as] you do not need a comprehensive definition of competition that fits all situations and applies to all kinds of economic behaviour. It is totally sufficient to identify certain acts of enterprises as interfering with undistorted competition… This indirect approach has the additional advantage that the rules are flexible enough to protect new forms of competition which were previously unknown and could not have been implemented into a concrete definition.[92]

The analysis so far clearly shows that some degree of flexibility should be applied regarding the term competition. It however also implicitly limits the type of claims that could be brought within a person-centred antitrust framework. By defining competition in line with both present and future conceptions of the term as economists understand it, we are invariably implying that an issue can only be flagged as an antitrust issue if it fits in with one or more of these conceptions. As such, no "interested" person would be allowed to represent for example, a strictly environmental issue as raising an antitrust concern if such issue cannot be linked to one or more of the conceptions of economic competition; a spade does not turn into a spear merely because the owner calls it a spear.

As such, it is expected that to raise an antitrust issue from any enquiry or dispute, such issue must satisfy some basic conditions which are: (1) the issue must relate to interaction between market participants; (2) the basis and the nature of such interaction must be economic; (3) the issue must relate to one of the above identified patterns of competition between firms. For instance, a policy initiative that promotes competitiveness in an industry does not necessarily raise competition issues even if it is at the expense of other industries.

The importance of these requirements can be brought to light by way of illustration: antitrust is not to be broadened to an extent such that politically-motivated policy which impacts on the competitiveness of an industry as against another is considered to constitute an antitrust concern. However, such issue might raise competition concerns where the so-called political decision is made by representatives of interested market participant especially where such decision is to their favour as against other firms that are unrepresented. This requirement also

[91] Bork (1978), p. 58.

[92] Fuchs (2012), p. 54.

shows that completely non-economic factors can only play an auxiliary role in antitrust analysis rather than being considered to constitute antitrust issues in their own right.

2.7 Conclusion

In this chapter, a cursory exposition of the person-centred approach has been given. In addition to evaluating this approach as against top-down accounts, this chapter emphasises the requirement of broadness. However, noting the dangers associated with overly broad laws, an attempt has been made to delimit the scope of the person-centred antitrust analysis. This is achieved by addressing the term "competition". The chapter stresses the need to remain open and to desist from following one conception of "competition" at the expense of another. It however succeeds in delimiting the scope of analysis by emphasising that an antitrust problem can only be said to have arisen when it involves *economic competition* in any of its ramifications.

References

Areeda P, Hovenkamp H (2006) Antitrust law: an analysis of antitrust principles and their application, vol 1, 3rd edn. Aspen, New York

Black O (2005) Conceptual foundations of antitrust. Cambridge University Press, Cambridge, p 8

Bork R (1978) The antitrust paradox. Free Press, New York, p 427

Froeb L, Kobayashi B (2001) Evidence production in adversarial vs inquisitorial regimes. Econ Lett 70:267–72

Fuchs A (2012) Characteristic aspects of competition and their consequences for the objectives of competition law – comment on stucke. In: Zimmer D (ed) The goals of competition law. Edward Elgar, Cheltenham, p 54

Greenfield L, Olsky D (2007) Treble damages: to what purpose and to what effect? Paper delivered at the workshop on cartel – comparative perspectives on practice, procedure and substance at the British Institute of International and Comparative Law, 2 February 2007

Hawk B (1998) Competition law implementation at present. In: Ehlermann CD, Laudati LL (eds), European Competition Law Annual 1997: the objectives of competition policy. Hart, Oxford p 353

Hayek F (1944) Road to serfdom. University of Chicago Press, Chicago, p 114

Joskow P (2002) Transaction cost economics, antitrust rules and remedies. J Law Econ Org 95:100

Knight F (1968) Immutable law in economics: its reality and limitations. Am Econ Rev 639–656

Kobayashi Y (1970) On competition. http://eprints.lib.hokudai.ac.jp/dspace/bitstream/2115/30639/1/2_P43-54.pdf

Korah V (1973) Book Review: *René Joliet* The rule of reason in antitrust law: American, German and common market laws in comparative perspective. Int Comp Law Q 22:188–189

López M (2002) Commission confirms its policy line in respect of horizontal agreement on energy efficiency of domestic appliances. Competition Policy Newsletter 1

Marsden P, Waller S (2009) Antitrust marathon: antitrust and the rule of law. Loyola Consum Law Rev 22:42

McGowan D (2005) Between logic and experience: error costs and United States v Microsoft Corp. Berkeley Technol Law J 20:1185
McNulty P (1968) Economic theory and the meaning of competition. Q J Econ 28:645
Meese A (2003) Price theory, competition and rule of reason. Univ Ill Law Rev 1:81
Monti G (2002) Article 81 EC and public policy. CML Rev 1065
Monti G (2007) EC competition law. Cambridge University Press, Cambridge, p 92
Moore H (1906) Paradoxes of competition. Q J Econ 20:211–230
Neven D (2006) Competition economics and antitrust in Europe. Econ Policy 741
Posner R (1976) Antitrust law: an economic perspective. University of Chicago Press, Chicago, pp 231–236
Posner R (1988) Comment: responding to Gordon Tullock. Res Law Policy Stud 2:29
Shin HS (1998) Adversarial and inquisitorial procedures in arbitration. Rand J Econ 29:378–405
Stigler G (1957) Perfect competition, historically contemplated. J Polit Econ 65:1
Stucke M (2012) What is competition. In: Zimmer D (ed) The goals of competition. Edward Elgar, Cheltenham, pp 30–31
Sunstein C (1996) Legal reasoning and political conflict. Oxford University Press, New York
Tullock G (1988) Defending the napoleonic code over the common law. Res Law Policy Stud 2:3–27
Vicker J (1995) Concepts of competition. Oxford Econ Paper 47:1, 1–23
Whish R (2008) Competition law, 6th edn. Lexis Nexis, London, pp 439–468 (Chapter 11)

Chapter 3
Antitrust Rights

3.1 Introduction

The preceding chapter reveals a peculiar drawback of the traditional modes of antitrust analysis which, as shown from a deconstructionist perspective, is that they fail to meet the requirement of *justice as inclusiveness*. In order to cure this defect, this thesis seeks to construct an alternative account termed the person-centred approach. So far, a broad overview of this approach has been given in the preceding chapter. While explaining the approach, due reference was made to the term antitrust right. It was emphasised that *antitrust right* is to be understood in the procedural context. In effect, to say that a person has antitrust right means that such person is entitled to procedural justice by being included in issues that involve or affect them. It was also stated that antitrust right does not countenance any particular normative usage of the term right as it merely means that we are bound to consider the interrelatedness of interests held by persons in any given instance.

There are two major reasons why the concept of right has been considered ideal for the person-centred exercise. First and foremost, this route accords with the procedural nature of this thesis. Secondly, it helps to situate all the theoretical bases for the person-centred approach within a single exercise—the exercise of antitrust right.

This chapter seeks to elucidate on the idea of antitrust right as used in this thesis. To flesh-out this account, this chapter is divided into three sections. Section 3.2 explores various accounts of right from which the account most suitable for this person-centred approach is chosen. In Sect. 3.3, I develop the account of antitrust right while in Sect. 3.4, I draw conclusions accordingly.

A. Al-Ameen, *Antitrust: The Person-centred Approach*,
DOI 10.1007/978-3-319-01724-2_3,

3.2 Accounts of Right

Wellman noted that our language of rights is lamentably vague and ambiguous.[1] This is because right is rather nebulous and generic term which has been used and can be used in multitudes of instances. This has led one commentator to note that "right can be used to express positions that have been worked out in accordance with normative principles, or non-normative policy instruments, or rights may be regarded as themselves constituting basic normative principles."[2] In effect, the variety of instances in which the term has been employed stirs a great degree of uncertainty when it comes to defining its purpose or contents.

In order to appreciate the context in which the term right is used here, different meanings of right will be explored. It is noteworthy that this thesis does not seek to evaluate the conflicting theories and to give an ideal meaning of right. The task rather is to ascertain and substantiate the account of right that fits the procedural agenda of this thesis.

Thus, different categories of right are hereby addressed after which the ideal account will be identified in Sect. 3.2.

3.2.1 Neutral Rights

There are theorists who imbue the concept of right with only legal contents. To them, the real usage of the term does not contain claims as to morality. In other words, they either disregard the impact of morality on the concept of right or they give it a rather insignificant room in their analysis. This group consider right to be a legal concept which is to be addressed neutrally.

Scholars who explain right through some form of neutral ideology include the likes of Raz, Waldron, Finnis and so on. For example, through his Source Thesis, Raz argues that legal right can only be established without reference to moral arguments.[3] He however contends that legal rights are legally recognised pre-existing moral rights and as such are protected interests which have legal backing. Rights are therefore merely names given to a collection of legal relations that are brought together on grounds that are not related to the moral meaning of right.[4] According to Waldron, legal rights (as a term) do not have a specific content or form. Thus, when we refer to legal right in different instances, there need not be anything that is common to the term in those instances. In a nutshell, the term legal right is more or less a homonymy.[5] Another example is Finnis' account of right. He

[1] Wellman (1995), p. 179.

[2] Halpin (1997), p. 210.

[3] Raz (1994), p. 250.

[4] Eleftheriadis (2008), p. 69.

[5] Waldron (1993), pp. 63–65.

argues that even though they may provide the conceptual apparatus through which a moral theory is expressed, rights in themselves do not constitute moral theory.[6]

3.2.2 Freedom-Based Right

Another category of theorists are those who base their idea of right on the non-consequentialist theory of freedom. There are also those who support a freedom-based account of right on the ground that there is need to protect the individual and the minority who are left out by consequentialist morals.[7] Lomasky, for instance, is of the view that right "stakes out chunks of moral turfs that others are forewarned not to trespass."[8] He also contends that rights are a kind of shorthand category for well-entrenched moral intuitions, principles, and standards whose aim is to support individualism as of paramount moral significance.[9] Also, Kantian philosophy of right provides that from the ultimate value of individual freedom comes the guiding universal principle of justice which requires that freedom of choice of each individual should co-exist with everyone's freedom in accordance with a universal law. In order for a person to possess a perfect right, there must be a corresponding perfect duty. The derived duty determines a person's moral obligation towards others as well as himself. This moral obligation originates from the causality in accordance with the law of reason (categorical imperative).

Another freedom-based account of right is Nozick's Libertarianism. He argues from the position of the "minimal state" that each person has absolute right to life and liberty, in the sense that no-one may justifiably interfere with another's life or liberty, except in cases of self-defence or legitimate punishment. Further, Nozick states that by going through certain procedures, we can come to acquire rights to property. However, the fact that we have these rights does not guarantee that they will always be respected. It is the task of the minimal state—the night-watchman state of classical liberalism—to protect us from each other and from external threat. The state is justified, thinks Nozick, only in so far as it protects people against force, fraud, and theft, and enforces contracts. Thus it exists to safeguard rights, and the state itself violates people's rights if it attempts to do any more than this.[10]

---

[6] Finnis (1980).

[7] Dworkin (1977).

[8] Lomasky (1990), p. 5.

[9] Lomasky (1990), p. 5.

[10] See generally Nozick (1974).

3.2.3 Welfare-Based Rights

To the consequentialists, a right either comes into existence or becomes enforceable where its application will lead to a specific result. For instance, utilitarian thought on right is modelled on the reasoning that right should exist where its outcome promotes the happiness of the majority even if the effect is that the interest of the minority is to be sacrificed. Within utilitarian thoughts, Halpin argues that there are different perspectives on how right interacts with aggregated pleasure.[11] He states that some utilitarian ideologies can be summed up as creating right through the objective of either maximising everyone's pleasure,[12] maximising everyone's pleasure so long as everyone gets an equal chance,[13] maximising everyone's pleasure so long as the pleasure of the worst off is maximised[14] or leaving everyone to maximise his own pleasure.[15]

The utilitarian ideology of moral rights also extends to the area of welfare economics. One of the purposes of welfare economics is to explore the impact of different policies on social welfare and to forge ways through which it can be maximised. One of the primary instruments for achieving this end is efficiency. By and large, Kaldor–Hicks and Pareto efficiencies represent the theoretical foundation for the economic analysis of rights. Regarding the role of efficiency in determining individual right, it could be inferred from Kaldor–Hicks that economic efficiency combines "a methodological individualism with a corporate substantive definition of the good".[16] Thus, while the "methodological locus of value" is the individual, the 'good' is based on the foundational principle of greatest happiness which maximises the aggregate sum of individual welfare for the society as a whole so that "each individual counts equally methodologically only, as an equal and a fungible addend in the summation of aggregate social welfare."[17]

Through its welfare orientation, the law and economics school employ the concept of right as an instrument for overcoming market failures. The pioneer work in this area is Ronald Coase's thesis on transaction cost.[18] This school of thought is modelled on two rules for assigning legal rights. The first is that based on the assumption of substantial knowledge, perfect rationality and absence of transaction cost and income effect, assigning legal entitlements in cases of two-party incompatible land uses will be neutral as to the goal of allocative efficiency. In other words, provided that exchange is available and that obstacles to exercising it are

[11] Halpin (1997), p. 251.

[12] This is the utilitarian conception formulated by Jeremy Bentham.

[13] See Dworkin (1977); Dworkin (1985), p. 359.

[14] See generally Rawls (1972). See also Daniels (1975); Halpin (1997), pp. 235–241.

[15] On Nozick as a utilitarian, see Halpin (1997), pp. 241–250.

[16] See Wright (1995), p. 161.

[17] Wright (1995), p. 161.

[18] Coase (1960), p. 1.

insignificant, rational co-operators will negotiate around inefficiencies.[19] Legal right is thus nothing more than a vessel for establishing a well-defined entitlement or negotiation point "which create a framework in which mutually advantageous bargains leading to optimal outcomes can be realized".[20]

Concerning the first rule, the real value of legal right does not rest on the initial distribution of entitlements. Put differently, the notion of right at a pre-transaction stage is worthless. Rather, its real value emanates from the unavoidable exchanges necessitated by the conflict in demand for the use of resources. This conflict, Coase argues, should be resolved by reference to which of the two conflicting uses has the greater social value. Expounding on this through the rancher-farmer analogy, Coase argues that if a rancher and farmer have different interest in a particular land—the rancher wants the land to allow the cattle to stray while the farmer wants it free from the cattle so that the crop can grow. This problem is not to be solved by reference to who had pre-existing rights but by ascertaining which of the two uses has greater value.

However, it should be noted that where the requirement of substantial knowledge, perfect rationality, and transaction cost and income effect are not met, the value of the first rule diminishes. As such, we would be unable to rely on the exchange process to overcome inefficiencies. In such instance, the second rule for assigning legal rights applies. Where the exchange process proves inadequate, the second rule requires that the court must allocate entitlements/rights efficiently from the outset. This, the court is meant to achieve by imagining what the exchange process would have been, had the assumptions under the first rule been intact. It is upon this "hypothetical Coasean market" that the court ideates a market paradigm to help it identify the efficient outcome it seeks to replicate.[21]

It is noteworthy that regardless of efforts to portray efficiency-based account of right as premised on a neutral account of legal right,[22] it would seem unduly laboured to dissociate the idea from utilitarianism,[23] and consequently from some form of morality.

Rights, under the law and economics paradigm, are primarily entitlements. Once entitlements have been assigned, the next task is to have them secured. Thus, in order to protect entitlement, Calabresi and Melamed set out a framework which explores three rules for securing rights.[24] They are property rules, liability rules and inalienability rules. Property rule protects an entitlement by enabling a right bearer to enjoin others from reducing the level of protection the entitlement affords him except he is willing to forgo it at a mutually agreed price. To protect a right through

[19] See Coleman (2003), p. 28.

[20] Coleman (2003), p. 28.

[21] Posner (2007).

[22] The law and economics school denounce the direct application of legal right in reaching an optimal level of resource deployment. See Posner (2007).

[23] Coleman (2003), ch 4.

[24] Calabresi and Melamed (1972), p. 1089. See also Epstein (1972), p. 209. See also Eleftheriadis (2008), p. 69.

liability rules means that a non-entitled party may reduce the value of the entitlement without regards to the right-holder's desires, as long as he compensates *ex post* for the reduction in value. The value of the compensation need not be the same as what the entitled party would have been willing to accept for the diminishment of his entitlement.[25] Where inalienability rule applies, transfers of any sort are prohibited.

In order to secure an assigned right in light of the Calabresi–Melamed framework, a choice has to be made between the available rules by assessing their Pareto optimality. Thus, if transaction costs are high, a property rule could be seen as likely to be inefficient. This is because transfer to more valued use requires negotiation which means that there is a potent possibility that as a result of lack of agreement, property rule may lead to entitlements being held by individuals who value them less. In a situation where transaction costs are high, Calabresi and Melamed are of the opinion that the liability rule may be better as individuals who value entitlements more than those on whom the rights are initially conferred can secure the entitlement without *ex ante* negotiations. This could be by compelling transfer to themselves and paying damages for the usurpation.

In order to forge an account of right premised on efficiency, institutions would have to choose the most appropriate of the alternatives open to them. Based on their framework, Calabresi and Melamed argue that it is the rule which conceives of right as an instrument for securing a level of well-being or utility that should be followed. This would most often require the application of liability rules.

3.2.4 Eclectic Account of Right

According to the neutral accounts, the term "right" has no fixed meaning. Moral accounts on the other hand view the concept either in terms of autonomy and control or as an instrument for securing a level of well-being or utility. Eclectic accounts give room for different interpretations of the term right. Of particular importance in this light is Coleman's account of right as it allows us to imbue the term with different meanings.

Coleman states that rights primarily entail entitlements. He states further that an adequate theory of institutional entitlement must address three different sorts of questions which are: what is the foundation of rights? What is the correct analysis of right? How might or ought a system of institutional right be enforced?

In order to answer the first question, Coleman recognises that the normative foundational bases which would normally shape our response are those which are freedom-based and those which are somewhat welfare-based. On the second question, Coleman distinguishes between the correct logical form for analysing right and correct content for right analysis. Scholars who view the question in light of the

[25] This is because the value is usually set by the relevant institution.

former are more concerned with ascertaining whether rights are or entail for example, interest, liberties or claims. Whatever we consider rights to entail, its form could be the same regardless of the foundational theory we align to. On the other hand, Coleman states that when we consider the correct way for analysing rights in light of its contents, our finding is bound to vary depending on the foundational or normative theory of right advanced. He asserts that:

> [a] theory of the content of right is a theory of their *constitutive elements*. And these elements are not constitutive of right as a matter of logical form, but rather as a matter of contingent fact. In any overall theory of institutional rights, the constitutive elements of rights are a function of the foundational theory.[26]

While the logical form of right represents the *syntax* of right, the constitutive elements represents the *semantics* of right. In Coleman's view, a proper analysis of right addresses both the syntax and semantics of rights. The relevance of these two sub-components of right analysis is that even if we disagree on what rights entail as a matter of logical form, we could still share the same opinion as to its content. However, if one is motivated by different foundational theories, their ideas as to the content of right are bound to be different. Emphasising this point, Coleman states that "different views of the purpose of institutional rights may require different theories of their content, while maintaining that certain features of rights may be necessary features of them which obtain irrespective of the range of various foundational theories."[27]

Regarding the question on the enforcement of right, Coleman states that reference need be made to institutional enforcement. At this stage, he states that "we want to know, for example, whether we ought to enforce or vindicate a particular set of claims by providing injunctive relief, tort liability and some combination of the two, or perhaps, by imposing criminal sanctions"[28]

In answering the questions as to the logical form of right, Coleman argues that rights are best understood as "conceptual markers" or "place holders", used to designate a subset of legitimate interests or liberties to be accorded special protection by law. He states that once an interest has been chosen, it enjoys a privileged status by being labelled a right or entitlement. The answer to the semantics of right rests on our application of property and inalienability rules which as part of the overall institutional theory of right, specify the meaning of right. Concerning enforcement, Coleman states that the approach we adopt might derive (though not necessarily) from the foundational theory.

In a nutshell, Coleman's account of right posits that:

> (1) All institutional rights are *necessary* conceptual markers designating certain legitimate interests or liberties as warranting a privileged status. (2) The privileged status is to be spelled out as follows: Each legitimate interest, for example, that is marked as a right is necessarily associated with, and in fact entails, some legitimate claims. In contrast, whether

---

[26] Coleman (2003), p. 34.

[27] Coleman (2003), p. 34.

[28] Coleman (2003), p. 34.

> or not a legitimate interest [which is] not marked as a right generates enforceable claims is a contingent matter. Rights however, entail legitimate claims. (3) The specific content of these claims is the function of the rule – property, liability or inalienability – applied to them. Therefore, I say that property rule and liability rule specify the content of right by generating specific legitimate claims from them. (4) The claims property and liability rules generate specify conditions of legitimate transfer. Thus, I refer to them . . . as constituting a 'transaction structure.' Though the claims given rise to by the rights within the domain of the transactions are a function of the transaction rules applied to them, (5) the choice of which rule or rules to apply depends on the foundational theory. That is, we cannot say whether a right's content should be given by a property or by a liability rule or by some combination of the two until we know what general purpose we want institutional rights to serve. (6) Finally, besides providing the basis for determining the content of rights, the foundational theory specifies the appropriate institutions for enforcing the claim these rights create. In this way, the foundation theory fuels the complete theory of institutional right. A commitment at the foundational level will suggest, though it will not strictly entail, certain views about the content and enforcement of rights. We should, therefore, expect that different institutional arrangements confer somewhat different institutional rights and suggest different mechanisms for their enforcement.[29]

3.3 Nature of Antitrust Right

Various accounts of rights have been identified in the preceding section. It now behoves that we forge a complete account of antitrust right. For our analysis of antitrust right to be truly complete, its associated elements and its defining core must be thoroughly substantiated. However, considering the barrage of theories on right, it would undoubtedly be challenging to fashion a universally acceptable understanding of antitrust right. The difficulty of the task results from the likelihood that we might end up with an array of (conflicting) antitrust expositions. Such problem can however be avoided by considering antitrust right to be nothing more than a broad procedure through which all antitrust-related claims and counterclaims can be established. Of all the accounts considered, it appears that Coleman's account of right is the closest as it merely raises the questions which trigger an implicit consideration of the different normative accounts of right. It also addresses the issue of enforcement. The associated elements and defining core of Coleman's right are hereby synthesised into the account of antitrust right. This is to be achieved by focusing on the three questions raised by Coleman which are; what is the foundation of rights? What is the correct analysis of right? How might or ought a system of institutional right be enforced?

[29] Coleman (2003), pp. 35–36.

3.3.1 *What Is/Are the Foundation(s) of Antitrust Right?*

Wellman in his thesis on right states that:

> [J]ust as a building rests on and is supported by its foundation and, ultimately, the ground on which it stands, so a legal action to claim a right, or any assertion that a legal right exists, rests on the reason or reasons that support it. Primarily, these are reasons found in judicial reasoning, legal norms and factual statements from which a court could validly conclude that some rights exist.[30]

The question about the foundation of antitrust right is synonymous to the technical and policy questions about the meaning and goal of antitrust. In chapter two, a similar question has been addressed the conclusion to which was that the definition of these relevant terms should be left broad enough to keep with the spirit of justice as inclusiveness, but at the same time confined to and addressed within the remit of economic competition. It thus should make one wonder why a similar question is asked differently. Though the questions ultimately lead to the same answer, this chapter sets in motion the operational perspective of the person-centred approach. Further, it gives us a unique avenue to consider the different usages of the term right in antitrust and to thus properly situate them within the person-centred framework. Finally, it reinforces the bottom-up nature of the overall exercise.

At this juncture therefore, the answer to the query about the foundation of antitrust right will commence with a conceptual analysis of accounts of right that has or could be potentially linked to present antitrust regimes. Particular reference will be made to Europe. This analysis is necessary so as to effectively dissociate such accounts from antitrust right.

3.3.1.i Usage of the Term Right in Europe

"Right" is not an unfamiliar term in the lexicon of EU law. Article 8(2) of the Maastricht Treaty declared that citizens of the Union shall enjoy the rights conferred by the Treaty and shall be subject to the duties imposed thereof. It has also been held that it is the duty of the national courts in each Member-state to uphold those rights.[31] However, the foundational core of European right remains unclear as the Union has continuously been evasive on the meaning of EU right. As such, scholars, in their attempt to make meaning of the term and to elucidate its foundation, have postulated differently about the basis of EU right. For instance, while some argue that right in EU law has a normative foundation[32] there are others who think that it is largely functional.[33] With regards to the former position, it is

---

[30] Wellman (1995), pp. 12–13.

[31] Case 106/77 *Amministrazione delle Finanze dello Stato v Simmenthal* [1978] ECR 629 para 16; Case C-213/89 *R v Secretary of State for Transport ex p Factortame Ltd* [1990] ECR I-2433 at para 19.

[32] Beljin (2008).

[33] Masing (1997) and von Bogdandy (2004) referred to in Beljin (2008).

expected that the specific regime indicates a legal norm necessitating such right. To support this contention, reference has been made to the Court of Justice's jurisprudence[34] whereby rights are determined by examining both the words and purpose of a provision.[35] On the flip side, those who think that EU right is based on functional motivations are of the opinion that EU rights is not so much about the interest of the individual as the grant merely mobilises the individual as an instrument for enforcing EU law.[36] In opposition to this reasoning, Beljin argues that it would be hard to substantiate a claim that EU rights are totally functionalist oriented as it does not explain why there are EU norms that grant no right at all.[37] However, grounding EU rights on functional orientation is no means inconceivable.[38]

The above expositions as to the foundation of European right should not be linked to the idea of antitrust right herein proposed. This reason for this assertion is expressed below.

3.3.1.ii The Foundation of Antitrust Right Deciphered

It has been noted that Coleman's account of right is primarily modelled on three questions—its foundation, its analytical core and its enforcement mode. In the assessment of the foundation of the term antitrust right, much effort has been put into ensuring that the term is not mistaken with the foundation of right, for example, as used in Europe. However, while this analysis helps to differentiate the concept of antitrust right, it does not go as far as identifying its real background. The task here therefore is to explain what we mean by the foundation of antitrust right by assessing different normative alternatives. The reason for considering these alternatives is to make it clear that rather than answering the question through one normative foundation or another, antitrust right is meant to keep open these different normative foundations without choosing between them ex ante.

[34] Cf. Case C-37/98 *Savas* [2000] ECR I-2927, paras 39, 46, 51ff and Joined Cases C-178/94, C-179/94, C-188/94, C-189/94, and C-190/94 *Dillenkofer and Ors v Germany* [1996] ECR I-4845, paras 34–36.

[35] Beljin (2008).

[36] "Right" in Europe is constantly linked to second-order principles such as subsidiarity and direct applicability. See Williams (2009), p. 552. Thus though *Van Gend en Loos* Case 26/62 [1963] ECR 1 signalled the birth of Union rights, its creation was as a result of an accident This is because the court was primarily concerned with whether certain provisions of the Treaty were directly applicable. In effect, it is correct to say that individual right "came into existence as a by-product of a provision's direct applicability." See Eilmansberger (2004), p. 1199 at pp. 1202–1203; von Bogdandy (2006), p. 38.

[37] There are rights based on functionalism. See Beljin (2008).

[38] For example, Case C-194/94 *CIA Security International SA v. Signalson SA and Securitel Sprl* [1996] ECR I-2201, para 48 wherein it was stated that right was granted in order to ensure the effectiveness on an EU legal act; Case C-253/00 *Muños and Superior Fruiticola* [2002] ECR I-7289, para 31 where right was granted in order to ensure fair trading and transparency of market in the Union.

Without much ado, it should be reiterated that term "antitrust right" herein introduced is a *sui generis* right, Hence, considering that the term antitrust right is deployed for the specific purpose of developing a comprehensive framework for the person-centred approach which invariably requires that different interests are accommodated, the question about the foundation of antitrust right cannot be set in advance, as a firm decision in one way or another might prejudice the interest of some.

To say that antitrust right is a *sui generis* right implies that the term has no strict link with any identified basis of right. To substantiate this assertion, I analyse antitrust right in light of foundations of legal rights has identified by Wellman.[39] First, he stated that legal rights can be grounded on legislation.[40] In this case, statutes explicitly establish a right and implicitly ground the complex Hohfeldian positions that constitute that right.[41] Second, the legal grounds of a right could consist of several laws that have established the Hohfeldian elements. A third way is where a legal right is derived from some prior right.[42]

The proposed antitrust right, being a *sui generis* concept, does not result from legislation so the first of the three possibilities does not apply. The question is whether it can be said that our proposed antitrust right is founded on several laws that align with Hohfeldian positions. If antitrust right is seen as constituting "several antitrust laws", it would amount to nothing more than a loose phrase for antitrust provisions such as Article 101 and 102 TFEU. A clear example of where the word right is used loosely is under consumer protection law. For instance, in Europe, though the original Treaty made no mention of consumer protection,[43] it soon became obvious that "consumer protection right" is simply an umbrella phrase for a couple of rights such as the right to protection against hazards to health and safety; the right to protection against damage to economic interests; the right to access to advice, help and redress; the right to information and education; the right to be consulted in the framing of decisions affecting the consumer's interests and so on.[44]

Based on this analogy, it should be noted that the idea of antitrust right should not be represented as merely reflecting different antitrust provisions. In fact, even though the term antitrust right is a loose term with no intrinsic legal meaning, it has a far greater effect than merely representing the different laws because, through the questions that it raises, it enables us to address different normative contents of antitrust by dealing with the substantive, procedural, theoretical, practical, and enforcement aspect of antitrust.

---

[39] Wellman (1995), p. 25.

[40] MacCormick (1977), p. 206.

[41] Wellman (1995), p. 25.

[42] Wellman (1995), p. 25.

[43] See Geddes (1995), p. 5.

[44] Geddes (1995), p. 5.

It is equally important that the concept of antitrust right is clearly distinguished from legal rights that are said to derive from prior rights. To say that a legal right derives from prior rights, the grounding right must be both temporarily and logically prior to the right it establishes. Wellman states that the grounding right must have been recognised in the law and it must somehow justify the inference to the new right derived from it.[45] Prior legal right can ground a derived right in two ways; one way is by showing that the derived right is a more specific form of the prior right on which it is grounded while the other is to ground a right on some prior right as a matter of necessity.

There is the danger that the idea of antitrust right might at some point be linked with present usage of right in specific jurisdictions such that antitrust right is considered to be a derivative of some underlying rights. This is quite likely because the term "right" is hardly novel within the jurisprudence of any legal regime. In Europe for instance, no attempt should be made to infer or ground antitrust right on the usage of the term right in *Courage v Crehan*[46] and *Manfredi*.[47] In *Courage*, the Court of Justice held that the Union's law is intended to give rise to right which becomes part of individuals' legal asset. The Court iterated further the prominence of European legal order and affirmed that the order has created rights and imposed duties on individuals. These rights, it was held, are not limited to instances where it is expressly granted by the Treaty. It also exists by virtue of obligations which the Treaty imposes in a clearly defined manner. Also in *Manfredi*,[48] the Court stated that following from the need to protect individual rights, any individual can claim compensation for the harm suffered where there is a causal relationship between the harm and an agreement or practice prohibited under Article 101 TFEU.

It would be wrong to strictly ground antitrust right on the usage of right as expressed in the above cases because the usage in these context are rather narrow, as such, they is unable to reflect the whole components of antitrust right. Moreover, it is dangerous to place the theory of antitrust right on such pre-existing right because it could be susceptible to any weakness present in such pre-existing right. For example, in Europe, *Courage* was able to substantiate a right from a competition law obligation by stating that right would be granted "once the conditions for the application of [Article 101(1) TFEU] are met and so long as the agreement concerned does not justify the grant of an exemption under [Article 101(3) TFEU] of the Treaty."[49] Following from the Treaty provisions on competition law, the Court of Justice was then able to derive a right through the obligation imposed on the institution in Article 3(1)(g) EC. It was said in particular that according to Article 3(1)(g) EC, Article 81 (now Article 101) of the Treaty constitutes a fundamental provision which is essential for the accomplishment of

[45] Wellman (1995), p. 25.

[46] Case C-453/99, [2001] ECR 1-6297.

[47] C-295/04 to C-298/04 *Manfredi v Lloyd Adriatico Assuricazione* [2006] ECR 1-6619.

[48] C-295/04 to C-298/04 *Manfredi v Lloyd Adriatico Assuricazione* [2006] ECR 1-6619.

[49] See para 22 of *Courage*.

the tasks entrusted to the Community [Union] and, in particular, for the functioning of the internal market. It is the importance of this provision, the Court emphasised, that "led the framers of the Treaty to provide expressly, in Article 85(2) [Article 101 (2) TFEU] . . . that any agreements or decisions prohibited pursuant to that article are to be automatically void."[50]

The problem at present however is that it is very debatable whether the competition law right which the Court had ostensibly linked to Article 3(1)(g) EC still exist considering that the TFEU has abolished this provisions and has brought in numerous changes which impact greatly on the institutions and functioning of the EU.[51] Thus, it might not be advisable to simply predicate antitrust right on such things as Treaty provisions and legislative intent especially where such underlying right is weak and could, as such, crumble at the slightest scrutiny. This is because the very foundation, which is built on layers and layers of assumptions, might leave us with an antitrust right that is vague, suggestive and haphazard.

So far, it has been shown that antitrust right should not be based on any of the three ways of creating legal rights as identified by Wellman. Rather, it is contended that to identify the foundation of antitrust right, it is more suitable to refer to jurisprudential expositions. It is therefore imperative at this juncture that we attempt to identify the ideal jurisprudential foundation for antitrust right. As it would be shown in paragraphs below, the ideal jurisprudential foundation for antitrust right is the capability approach as it enables us to effectively use the concept of antitrust right to conduct a comprehensive analysis of the person-centred approach whilst also maintaining the strictly procedural form. It does this by helping us maintain the neutrality required for building a framework that could potentially accommodate and (at least, occasionally) vindicate different interests.

To justify the reference to capability approach as the foundation of antitrust right, one has to consider the alternative normative bases which are then to be evaluated against each other.

A common underlying point should be noted—that is, as stated by Coleman, what is considered to be the foundation of right is shaped by the perceiver's inclination either towards freedom or welfare. This means that the different normative points that may exist would be based on either one or both ideals. The way one associates the idea of antitrust right to either of these ideals is of great importance as it has the tendency to affect our idea and definition of even germane terms such as competition itself. Where it aligns to one foundation at the expense of others, its definition of competition will be effectively skewed to that foundation, meaning that the definition of antitrust right would be exclusive to that foundation and can thus be pre-determined through doctrines deriving from such foundation. This is the more reason why the person-centred approach requires that much care is exercised

---

[50] See para 22 of *Courage*.

[51] See e.g. Riley (2007). Contra Lord Leach of Fairford in European Union Committee and House of Lords (2008), p. 218, para 9.15.

to ensure that the ideal jurisprudential foundation does have a normative undertone which would invariably narrow the interpretation of antitrust right.

Conclusively therefore, in light of the pure procedural nature of the exercise, the question about the foundation of antitrust right would have to be left unspecified.

3.3.2 How Should Antitrust Right Be Analysed?

Given that the conclusion in the preceding part is that the foundation of antitrust right is to be left unspecified, it is important to consider how the conceptual analysis will proceed. This leads us to the question of how antitrust right is to be analysed. It would be shown here that the role of the person-centred approach is merely to provide a platform for the conceptual normative analysis which might be conducted by interested parties. In other words, the way to analyse antitrust right is by accommodating the different normative analysis of antitrust right. I also take time in this part to dissociate manner in which person-centred account seeks to achieve inclusiveness from other transcendental accounts which claim to combine different normative accounts of right.

As it has been reiterated in this thesis, specific antitrust theories and norms are undergirded by their own individual foundations which ultimately determine the interests that they choose. For instance, efficiency proponents would argue that antitrust subjects are better-off with an efficiency-based antitrust regime. It is this inclination towards efficiency that perhaps led some scholars to challenge the application of Article 101(3) in some cases as they considered that since the provision was either redundant or aimed at something else other than efficiency, it fails to withstand critical analysis. This is because, as they argue, an agreement would either restrict economic welfare, improve it or would have no effect on it.[52] In the same vein, if ordoliberalism is applied in establishing the interests of antitrust subjects, it is needless to emphasise that there will be categorical preference for freedom as the ideal foundation for antitrust analysis. For example, staunch ordoliberal theorists are not pleased with the continued reference to efficiency in Article 101(1) and (3) analysis since freedom should not be compromised, not even for productive efficiency gains.[53]

With regards to the central position in this thesis (which is that plural interests should be vindicated), the appropriate foundation of antitrust right is that which covers the wide range of interests and consequences that could truly enhance the position of antitrust subjects. This requires that the foundation of antitrust be broad enough. Thus, as stated above and as would be substantiated later,[54] the capability approach could serve as an ideal framework for ascertaining the foundation of

[52] Nicolaides (2005), pp. 123–124.

[53] Moschel (1989), p. 150.

[54] See Chap. 4 below.

antitrust right in specific cases as it provides antitrust regimes with the requisite platform upon which they could truly reflect the diverging interests of antitrust subjects.

Using Europe as example, it has been shown that the idea of antitrust right should be dissociated from the pre-existing usage of right in European jurisprudence. Coleman's account of right allows us to define antitrust right broadly. It however does not, by itself explain antitrust right. Thus, working through the flexibility of Coleman's syntax and the semantics of right, the Capability approach will be applied as it sits well with the concept of antitrust right given that they both accommodate plurality of interests. At this juncture, it is necessary to address the properties of antitrust right—if the term is to be used in exploring plural interests, does it mean antitrust right can be wielded solely as a sword or as a shield? Does it mean that antitrust right is a convenient term devoid of legal content and as such cannot ground an action or serve as a defence on its own right? These issues will be addressed as I detail the syntax of antitrust right.

3.3.2.i Syntax of Antitrust Right

The syntax of right is simply the logical form of right. A theory of the logical form of right seeks to specify the necessary features or properties of rights. As a matter of necessity, all institutional rights possess peculiar features.[55] Hohfeld sought to analyse legal rights by identifying the likely features that they could be comprised of. In his analysis, Hohfeld was of the opinion that its basic components, that is, "right" and "duty" have often been misused. He attempted thus to explicitly analyse legal right by disambiguating these components. He did this by presenting four kinds of right and four kinds of duty in an exact logical structure[56]—Hohfeld stated that right is a vague term which, in ordinary legal use, indiscriminately covers such things as claim-right, privilege, power and immunity. Opposite to generic usage of right is duty. When duty is put into more specific form, we have duty, no-duty, liability and disability. In substantiating the form of legal rights, specific form of rights bring about jural correlatives; Right, privilege, duty and no-duty are interrelated. As such, where x has a claim-right against y, then y would have a correlative duty to x. Also, if x has the privilege to do p, it means that x has no duty not to do p. Similarly, power, immunity, disability and liability are logically interrelated so that if x has a power against y, it is to be understood as y being under a liability to x in the matter. If y has no such liability, then y is immune to the relevant exercise of power. If y has such immunity, then x has a disability of exercising the power against y.

As a result of the different forms in which legal right could appear, a query that we might have to grapple with concerning the syntax of right is how we are to determine what exactly makes them all "rights". Here, there are primarily two

[55] Coleman (2003), p. 34.

[56] See generally Hohfeld (1917), pp. 710–770. See also Gorman (2003), p. 88.

schools of thought—the benefit or interest theory of right and the choice or will theory. Another relevant one is the theory of right as sanction.[57] It has been said that the difference between the two is best explained by returning to the issue of "correlativity".[58] Simply put, should a claim-right implicate a duty and vice versa? On the benefit theory, Raz, for instance, states that one has a right (1) if he is an intended beneficiary and; (2) if that person's interest is sufficient reason for holding another to be under a duty.[59] Regarding the choice theory of right, H.L.A Hart is very prominent. According to Hart, the essential feature of a duty which yields a right is that the person to whom the duty is owed is able to control the performance of that duty.[60] As such, he argues that it is inappropriate to speak of a right correlating with a legal duty where the beneficiary of the duty can exercise no choice over its performance. Finally, opinion of jurisprudents such as Ross, Stoljar, Feinberg and Austin on right can be summed up as meaning that claims can only be converted to right by virtue of such claim being linked to sanctions.[61] In the context of legal right, this means that the presence of a sanction upholding and enforcing a claim is essential to that claim's being a right. In the context of moral right, it is believed that moral claim amounts to moral right only if that claim ought to be upheld by sanction.[62]

If the logic of legal right is to be considered in the context of our analysis of antitrust right, we might be tempted to undertake a thorough exercise into the strength of antitrust right; it might trigger our curiosity in ascertaining whether antitrust right truly brings about a right in terms of the benefit theory or more specifically, according to Raz's account. Antitrust right can also be checked against Hart's choice or will theory. For example, do antitrust subjects have a choice as to whether hardcore cartel violation should be punished or accepted in specific instances? If they have no power of choice, can it really be said that there could be anything like antitrust right in the context of Hart's theory?

In the context of right as a derivative of a sanction, one might assess if antitrust right truly falls within the syntax of right by analysing its foundation and application. Thus, where we seek to identify the syntax of antitrust right through the sanction theory, it would be hard or impossible to identify antitrust right particularly when addressing antitrust issues which allows for the granting of for instance, exemptions as a result of efficiency benefits. This is because in such cases, the defendant may not be sanctioned for their restrictive or (potentially) abusive behaviour. Failure to sanction weakens any claim of right under the sanction theory.

Based on its procedural nature, the idea of antitrust right that is proposed in this thesis requires that we desist from subjective theoretical exposition of the syntax of

[57] See Jones (1994), p. 39.

[58] Jones (1994), p. 26.

[59] Raz (1986), p. 166.

[60] Hart (1982).

[61] Jones (1994), p. 39.

[62] Jones (1994), p. 39.

antitrust right. Rather, antitrust right should simply be understood as a "conceptual marker". In putting forward their proposition on right, Coleman and Kraus[63] attempted to build the entitlement model in consonance with the Hohfeld's scheme. They argue that rights are merely preliminary and incomplete markers for the allocation and protection of resources. Following from their explanation that rights are merely "conceptual markers" or "place holders", they state further that "as a matter of logic or necessity, legal rights are neither protected domains of autonomy nor levels of protected welfare." Thus, "[t]heir content is a contingent matter depending on the foundational theory". As such, legal rights remain neutral while the chosen foundation theory in individual cases provides the required normative basis.[64] In effect, "[w]hen interests or liberties are marked as rights, it is only as if an asterisk has been placed on them. The right that secures them is as yet (analytically) content-free."

If this Coleman's account is applied in ascertaining the syntax of antitrust right, the result is that the analysis of the syntax of right would be less convoluted. It would also respect the plurality and flexibility required for the enterprise as the syntax in every particular case will be determined by what is considered to be the particular theoretical foundation of antitrust right in specific instances. Antitrust right is thus not a concept to be wielded in any practical sense.

3.3.2.ii Semantics of Antitrust Right

It has been stated that antitrust right is analytically content free. However, when claims and counter-claims are raised by interested parties, their usage of right would have to be imbued with contents. The issue about the semantics of antitrust right is therefore about how these normative accounts of right figure within antitrust right.

Where claims and counter-claims are made, right arguments often take the form of either or a combination of property rules, liability rules and inalienability rules. There is the tendency to imbue right with meanings that reflect our ideological stance. For instance, some scholars address the semantics of right from a utilitarian perspective. In this case, the meaning of antitrust right may be predicated on the framework that, for example internalises the net inefficiencies in the market.[65] Also, right claims and counter-claims could be made from a classical liberal perspective. For instance, White is of the opinion that antitrust right does not figure in the semantics of right.[66] Basing his arguments on Kantian idea of right, he emphasises the relevance of freedom and the correlative nature of rights and duties. He thus argues that antitrust is a violation of property rights with no parallel

[63] Coleman and Kraus (1986), p. 1335.

[64] Coleman (2003), p. 18.

[65] Kaplow and Shapiro (2007), p. 94. Kaplow (2012), pp. 3–26.

[66] See generally White (2007), pp. 161–190.

justification. White's conclusion in effect is that antitrust laws are baseless as there is no initial violation of property right which they can be said to protect. Bolstering his arguments with reference to Kant's political theory, White argues that law is only meant to enforce citizens' clearly defined rights against each other rather than to promote a consequentialist end such as welfare maximisation. He argues that Kantian philosophy presupposes freedom which naturally requires a corresponding duty on individuals, not only to perfect their own freedom, but also to avoid injuring the freedom of others. This order is to be sustained through the categorical imperatives which ground either perfect or imperfect duties. While perfect duties will ground legal responsibilities and thus create corresponding rights, imperfect duties are those that, even though may be desirable, cannot impose legal responsibilities. Example is the duty of beneficence. White's claim is that competition law provisions require companies to be beneficent which thus mean that antitrust duties are imperfect and as such could not give rise to legal rights. In conclusive term, he asserts that antitrust laws are not firmly grounded at least in the light of Kantian right.[67]

Similarly, one could infer from the libertarian position held by Armentano that antitrust right has no room in the semantics of right. He is of the view that activities such as price discrimination, tying and price-fixing do not violate any property right in the ordinary use of the term, "yet their regulation or prohibition by the state violates the property rights of the market participants." He argues further thus that "[f]rom a strict libertarian or natural right position, antitrust laws are inherently unjust." A liberal account that accords with antitrust right is the theory of economic freedom. Here, the right is against the distortion of the competitive process which is to be protected through property rules.

As it can be inferred from Coleman, one thing that must be acknowledged is that whether we choose to see antitrust through either efficiency or the classical ideas deriving from Kant, libertarianism or economic freedom, our ideological preferences cannot fully reflect what it means to have antitrust right. It should be noted that whatever position we choose to follow is merely a contestable normative assertion connecting a particular normative theory to the idea of antitrust right. As such, when anyone of these theories is applied to the antitrust exercise, it would be merely normative and not analytic of antitrust right. These theories are, at best, supportable by substantive argument rather than taking the form of "linguistic convention"[68] of the very idea of antitrust right.

Based on the imperfections of substantiating the semantic of right strictly through liability, property or inalienability rule etc, it becomes clear that none of the individual semantic interpretations can give a complete account of what it means to have antitrust right. In essence, a true analysis of the semantic of antitrust right might require a platform that accommodates all the rules.

[67] Armentano (1985), p. 927. See generally, Armentano (2007).
[68] Coleman (2003), p. 38.

In light of the overall idea of inclusiveness, we might think that the right option is to combine the different normative interpretations of these rights. If one merely wants to combine the incidence of liability rule and property rule, we might for instance want to ascertain the semantics of antitrust right through a flexible account of either property rule or liability rule. A flexible account of liability rule that comes to mind is the theory of indirect utilitarianism. This theory, it has been said, holds out the best prospect for reconciling welfare rights and liberal rights.[69] Indirect utilitarianism rests upon the idea that institutions are often more successful in promoting utility by pursuing secondary principles formulated in non-utilitarian terms as opposed to attempting the direct pursuit of utility itself.[70] The problem with this approach though is that it is difficult to conceive its steady application in competition law. Except for instances where there is likely to be a convergence of opinion and outcome (for example, hardcore cartel infringements) regardless of the meaning imbued into antitrust right, there could hardly be a complimentary outcome in the more complicated areas. Jones was sceptical about the rule as he doubted whether utilitarianism, even in an indirect form, would always deliver and respect those rights which we believe ought to be delivered and respected. He thereafter asserts that "[i]n any goal-based theory, no matter how sophisticated, values and institutions will be recognised and upheld only to the extent that they promote the favoured goal of the theory. It is hard therefore to entirely eradicate the fear that, at some point, [liberal] rights will be the sacrificial victim of utility [based rights]."[71]

What is truly needed in order to ascertain the semantic of antitrust right is an account that, at the pre-violation stage makes no obvious choice between liability rule and property rule. Such account, by and large, ensures the plurality necessary for the person-centred approach. For an ideal account of the semantic of right, Coleman's position should be adequate. To Coleman, the task concerning the semantics of right is about the content of right. To re-iterate, he states that the specific content of legitimate claims that derive from rights is the function of the rule—property, liability or inalienability—applied to them. In other words, he argues that property rule and liability rule specify the content of right by generating specific legitimate claims from them and as such, the claims property and liability rules generate specify conditions of legitimate transfer.

Further, it is necessary to specify more concretely the content of antitrust right. Prior to specifying the content and meaning of antitrust right, the only thing that could be firmly stated is that entitled persons have legitimate claims, for instance, against abuse of dominance or to exploit their dominance. What is unknown however is the precise nature of the claim. In order to move beyond conceptually marking a claim as a right, the rules for generating particular and fully specified legitimate claims from rights (through the application of property, liability and

[69] Jones (1994), p. 59.

[70] Jones (1994), p. 59.

[71] Jones (1994), p. 61.

inalienability rules) need to be specified. The capability approach allows interested parties to move beyond the conceptual marker as they are allowed to generate particular contents for those rights from their own individual normative standpoint which might be reflected in different ways (i.e. through the general provisions, exceptions, exemptions etc).

Because of the peculiarity of antitrust, the specific description of claims could boil down to hypothetical transfers amongst antitrust subjects. For instance, we might have to consider transfers between consumers and suppliers—should the consumer be granted a right or should the supplier be held to be under no duty? The specific claims that are given rise to by antitrust rights are to be derived from norms or rules governing the term of legitimate transfer of rights and duties. These norms which are influenced by either efficiency thought, economic freedom etc, consequently find their way into the capability approach. By accommodating different norms, capability approach can be termed as the person-centred antitrust regime's transaction framework. In other words, the capability approach is the framework which contains normative claims of antitrust subjects.

This conclusion is in line with Coleman's position. He said that by generating claims entailed by right ownership, property, liability and inalienability rules (as well as a combination of them) specify the content of rights over a domain of transfer.[72]

The semantics of antitrust right depends on the scope and theoretical options within the capability framework as well as the practicality of those options. It is the practical aspect (that is, the fine line between what is desirable and what is feasible) that implicates the decisional frameworks and the enforcement priorities into the semantics of antitrust right.

3.4 Enforcing Antitrust Right

Having noted through the analysis of the syntax and semantics of antitrust right that it is a bare concept that allows us to carry out the person-centred analysis, the simple conclusion that could be drawn is that antitrust right is akin to antitrust as a field, the only difference being that it affords us the route for a fresh approach. Thus, when we talk of enforcing antitrust right, it means nothing more than enforcing antitrust violations—once a specific antitrust issue has been assessed (in light of the framework for ascertaining the foundation of right as well as for identifying the syntax and semantics of right) and a conclusion has been reached or there exists a prima facie case to suggest the presence of a violation, we automatically move to the enforcement stage. The phrase "enforcement of antitrust right" simply refers to the enforcement of (alleged) antitrust violations either through private or public enforcement or both.

[72] Coleman (2003), p. 37.

That enforcement is important for antitrust as a field (and in this context, antitrust right) should go without saying. What is the essence of a right that cannot be enforced? What can we make of antitrust right without a thorough elucidation of its enforcement? A firm account of antitrust right with no corresponding position on enforcement, metaphorically speaking, renders antitrust a clawless paper tiger. Considering that it is settled that any respectable antitrust regime should have a firm position on enforcement, the tricky task will be to ascertain the form which the enforcement should take. As it must have been observed above, the form of enforcing institutional rights is likely to follow from the foundational theory. It is thus the foundational theory that specifies the appropriate institutions for enforcing the claim these rights create and by so doing, the foundational theory fuels the complete theory of institutional right. Coleman opined thus that a commitment at the foundational level will suggest certain views about the content and enforcement of rights. He however acknowledges that the enforcement modality might not strictly entail the foundational theory.

To enforce antitrust right, it is required that, first, the enforcement process must be unclogged from practical and legal hurdles. Secondly, enforcement must accommodate plural interest en route enhancing the position of antitrust subjects.

Taking European framework as the institution of reference, one could observe that great efforts have been and are still being undertaken in order to meet the first requirement at both public and private levels. Perhaps, the value of an unclogged enforcement process to the idea of antitrust right will be better understood through a brief exposition of the developmental process (at both public and private level) in Europe.

Concerning legal hurdles, a clear example could be made of public enforcement. So as to stamp out anti-competitive practices, the Commission sought to oversee the enforcement of competition law Europe-wide through Regulation 17/62.[73] Though the Commission had steadily improved on its enforcement over the years, its activities were still generally regarded as inadequate particularly when one considers the enormity of the market. For instance, to relieve itself of the heavy workload, the Commission, in its Article 101 enforcement, issued "comfort letters" for good 40 years and did an average of mere four formal exemptions per year since 1979.[74] The problem in enforcement at that time was as a result of legal hurdles which limited enforcement initiative to the Commission particularly as regards the present Article 101(3) TFEU. Sensing the need to improve on the task of antitrust enforcement, the Commission identified the major structural deficiencies in its system and then came up with a functional structure called Modernisation.[75] The reform decentralised the enforcement of the Community's competition law so that

[73] This would have been legitimate at the time where national hegemony was more prevalent. The idea of centralisation worked at the time because there were just six members and because the members perceived the need to create a competition culture.

[74] Jones (1999).

[75] Regulation 1/2003 OJ [2003] L 1/1, [2003] 4 *CMLR* 551.

national competition authorities could have a fair share of enforcement responsibilities.

Regarding practical hurdles, the private aspect of European antitrust enforcement illustrates the point. As far back as 1961, a legal base for private actions could be inferred as European Parliament unequivocally expressed its view on the value of private actions and the role it could play in ensuring that the aims of competition rules are met.[76] The legality of private actions in competition law was even further strengthened by the decisions in *Courage* and *Manfredi*. This decision notwithstanding, the study revealed that there was "total underdevelopment"[77] with regards to the institution of private actions by private parties. It was observed by the Commission that the poor state of private antitrust enforcement is traceable to: the rarity of collective actions; the difficulty of establishing fault; the difficulty of discharging a high standard of proof; limited power of courts to order presentation of documents; lack of binding effect of decisions of competition authorities and national courts; the complexities involved in quantifying damages; the problem of passing-on defence and indirect purchaser claims; and the meagre amount of damages granted. In order to reduce these practical problems, the Commission has proposed a White Paper on damages action.[78]

Till this point, it does appear that Europe might meet the primary condition for enforcement if it is to adopt the idea of antitrust right proposed in this thesis. It is however left to be seen whether the Union's antitrust enforcement can meet the core aim of the person-centred approach, that is, to give due consideration to the interests of antitrust subjects whilst striving to meet institutional objectives.

While one can easily identify with the requirement that antitrust enforcement regimes should unclog their mechanisms of practical regimes, it is less clear how the second requirement (that enforcement activities should respect plurality of interests) can be achieved. This is because we are more likely to identify ideal enforcement objectives through our subjective inclinations. With regards to the ultimate requirement of broadness deriving from the person-centred approach, we could assess responses deriving from the debate about the best enforcement modality in a particular case. We might for instance disagree on the appropriate institutional objective—is it deterrence or efficiency?[79] Concerning private actions, we

[76] See the Deringer Report for the European Parliament. Also, in 1966, the Commission published a specific study examining the remedies in national laws for damage caused by infringement of competition rules see La Reparation des Consequences Dommageable d'une Violation des Article 85 et 86 du traite Instituant a CEE, Series Concurrence No. 1 (Brussels, 1966) referred to in XIIIth Report on Competition Policy 1983.

[77] See study on the conditions of claims for damages in case of infringement of EC antitrust rules, available on the Commission's website at: http://europa.eu.int/comm/competition/antitrust/others/private_enforcement/index_en.html.

[78] White Paper (2008). There has however been little or no development in this respect since White Paper was published.

[79] See Becker (1968), p. 169; Landes (1983), p. 652 contra Wils (2008), p. 56. For a middle-way position see Calvino (2007), p. 320.

might be saddled with the task of ascertaining whether the positions of antitrust subjects are better enhanced where parties are taken as mere instruments for attaining institutional goals or whether the positions of antitrust subjects are better enhanced where private claims are vindicated for their own sake (for instance, as a matter of corrective justice).[80] Overall, our idea of the appropriate enforcement modality seems to derive from our idiosyncratic idea of what is good or right.

We could also assess subjective responses to the issue concerning the relationship between public and private enforcement. Lawyers and economists debate whether: public enforcement is enough; whether private actions should be discouraged;[81] whether private action can substitute public enforcement; or whether it complements public enforcement.[82] So far, the debates about the appropriate enforcement institutions have been undertaken on the basis of their optimality. The various interpretations we have are subjective because they define "optimality" through their own lens. Even where we proceed from the same definition of optimality, controversies still arise as to what enforcement modality or combination of modalities is optimal.[83] The question is, should our discourse be streamlined to optimality?

Another issue upon which we can assess subjective responses is about the appropriate mechanisms and instruments for enforcing antitrust. The propriety of applying particular enforcement tool or a combination of them has been hotly contested.[84] In private antitrust, the nature and value of class actions has been debated.[85]—for instance, it has been considered whether the easing of the requirement of fault will enhance or endanger the position of antitrust subjects; whether the manipulation of burden and standard of proof will be helpful or whether it is more likely to be counter-productive; if the value of discovery process to the enforcement enterprise can be ascertained etc. One thing that is common to all these debates is that the instruments and mechanisms are continuously debated and assessed on how effective they are, whereby "effectiveness" is defined subjectively. The question here as well is whether we should only assess these issues on the account of their effectiveness.

It can be argued that the present modes of analysing antitrust enforcement do not really take account of plurality—the debates about the appropriate enforcement modality, the debates that address the relationship between public and private enforcement on the platform of optimality, and the debates about the appropriateness/effectiveness of enforcement tools fail to pay attention to the need to accommodate plural interests. It is therefore imperative that a fresh insight into addressing enforcement queries which takes account of the issue of plurality is introduced. It is

[80] See e.g. Al-Ameen (2009), pp. 327–346.

[81] See e.g. Wils (2003), p. 473; McAfee and Vakkur (2004), p. 1; Boumal and Ordover (1985) p. 247.

[82] McAfee et al. (2008), pp. 625–71.

[83] Al-Ameen (2010), pp. 81–102.

[84] For example we assess whether criminalisation is appropriate see Wils (2007).

[85] Congedo and Messina (2009), pp. 163–189.

hoped that substantial debates would arise on how we could best attain *incremental enforcement* of antitrust right.

3.5 Conclusion

It is contended in this chapter that since the person-centred approach takes a bottom-up perspective to antitrust, it will be ideal to develop the account through the idea of right. Coleman's account of right was chosen as it fits with the pure procedural agenda of this thesis. Importantly, it helps to illuminate the person-centred approach through the eyes of antitrust subjects. The account of antitrust right, through Coleman's questions, also affords us the room to give a holistic exposition of antitrust. Above all, the account of antitrust right helps us to situate and develop the major components of the person-centred approach.

References

Al-Ameen A (2009) Restitutionary remedy in competition law: a bull in a China shop? World Competition Law Econ Rev 32:327–346

Al-Ameen A (2010) Antitrust fines: seeking justice. Competition Law Rev 7:81–102

Armentano D (1985) Efficiency, liberty and antitrust policy. CATO J 4:927

Armentano D (2007) Antitrust: a case for repeal, 3rd edn. Ludwig Von Mises Institute, Alabama

Becker G (1968) Crime and punishment: an economic approach. J Polit Eco 76:169

Beljin S (2008) Right in EU law. In: Prechal S, van Roermund B (eds) The coherence of EU law: the search for unity in divergent concepts. Oxford University Press, Oxford (Chapter 5)

Boumal W, Ordover J (1985) Use of antitrust to subvert competition. J Law Econ 28:247

Calabresi G, Melamed D (1972) Property rules, liability rules and inalienability: one view of the Cathedral. Harv Law Rev 85:1089

Calvino N (2007) Deterrent effect and proportionality of fines. In: Ehlermann CD, Atanasiu I (eds) European competition law annual: enforcement of prohibition of cartels. Hart, Oxford, p 320

Coase R (1960) The problem of social cost. J Law Econ 3:1

Coleman J (2003) Market morals and law. Oxford University Press, New York, p 28

Coleman J, Kraus J (1986) Rethinking the theory of legal rights. Yale Law J 95:1335

Congedo P, Messina M (2009) European 'class' action: British and Italian points of view in evolving scenarios. Eur Dir Priv 1:163–189

Daniels N (1975) Reading Rawls. Blackwell, Oxford

Dworkin R (1977) Taking right seriously. Duckworth, London

Dworkin R (1985) A matter of principle. Clarendon, Oxford, p 359

Eilmansberger T (2004) The relationship between rights and remedies in EC law: in search of the missing link. Common Mark Law Rev 41:1199

Eleftheriadis P (2008) Legal rights. Oxford University Press, New York, p 69

Epstein R (1972) A clear view of the Cathedral: the dominance of property rules. Yale Law Rev J 106:209

European Union Committee, House of Lords (2008) The Lisbon Treaty: an impact assessment 10th Report of Session 2007–08, vol 1. Stationary House Limited, London, p 218

Finnis J (1980) Natural law and natural rights. Clarendon, Oxford

Geddes A (1995) Protection of individual rights under EC law. Butterworth, London, p 5

Gorman J (2003) Right and reason: an introduction to the philosophy of rights. Acumen, Chesham, p 88
Halpin A (1997) Rights and law analysis & theory. Hart, Oxford, p 210
Hart HLA (1982) Essays on Bentham: studies in jurisprudence and political theory. Clarendon, Oxford
Hohfeld W (1917) Fundamental legal conceptions as applied in judicial reasoning. Yale Law J 26:710–770
Jones P (1994) Rights. MacMillan, Hampshire, p 39
Jones C (1999) Private enforcement of antitrust law in the EU, UK and USA. Oxford University Press, New York
Kaplow L (2012) On the choice of welfare standard in competition law. In: Zimmer D (ed) Goals of competition law. Edward Elgar, Cheltenham, pp 3–26
Kaplow L, Shapiro C (2007) Antitrust NBER working paper No. 12867, p. 94
Landes W (1983) Optimal sanctions for antitrust violations. Univ Chicago Law Rev 50:652
Lomasky L (1990) Persons right and the moral community. Oxford University Press, New York
MacCormick N (1977) Rights in legislation. In: Hacker P, Raz J (eds) Law, morality and society: essays in honour of H.L.A. Hart. Oxford University Press, Oxford, p 206
Masing J (1997) Die Mobilisierung des Bürgers für die Durchsetzung des Rechts. Duncker & Humblot, Berlin
McAfee P, Vakkur N (2004) The strategic abuse of antitrust laws. J Strategic Manage Educ 1:3
McAfee P, Mialon H, Mialon S (2008) Private v public antitrust enforcement: a strategic analysis. J Public Econ 92:625–71
Moschel W (1989) Competition policy from an Ordo point of view. In: Peacock A, Willgerodt H (eds) German neo-liberals and the social market economics. Macmillan, London, p 150
Nicolaides P (2005) The balancing myth: the economics of article 81 (1) and (3). Legal Issues Econ Integr 32:123–124
Nozick R (1974) Anarchy, State, and Utopia. Basil Blackwell, Oxford
Posner R (2007) Economic analysis of law, 7th edn. Aspen, New York
Rawls J (1972) A theory of justice. Oxford University Press, Oxford
Raz J (1986) The morality of freedom. Clarendon, Oxford, p 166
Raz J (1994) Ethics in the public domain. Clarendon, Oxford, p 250
Riley A (2007) The EU reform treaty and the competition protocol: undermining EC competition law. Centre for European Policy Study Brief 142
von Bogdandy A (2004) In: Grabitz E, Hilf M (eds) Recht der EU. München, Beck
von Bogdandy A (2006) Constitutional principles. In: von Bogdandy A, Bast J (eds) Principles of European constitutional law. Hart, Oxford, p 38
Waldron J (1993) A right to do wrong. In: Waldron J (ed) Liberal rights. Cambridge University Press, Cambridge, pp 63–65
Wellman C (1995) Real right's. Oxford University Press, New York, p 179
White M (2007) A Kantian critique of antitrust: on morality and microsoft. J Private Enterprise 22:161–190
Williams A (2009) Taking values seriously. Oxf J Legal Stud 3:552
Wils W (2003) Should private antitrust enforcement be encouraged in Europe? World Competition Law Econ Rev 26:473
Wils W (2007) Is criminalization of EU competition law the answer? In: Ehlermann CD, Atanasiu I (eds) European competition law annual 2006: enforcement of prohibition of cartels. Hart, Oxford
Wils W (2008) Efficiency and justice in European antitrust enforcement. Hart, Oxford, p 56
Wright R (1995) Right, justice and tort law. In: Owen D (ed) Philosophical foundations of tort law. Oxford University Press, New York, p 161

Chapter 4
Capability Approach: The Framework for the Person-Centred Analysis

4.1 Introduction

The prevailing accounts in antitrust have been shown to be deconstructible primarily because they are not broad enough to meet the requirement of justice as inclusiveness. It is thought therefore that if the herein constructed person-centred approach is to withstand the scrutiny of post-modern deconstruction, there need to be a procedural and conceptual platform that can intelligibly accommodate conflicting interests. Hence, the need to introduce the capability approach.

The person-centred approach rests on the idea that antitrust subjects should be the focal point of antitrust analysis. This approach, it is believed, will allow us to address real issues that concern antitrust subjects by requiring institutions to take account of the various interests held by different relevant persons in specific instances. On the part of the antitrust subjects, an antitrust institution that takes the interests of persons seriously is unlikely to have legitimacy concerns as it is likely to be perceived as just. In a nutshell, antitrust institutions should seek justice as inclusiveness. This inevitably requires a broad scope for antitrust.

It can be deduced from the foregoing that we should not structure our analysis merely for the convenience of antitrust authorities/courts or strictly on what institutions consider to be important. This however does not mean that the person-centred approach disregards the role of established institutions. Rather, it gives the relevant institutions a broader task. A broad framework is essential if the various interests held by different persons are to be taken into consideration. This same effect is not attainable under a narrow regime.

Their flaws (to wit, that they are mistaken and incomplete) notwithstanding, the prominent antitrust theories achieve one thing which eludes a plural regime—their focus on predetermined and homogenous linear order means that they can avoid the problem of non-commensurability that often befalls the valuation of heterogeneous objects.

The overall idea behind the capability approach however has to be addressed in light of suspicion often harboured by neoclassical thinkers about the balancing of

DOI 10.1007/978-3-319-01724-2_4,

plural factors. While the balancing dilemma raise genuine concerns, it appears that the capability approach may be insulated from such concerns as it is premised on the idea that we could consider plural factors without referring to their values in order to include them and to decide between them. Moreover, in the context of antitrust, strict focus on a single factor is not an option as it has been observed in Chap. 1 that any such sole factor would be found to be insufficient and mistaken[1] which in effect means that "social evaluation may be starved of useful information and good argument."[2] Hence, we cannot disregard the fact that it is impossible to reduce all things that one might have reason to value into one homogeneous magnitude.[3]

Following from the assertion that broadness in antitrust is inherently inescapable, it is pertinent to pay closer attention to what such broad-based antitrust regime should entail and how it should work. In this chapter, I set out the broadness conditions for the person-centred approach. I then test selected theories and approaches against these requirements. Ultimately, I show preference for the capability approach.

The remainder of this chapter is divided into six sections. In Sect. 4.2, details of the person-centred conditions of broadness is given. In Sect. 4.3, I test the major antitrust theories against these requirements. Section 4.4 tests the more unconventional "eclectic" theories (one of which is the capability approach) against this requirement. In Sect. 4.5, I focus on the capability approach. Section 4.6 illustrates how the capability framework would achieve the requisite broadness vis-à-vis the other theories. I conclude accordingly in Sect. 4.7.

4.2 Broadness Conditions in the Assessment of Wellbeing

The primary motivation behind this thesis is to fashion out an account of antitrust that will meet the requirement of "justice as inclusiveness". The idea of "justice" herein referred to is measured by the extent to which such account accommodates plural interests. It is inescapable therefore that the person-centred approach be applied broadly enough to accommodate these interests.

At this juncture, it is imperative to break down the broadness requirement into sub-components in order to ensure that it truly reflects plurality of interests as envisaged by the person-centred approach.

To begin with, in order to avoid conceptual confusion in our person-centred analysis, it is necessary to make conscious effort to set clear the contextual meaning of the broadness requirement. Hence, so far as this approach to antitrust primarily

---

[1] See Chap. 1 above.

[2] Sen (2009), p. 242.

[3] Berlin (1997) and Williams (1973, 1985). In fact, it has been argued that there is much diversity even in utility which is the very basis of neoclassical thoughts. See Sen (1980–1981).

advocates that interests of persons should be the focal point of antitrust analysis, the first requirement of broadness is that the terms "persons" and "interests" should be interpreted in a way that is ultimately inclusive such that the "interests" and the "persons" holding such interests must not be unduly restricted. In essence, "persons" must not be understood as referring merely to a class of persons. Rather, it should refer to the whole range that could be interested or be affected by the state of competition in any given market. In the same vein, interests (which invariably relate to wellbeing) must not be defined narrowly.

"Interests" here can be equated to wellbeing in the general sense. Most antitrust institutions recognise and even emphasise the role of interest/wellbeing for antitrust. For example, the General Court in *Österreichische Postsparkasse* noted with regards to the role of EU competition law that "it should be pointed out . . . that the ultimate purpose of the rules that seek to ensure that competition is not distorted in the internal market is to increase the *well-being* of consumers."[4] With emphasis on wellbeing/welfare, Europe's recognition of the welfare aspect of competition law is also apparent from the *Glaxo* case.[5]

The recognition notwithstanding, it is still imperative to define interests/wellbeing particularly as it is subject to diverse meanings under different antitrust theories. For example, considering present trends particularly in light of the often advocated "more economic approach", there is a tendency to take a narrow view of what amounts to interest/wellbeing. Thus, for the purpose of the person-centred approach, wellbeing must not be given a narrow meaning. Mere broadness will also not be adequate. Rather, broadness under this approach is to be reached by focusing on the interests/well-being of each person as a unit rather than as an aggregate. The inescapable diversity of interests mean that antitrust must also be broad.

The requirement that "persons" should be understood as referring to diverse groups rather than a specified group appears to be particularly demanding especially when one considers that most antitrust regimes seem to narrow the scope of "persons". For instance, we could consider the European position as expressed by the General Court in *Österreichische Postsparkasse*. Confirming the role of competition law in ensuring wellbeing, the Court particularly narrowed the scope of persons to the consumers as opposed to persons in general. The same can be said of the position of the General Court in *Glaxo* where the final consumers were identified as the relevant persons in antitrust analysis. However, as it has been stated earlier,[6] it is quite debatable that the usage of the term "consumer" actually accommodates a broader definition beyond consumers within a specific product market as the exact import of Article 101 and 102 TFEU remains unclear. Moreover, there are good reasons to suggest that "persons" should not be limited to

[4] Cases T-213/01 and T-214/01, *Österreichische Postsparkasse AG v. Commission* and *Bank für Arbeit und Wirtschaft AG v. Commission* [2006] ECR II-1601, para 115.

[5] Despite their differences, both the General Court and the Court of Justice recognised the welfare aspect of competition law.

[6] Above, Chap. 1.

selected groups. For example, most scholars and practitioners would agree that abusive use of dominance should be prohibited. However, when faced with a unique case of bilateral monopoly, it might be difficult to identify the "persons" whose interests should be protected. If "persons" are conceived strictly in terms of consumers[7] such that we simply seek for our antitrust regime a state (on our Marshallian demand curve) where the consumer welfare is equal to the consumer surplus while totally disregarding producer welfare, then we might be blinded to the monopsony power[8] of strong consumers even where the exercise of such power raises anti-competitive concerns. In such scenario, we can avoid the conceptual problem by applying a more general definition of "person".[9]

There are a good number of reasons why institutions should be wary of narrowing their focus as it could have grave effect from the policy initiation stage to the implementation stage. For instance, focus on consumer welfare means that preference will always be given to type I error as against type II error when in fact a more detailed evaluation of specific cases might have led us to risk type II errors and not type I. Other justifications have been given in preceding chapters.

The second and third requirements build on our interpretation of "interests". By saying that "interests" should be understood in their heterogeneous context, it partly means that antitrust institutions should understand and accommodate different interests held by different persons or groups. At the macro-level, rather than taking a simplistic approach by relating interests to the type of market (such as interests linked to different forms of free markets), a more ingrained approach should be adopted in identifying interests. For instance, we might factor into an institution's competition policy the impact of an isolated behaviour on a wide range of interests within the community spanning from businesses to social groups and so on. They should be able to demand that their interests be considered as long as they are affected by and sensitive to competition policy concerns. This kind of reasoning implies a broader scope which includes different shades of interests held by consumers, labour union, legal profession, economists, big businesses, small businesses, export industries, importers and so on.[10]

Third, interests also refer to the diverging interests which a single antitrust subject or a section of them may deem worthwhile in specific cases. Using consumers as example, our acceptance that the interests, which a set of consumers (or a single consumer) may hold are plural and diverse, would have fundamental impact on the way we perceive antitrust concerns. By recognising plurality, we will

---

[7] This applies where, for example, consumer welfare is defined as buyer's well-being—that is, the benefits a buyer derives from the consumption of goods and services. See Orbach (2010).

[8] On monopsony and buyer power, see generally the OECD Competition Committee Policy Roundtable Monopsony and Buyer Power 2008 [http://www.oecd.org/dataoecd/38/63/44445750.pdf].

[9] This could be by taking the suppliers as relevant antitrust subjects. For instance, in the context of monopsonistic market, the US Court in *Weyerhaeuser* identified the sellers as consumers. See *Weyerhaeuser Co v Ross-Simmons Hardwood Lumber Co.*, 549 US 312 (2007).

[10] See Doern (1996), p. 23.

realise that substantiating the interests of a minute unit or even a person may be more complicated than it initially appears. For individual cases, general assumption cannot be made regarding the interests held by a certain group (such as consumers). We have to specifically query—what interests? Which consumers?[11] A single case might spring up different interests between an erstwhile uniform set of consumers. Drawing analogy from the merger case of *Tetra Laval/Sidel*[12] where, even though the consumers could be sub-grouped as customers as they were all into the business of bottling liquid foods, their concerns about the possibility of leveraging strategies that might result from the proposed merger depended heavily on the sort of food a particular customer was concerned with and the nature of offer they received. In sum, while some seemed to prefer the merger because the efficiency gains facilitated their business, others were, to varying degrees, sceptical and hence against the merger because of the negative impact they believed it could have on their business.

The EU *Intel* decision[13] is another example. In this case, one of the issues to be determined was whether the benefit made out to consumers by Intel amounted to an anticompetitive practice against competitors. If we look strictly at consumers perception of harm,[14] we might find it difficult to justify the sanction imposed by the Commission on Intel especially where one thinks that the preferences of buyers is the only good measure of economic well-being. This is because it is possible that consumers do not, in fact, perceive any harm from the behaviour of Intel. If we are solely concerned with perceived harm, we have to grapple with the submission of the Consumer Association which was that most individual consumers do not really care whether Intel is built into their computer or not.[15] We cannot hold such a narrow view of consumers' interests as it has been argued, for example in relation to consumer perception, that from the standpoint of society, willingness of consumers is not necessarily a good measure of consumer harm or benefit.[16] Further, if we limit the meaning of interest to consumer choice, we might find it difficult to justify the sanction against Intel where it is confirmed that individual consumers are particularly less concerned with having computers with alternative processors or that they even prefer to be locked into computers with Intel as it saves them from incurring searching cost and also reduces confusion.

Hence, it could help our antitrust analysis to for instance, acknowledge that a single consumer might be simultaneously interested in conflicting outcomes

---

[11] Sibnony (2009).

[12] Case No. COMP/M. 2416—Tetra Laval/Sidel.

[13] Commission decision of 13 May 2009, relating to a proceeding under Article 82 of the EC Treaty and Article 54 of the EEA Agreement (COMP/C-3/37.990—Intel), D(2009)3726 final.

[14] Especially where one considers the definition of consumer surplus given by Mankiw which simply requires that we measure "the benefit that buyers receive from a good *as the buyers themselves perceive it*." See Mankiw (2008), p. 142 (emphasis in original).

[15] For example see the opinion of the Federation of Consumer Associations in *Intel* Decision, para 1611.

[16] Mankiw (2008), p. 142.

deriving from a particular market conduct. To illustrate this point, a consumer may hold diverging interests which may result in conflicting conclusions (both positive and negative) towards a particular conduct which results in parallel trade. Such individual may want the immediate benefits that are derivable from the parallel trade such as lower prices but at same time they might be concerned with the likely long term loss such as less innovation.

Fourth, great care must be taken to avoid masquerading ideas deriving from specific schools of thought as those which antitrust subjects hold. Thus, for broadness to be achieved, it is imperative to take note of real interests rather than grand propositions about persons' interests.

The fifth requirement is that antitrust regimes should desist from enmeshing antitrust in the fallacy that interests of persons' can be ranked on an *ex ante* basis. Considering the illustration above about parallel trade and coupled with the fact that institutions are to focus on real person and not the idea of persons, it should be noted that the interests of a single antitrust subject is likely to be too complicated to allow for *ex ante* prioritisation. Thus, it would be inappropriate, in light of the person-centred approach to set an *a priori* fixated ranking, for instance, between the short term benefit such as price increase and the long term loss such as loss of innovation. It must not be taken for granted that specific issues in individual cases may vary the preferences of antitrust subjects.

Conclusively, the above stated requirement should guide our antitrust analysis when applying the person-centred approach. They are summarised as follows:

(i) The nature of person's and their interests must be viewed in plural term
   - "Interests" cannot be strictly defined and as such we must evince plurality in our meaning of wellbeing
   - The "persons" must relate to a wide range of persons and not a section or group such as consumers

(ii) The plurality represented by interests should be understood as different interests held by different persons or groups
(iii) Plurality of interests should also be understood as meaning different interests which a single antitrust subject or a section of them may deem worthwhile in specific cases
(iv) Focus of antitrust institutions should be on the real interests held by persons', not the idea of the interests they should hold
(v) We cannot suppose that an antitrust subject or a class of them will have a set and universally predetermined preferential ranking of the interests that they deem worthwhile

4.3 Testing Theories Against the Requirements of Broadness

Economists and legal scholars have developed theories which guide antitrust analysis. The field however continues to evolve as fresh insights are brought to modify or replace old ones. The proposed person-centred approach is not a full blown theoretical construct on antitrust. It merely details the bottom-up perspective. This means that antitrust theories continue to have their relevance in antitrust analysis. However, the person-centred approach requires an assessment of these full scale and partial theories against the requirement of broadness. I start by detailing the theories and then checking their compliance with the broadness requirements set out above. For the purpose of analysis, focus is placed on theories which are either pervasive or contemporary. As such, I limit my analysis to total welfare, wealth transfer (consumer welfare), consumer choice, behavioural law and economics, public policy and economic freedom.[17] Each of the requirements on broadness will be flagged by their corresponding roman numeral.[18]

4.3.1 Total Welfare

According to Bork, competition policy should be guided by basic economic analysis, "otherwise the law acts blindly upon forces it does not understand and produces results it does not intend."[19] This approach to antitrust is the product of the so-called Chicago school. To Bork and other member of this school, antitrust can be summed up as the effort to "improve allocative efficiency without impairing productive efficiency so greatly as to produce either no gain or a net loss in consumer welfare."[20] The two types of efficiency—allocative efficiency and productive efficiency—primarily recognised by this school[21] are explained briefly.

---

[17] Though the list is not exhaustive, these theories represent a cross-section of antitrust thoughts.

[18] For instance, requirement i(a), requirement ii etc.

[19] Bork (1978).

[20] Bork (1978), pp. 90–91.

[21] These categories of efficiency are regarded as static. Bork particularly does not think we should consider dynamic efficiency in antitrust analysis. He argued that "the propriety of 'progressiveness' as an antitrust criterion is not obvious ... Progress ... is obviously not costless to consumers. It requires the devotion of resources to research and development that would otherwise be devoted to the production of other goods and services. Progress will occur even without special consideration by the law, but the rate will be that which consumers choose by the degree to which they make it profitable to engage in the activity of producing progress. Courts have no criteria for establishing compromise deviations from consumer welfare here." See Bork (1967), p. 251.

4.3.1.i Allocative Efficiency

The economists' concern for the efficient allocation of resources emanates from the concept of cost.[22] The value of the concept of cost (opportunity cost) stems from the fact that the use of a resource in the production of a good precludes its use in the production of an alternative good. It means therefore that the cost of resources to society is its value in the best alternative use.[23] Where resources are put to the best alternative use, a market is likely to attain allocative efficiency as its output will be maximised. This however fails to materialise where scarcity is contrived. Such contrivance can arise where firms find it profitable to reduce output because the increased price more than compensates for the lost sale. They thereby raise the cost the society pays for such resource, hence rendering the market's allocation mechanism inefficient. In event, the consumer is worse off as he pays more for less. He could also be in a situation where, because he has been charged a value above cost which he did not pre-empt, his needs go unsatisfied.

4.3.1.ii Productive Efficiency

Productive efficiency is a firm-specific way of ascertaining efficiency. Like allocative efficiency, cost is one of the key factors for aiming at productive efficiency.[24] The difference however is that cost is not construed in terms of opportunity cost. Rather, it is the scale of operation that determines the resulting efficiency. In identifying the scale of operation through cost analysis, it is believed that to some extent cost determines price, "that price determines market share, and that all these together determine the profitability of the firm."[25] The material efficiency effect attributable to productive efficiency is the presence of economies of scale, economies of scope, and efficiencies from synergies such as cost savings.[26] Efficiency gains emanating from a firm's scale of operation can also be ascertained by identifying the between-firm efficiencies. These efficiencies can be found where agreements increase the number and quantity of transactions between firms which may help to solve free-rider and hold up problems.[27]

---

[22] Hay and Morris (1979), p. 37.

[23] Hay and Morris (1979), p. 37.

[24] This cost-related aspect can be referred to as Cost efficiency. See European Commission (2004), *Guidelines on the application of Article 81(3) of the Treaty*, OJ C 101 27/4/2004, or Within-Firm efficiency. See *Practical Methods to Assess Efficiency Gains in the Context of Article 81(3) of the EC Treaty Final Report* by Copenhagen Economics published on 21 April 2006 2208 DG Enterprise and Industry, 56.

[25] Hay and Morris (1979).

[26] Cost savings either through the combination of existing assets that reduces cost by avoiding duplication or the presence of better production planning, reduced inventory or improved capacity utilisation. See Guidelines on Article 81(3) para 68.

[27] European Commission Guidelines on Vertical Restraints, OJ C 291, 13.10.2000, 1–44.

In the context of antitrust, productive efficiency is considered important because it increases social wealth over the whole range of output.[28] The total welfare model is concerned about productive efficiency as it values any cost savings associated with the practices at issue since the efficiencies that affect marginal cost of production also tend to affect ultimate price.[29] It is possible to take account of productive efficiency. This is because, under certain assumptions, the efficient solution under this approach is achieved through equilibrium prices at the intersection of the demand and supply curve.[30]

In sum, allocative efficiency is achieved when resources are distributed among alternative uses such that the goods and services it produces are those most highly valued by consumers.[31] Regarding the relationship between allocative and productive efficiency, total welfare is achieved where the sum of consumer surplus and producer surplus is maximised. This occurs where price is equal to marginal cost.[32]

At this juncture, the total welfare standard will be tested against the person-centred approach's five requirements on broadness.

On requirement i(a) which calls for a plural understanding of the concept of welfare, the total welfare model fails because the efficiency goal has a rather limited scope. The Chicagoans' interpretation of "maximise welfare" has a thin meaning as it relates to utility.[33] It is thus unsuitable for a general conception of wellbeing.[34] Even more serious is the cognitive argument against total welfare. It has been contended that the Chicago idea of "welfare" is not welfare in the intuitive sense let alone that it meets the general conception of wellbeing. Black argues that where Pareto optimality is conceived in terms of utility, "welfare" cannot mean "utility", for to say that no one's utility can be increased unless someone else's utility is decreased does not imply that utility is maximised in any intuitive sense.[35] This means that the cognitive argument for total welfare is not expansive enough as it is unlikely to cover utilitarian ideals even if it is conceptually possible to achieve utilitarian goals through total welfare.

Suppose we concede that the interpretation of welfare is to be limited to its economic meaning, total welfare still fails this narrower threshold as its strict focus on efficiency renders it inadequate in analysing economic welfare. This is because

---

[28] Brodley (1987), pp. 1020 and 1027.

[29] Areeda and Hovenkamp (2000), pp. 106–107.

[30] This implies that price is equal to marginal cost. It is the point at which consumer and producer surplus are maximised.

[31] Brodley (1987), pp. 1025 and 1027.

[32] Bishop and Walker (2002), p. 25.

[33] According to Black, to say that a person is better or worse off is to say that his utility increases or decreases and that utilities are commonly understood to be numerical values of a utility function that represents a person's preference, and his preference to be revealed in the choice he makes. Total welfare theorists also believe that welfare and its maximisation do not have independent meanings. See Black (2005), pp. 35–39.

[34] See Black (2005), p. 36.

[35] See Black (2005), p. 38. This position can however be contrasted with arguments which seem to link total welfare to utilitarianism. See e.g. Posner (1979), pp. 103–140; Posner (1980), p. 243.

the issue of economic welfare has been shown to include not only efficiency concerns but also distribution concerns. It also fails because it tends to relate benefits and burdens strictly to price.[36] Thus, in relation to the scope of wellbeing, it can be conveniently concluded that the total welfare standard fails to meet the person-centred requirement.

With regards to requirement i(b) which is about the broadness of the term "persons", it is arguable that total welfare model is somewhat broad. This possibility stems from the fact that it requires neutrality in antitrust analysis. In other words, there must be a clear attempt to desist from making value judgement between consumers and producers.[37] This is in fact the primary function of allocative efficiency which is that it is impossible to make any normative statement about the preferability of an efficient allocation *A1*, based upon distribution *D1*, compared to an efficient allocation *A2*, based upon another distribution, *D2*. In some sense, broadness is attained since the scope of persons who benefit from the resource distribution is not determined *ex ante*. This means that different interests (in this context, consumers and producers) are well within the definition of "persons" all of whom will benefit (either directly or indirectly) from the net welfare effect. There are however strong reasons to suggest that the promise of neutrality is a facade and that in fact, the total welfare approach which often advocates minimalist interference is primarily geared towards producer surplus because of its blindness to distributive injustice[38] and as such follows a narrow meaning of "persons". This likelihood remains strong despite contrived explanations that consumers also benefit through their shareholdings.[39] Moreover, even if the total welfare standard is value neutral, its broadness cannot go far enough because of the exclusive focus on price and efficiency.

On requirement ii which is that "plural interests" should be understood as different interests held by different persons, the total welfare model fails as it is unconcerned about the interests of persons; where in a particular instance, a person's interest is recognised, it is merely derivative of the primary focus on efficiency. Thus, built on the Kaldor–Hicks or wealth maximisation principle, this model can be primarily faulted on the ground that it allows for a range of uncompensated redistribution between individuals and businesses[40] because the broad range of interests are totally ignored.[41]

[36] This is the case when analysis is done through the price theory in general and more specifically on wealth maximisation.

[37] Bishop and Walker (2002), p. 24.

[38] Boadway and Bruce (1984), p. 62, fn 22; Buchanan (1985), p. 9.

[39] Bork (1978).

[40] See Scitovsky (1941), p. 77.

[41] Those who argue from the standpoint of liberal right also sense the deficiency of the efficiency thoughts because where ideas of liberal rights are prevalent, society is not allowed to balance the positive effect on one person with negative effects on others as each person is allowed to decide according to his or her own preferences. See Sen (1970), p. 152. Such right should be protected even if the well-being of others or the total welfare is reduced. See Kerber (2008), p. 105.

Regarding requirement iii which is that plural interests should mean different interests held by a single antitrust subject or those held by a group of antitrust subjects, the total welfare model fails because of its strict focus on the idea of rational choice. This theory builds the notion of an "economic man" who focuses solely on utility. Conceived in terms of price, a person's interest has to be explained through the homogeneous price-related proxy.

On requirement iv which is that focus should be on real interests held by persons rather than the idea of interest which specific schools of thought tend to attribute to persons, total welfare school is flawed because of its foundation in rational choice theory. Even where it advocates consumer welfare, this approach fails as well because it is based on the idea of the consumer rather than on real consumers.[42]

Hence, unlike the idea of "homo economicus", contemporary approaches have shown through empirical studies that real persons do not engage in unbounded pursuit of self-interest; their interests are more diverse and must be recognised as such.[43]

Concerning requirement v which is that interests of a person cannot be predetermined through a universal preferential ranking, total welfare fails because it seeks *ex ante* consistency of choice through the idea of rationality by mechanically seeking any state that is allocatively efficient in the relevant market over and above any other state.

In conclusion, the total welfare approach fails irredeemably as the sole proxy for antitrust analysis under the person-centred approach.

4.3.2 Wealth Transfer

From the total welfare point of view, antitrust assessments should be strictly based on efficiency concerns as it is certain that problems will arise where attention is to heterogeneous factors. The concerns it generates, to them, can be avoided by focusing on the single goal of efficiency. The success and popularity of the efficiency thoughts was aided by the perceived lack of sophistication in antitrust at the time. However, as noted by the wealth transfer school, the lack of sophistication that attended antitrust analysis before the Chicago revolution was not solely based on the fact that antitrust regimes pursued more than one goal. Antitrust could still be rational with more than one goal.[44] In other words, they argued that having more than one goal in antitrust and having a rational antitrust regime are not mutually exclusive ideals. Based on this finding, it thus became necessary to assess the validity of the total welfare standard in its own right rather than strengthening the efficiency argument primarily by reference to some "unsophisticated"

[42] Fox (2008), p. 1.

[43] For example see below behavioural law and economics.

[44] Lande (1989), p. 631.

alternatives. As such, it was necessary to assess the total welfare standard (which is solely premised on efficiency) with well though-out theory of antitrust which accommodated more than one goal. This revelation triggered the debate between sole efficiency goal and antitrust goals that included not only efficiency but also wealth transfer.[45] The efficiency model was thus said to be particularly faulty as it failed to address distributional issues thereby disparaging the interests of those whom it should ordinarily protect. Even though efficiency proponents will recognise that redistributions which arise not as a result of better performance, but through restraints of competition and market power should be prevented, they argue notwithstanding that legal rules and regulation should focus only on efficiency effects. Distributional concerns, they say, should be dealt with through means such as taxation and social policy.[46]

The wealth transfer model seeks to protect consumers and as such seems to be the approach more deserving of the often misused phrase of consumer welfare. Proponents of this approach argue that competition law and policy should aim at enhancing consumer welfare by preventing or correcting the transfer from consumers to businesses. This model is based on the reasoning that antitrust law and policy has to be regarded as arising out of repeated interaction and coordination between two large interest groups the result of which leads to a political bargaining between consumers and producers.[47] This background presupposes that the selection of competition policy objectives has to be regarded as a result of the bargaining process. Thus, if one takes it as axiomatic that consumers usually have a weaker position in the process of bargaining, lobbying and litigation, then a pro-consumer policy objective seem justified as the resulting wealth transfer standard can be seen somewhat like a "rebalancing" measure.[48]

As a result of its focus on the benefits to consumers, the wealth transfer standard does not accept instances where a firm's practice generates allocative efficiency benefits while reducing consumer surplus[49] as this undermines consumer confidence. According to proponents of this standard, unlike the total welfare which is not compatible with the Pareto criterion because it allows for redistribution between consumers and producers in the balancing of positive and negative effect between different persons,[50] the wealth transfer standard can be derived from the Pareto criterion because it stipulates that no one should be worse off. For instance, the

---

[45] Lande (1989), p. 649.

[46] See e.g. Kaplow 2012, pp. 3–26; Kaplow and Shavell (1994), pp. 667–681.

[47] Baker (2005), p. 2.

[48] Cseres (2006), pp. 121 and 127–128.

[49] Consumer surplus is the difference between consumer reservation price for a commodity and the price they actually pay for it.

[50] This balancing activity is incompatible with Pareto because the Pareto criterion assumes that no interpersonal comparison of utility is possible between different persons. As such, there is no way to balance different interests. In effect, total welfare cannot be derived from the Pareto criterion and neither can it be derived from the goal of allocative efficiency. See Kerber (2008), p. 105.

criterion that consumer surplus should not be reduced can be seen as an application of the Pareto criterion.[51]

There are different variants of the wealth transfer standard. One of it is the consumer interest standard which emphasises the role of price, service quality and choice in welfare analysis.[52] Its primary focus is on the impact of business behaviour on end users. The competitive effect to be considered could either be direct or indirect as the consequences are transmitted down the distribution chain.[53]

There is some measure of broadness in this approach especially when one compares it with the total welfare standard.[54] However, testing the wealth transfer standard against requirement i(a) which calls for a plural understanding of the concept of welfare, it becomes evident that this standard is not quite as broad since it is still addressed through price. For requirement i(b) which is about the broadness of the term "persons", the wealth transfer model can be particularly faulted because of its bias for consumers rather than focusing on persons as a whole. Instances abound where the assertion that consumers are generally in a weaker position can be shown to be incorrect particularly in highly competitive markets where there is a high potential for consumerism. With regards to requirement ii which is that "plural interests" should be understood as different interests held by different persons, it is likely that the wealth transfer account would fail; one just needs to consider the reasoning of the General Court in *Glaxo* (where it merely took into account the interest of consumers and failed to recognise the interest of pharmaceuticals to prevent arbitrage practices) in order to appreciate this possibility. Concerning requirement iii which is that plural interests should mean different interests held by either a single antitrust subject or those held by a group of antitrust subjects, this approach fails because consumers' interests could be over and above price-related concerns. Finally, on requirement v which is that interests of a person cannot be predetermined through a universal preferential ranking, this approach fails because it is premised on an assumed political bargain between consumers and producers whereby the latter have the upper hand. Thus, in contradiction to the requirement against *ex ante* preferential ranking, wealth transfer standard presupposes that in order to redistribute, the interests of consumers would always be ranked over and above other interests.

Conclusively, though the wealth transfer standard signals an improvement and hence relatively superior to the total welfare approach in terms of broadness, it is still seriously inadequate in terms of the broadness required under the person-centred approach.

---

[51] Kerber (2008), p. 105.

[52] Buttigieg (2009), p. 1.

[53] Buttigieg (2009), p. 1.

[54] Consumer welfare can be said to be broader than total welfare if one considers that the former accommodates redistribution goals together with efficiency claims. It should however be noted that total welfare can be considered to be broader in certain respect particularly when assessing antitrust subjects. See Arezzo (2008), p. 43.

4.3.3 Consumer Choice

The consumer choice approach is quite similar to the consumer interest approach and consequently the wealth transfer standard. However, the former seem to develop further the need to address non-price competition. The primary objection of the consumer choice approach, as identified by Averitt and Lande, is that price theory based antitrust law and policies are unable to handle important issues of non-price competition.[55] This is despite the fact that institutions applying the price theory often attempt to address non-price issues indirectly. The scholars argue that these institutions often seek to achieve this by folding the non-price objectives into the price analysis in the form of quality adjusted prices, or by assuming that markets that are price competitive will also be competitive for non-price preferences. This notwithstanding, proponents of the consumer choice approach contend that such indirect consideration of non-price issues is rather awkward and, as such, should not be encouraged.

Under the consumer choice approach, antitrust law protects a competitive array of options in the marketplace, undiminished by artificial restrictions. Proponents of this approach suggest that the role of antitrust should be broadly conceived as protecting all the types of options that are significantly important to consumers. These options, they argue, are not limited to price but also innovation, quality and other forms of non-price competition. As such, antitrust violation should be understood as activities that unreasonably restrict the totality of price and non-price choices that would have been otherwise available.[56] Thus, what this approach does is to prohibit business conducts that harmfully and significantly limit the range of choices that the free market, absent the restraints being challenged, would have provided.

The consumer choice approach is broader than both the total welfare and wealth transfer models as it furthers the allocative, productive and dynamic efficiency goals[57] as well as the (wealth transfer model's) consumer effect. It goes beyond the total welfare[58] and wealth transfer model because, coupled with its focus on choice, it places true emphasis on innovation.[59] This perspective on antitrust is of great

[55] Averitt and Lande (2007), p. 175.

[56] Averitt and Lande (2007), p. 182.

[57] Averitt and Lande (2007), pp. 186–187.

[58] It is thought that this model gives only limited attention to the factors of innovation. Rather, efficiency defences are almost always cast in terms of whether the practice will lower costs. As such, whether the practice might raise or lower the rate of innovation in products is usually only an afterthought. See Porter (2001), pp. 919 and 958.

[59] See Porter (2001), p. 187. Orbach asserts that thinkers such as Bork underestimated the significance of law to innovation and overestimated the significance of consumer preferences. See Orbach (2010), p. 23.

value as there is a widespread undisputed empirical fact that technological progress is the most important determinant of long term economic growth.[60]

In line with the consumer choice theory, evolutional innovation economists argue that competition policy should take due account of dynamic factors.[61] This is because in a dynamic competitive environment, businesses compete not only on the basis of price, but also by carrying out R&D. Hence, businesses are encouraged to innovate where they are able to supply products which no other firm is able to supply.[62] There is empirical evidence to support this claim.[63] The strive for productivity in the midst of competitors means that a firm will take steps to develop new products, services and technologies at the lowest possible cost. The welfare benefit deriving from this sort of efficiency is that consumers are spoilt with choices and they can get better products at a lower price. However, the benefits to both the firm and the consumers may be lost if the value of dynamic efficiency is not recognised. Schumpeter regarded competition as a process of "creative destruction" in which innovative activities led to new markets, new industries and the death of old markets and industries. On this basis therefore, unless competition policy recognises its value, dynamic efficiency may be constrained as businesses are not likely to invest if there is little or no expected profit from bringing a new product onto the market.

It appears that the consumer choice approach fails on account of broadness just as the wealth transfer standard notwithstanding its relative improvements. Thus, even though it promotes vividly that a wide range of choice be considered, the idea of choice is still narrowed to consumers[64] instead of antitrust subjects in general. Moreover, one could sense that the big claims regarding the need to focus on non-price analysis might not have much practical impact as the consumer choice approach appears to be rather too subtle on price theory. As such, institutions applying it may be ready to sacrifice non-price based choices. For instance, it may accommodate diminutions in choices on the ground that antitrust law does not require that the number of options be maximised.[65]

---

[60] See Kerber (2008), p. 98. Orbach confirms that at present, it has been established that "legal regimes affect innovation and that the rate of innovation is affected by many variables and strategic decisions" such that "consumer choice and preferences constitute only a subset of variables in this vector." Orbach (2010), p. 23.

[61] On competition as a dynamic process of innovation and imitation, see Clark (1961). It could also be seen as a knowledge-generating process of parallel experimentation. See Hayek (1978), p. 179.

[62] Bishop and Walker (2002), p. 36.

[63] See Ahn (2002).

[64] Under this model, consumers are normally ultimate consumers as well as entities engaged in purchase transactions, including corporations buying intermediate industrial goods. See Averitt and Lande (2007), p. 183.

[65] Under this model, consumers are normally ultimate consumers as well as entities engaged in purchase transactions, including corporations buying intermediate industrial goods. See Averitt and Lande (2007), p. 184.

4.3.4 Behavioural Law and Economics

According to the behavioural law and economics school, the goals of antitrust and the ideal methodologies for analysing business conducts can only be correctly determined if we model antitrust law and policy on *actual human behaviour* and not on the idea of *economic man*. Thus, rather than analysing competition issues on the basis of false, narrow and strict conception of the individual (such as those based on the rational choice theory), the behavioural law and economics model moves away from the remits of rationality by arguing specifically against it. The central position of this school is that our actions, reaction and expectations concerning specific market behaviours are unlikely to follow a set rational pattern as there are always biases and errors that lead to predictable irrational behaviours.[66]

Arguing against the traditional assumption regarding the consistency of human rationality, the behavioural law and economics school seeks to establish that humans can be irrational with regard to their market behaviour. They support this conclusion with insights from psychology. Their finding thus is that humans are largely boundedly rational. In essence, we should not expect a consistent pattern of choice between different or even the same individual as people are at different times influenced by different factors and sentiments. For example, most persons do have limited cognitive resources and are often affected by emotions and motivations such that they are influenced to take a course of action or react in a particular way, for instance, because of the ease at which they could recall a particular related consequence or event rather than engaging in objective and rational analysis.[67]

With regards to the impact of behavioural economics on the nature of antitrust analysis, it means that there is need to be suspicious of the idea of rationality. One should thus proceed from the understanding that since in real fact, humans do not always reason correctly in terms of maximising their welfare (regardless of the standard of welfare they consider ideal), we have to modify the assumptions of antitrust so that we can successfully tackle anti-competition concerns. From this perspective, there is a suspicion that the likelihood of type I and type II errors are rife where market behaviours are assessed on the basis of rational choice. As such, by taking into account real behaviours and reactions of relevant antitrust subjects, we can provide a better description of market dynamic and also provide more effective prescriptions for competition policy.[68]

This approach (in general and its application in competition law in particular) is still developing. Notwithstanding, there are clear signs on how it can promote broadness. To showcase how the behavioural thought generates vast thinking and consequently accommodates broad reasoning, we just need to take a look at the four conceptions of competition arising from four assumptions of the relative rationality

[66] See Mitchell (2002).
[67] This is called availability heuristics in behavioural psychology.
[68] Tor (2004).

of firms and consumers as analysed by Stucke.[69] He gave four exhaustive analyses in four different scenarios. First, he identifies the ideal way of analysing antitrust issues where both the firms and consumers are rational. Second is where rational businesses interact with boundedly rational consumers. Third is where boundedly rational firms interact with rational consumers and finally, where boundedly rational firms interact with boundedly rational consumers.

It must however be noted that its likely value to the idea of broadness notwithstanding, it is still difficult at this stage to fully assess the extent to which the behavioural law and economics approach could be broadened beyond the realms of economic thought. There is however a likelihood that this approach might fail as it appears that its value is limited to the operational concerns; broadness is achieved not in terms of policy considerations but when assessing the economic impact of firms' behaviour.

4.3.5 General Equilibrium and Public Policy

Based on economic and non-economic reasoning, arguments have been made that antitrust regimes should look beyond the welfare theories addressed so far. This line of thought advocates in general that some broader effects aside from the traditional efficiency and freedom-based considerations can be applicable in antitrust. This category of thought can be sub-grouped into economic and non-economic aspects. Economic justification for this broader scope is based on the general equilibrium theory (otherwise referred to as the theory of second best) while the non-economic justification has been premised on public interest.

To neatly establish the economic justification, it is important to appreciate the difference between the partial equilibrium theory and the general equilibrium theory and to show how they affect antitrust analysis. The partial equilibrium analysis focuses on a subset of the economy which is often referred to as the "relevant market". This is the basis upon which the hitherto addressed welfare standards are based.[70] On the other hand, the general equilibrium approach looks at the market as a whole. For example, here, the requirement of allocative efficiency will be that the model of perfect competition is fulfilled by all markets such that the decentralised optimising behaviour of all agents will lead to an efficient allocation throughout the entire economy. For instance, the market could meet the Pareto criterion without the necessity of state intervention. It is expected that the market aligns with the assumption of perfect competition and desists from deviation otherwise it would lead to some kind of allocative inefficiency.

---

[69] Stucke (2012), pp. 27–52.

[70] Orbach (2010), p. 6.

Under the second best theory, competitive equilibria are Pareto efficient. However, rather than seeking to achieve this state by solving market failures in isolated markets, it is believed that efficiency of market equilibria is an all-or-nothing proposition.[71] As such, unless all conditions can be satisfied in a market, there is no guarantee that remedying separate market failures will improve efficiency. It is thus expected that in assessing the Pareto state (allocative efficiency) in the market in question, due account should be taken of the impact of such behaviour on other markets.[72] We therefore need not restrict our analysis to an isolated market. Where there are substantial gains to other markets, it could for instance mean that such behaviour is considered to be outside the purview of typical competition concerns.[73] It appears that this reasoning was applied in *CECED*[74] where the Commission exempted an agreement between virtually all the European importers and manufacturers of domestic washing machines to stop importing or producing the least energy-efficient machines, thereby reducing the pollution emissions from power generation. The Commission was convinced that the environmental benefits for society trumped the likely increase in cost arising from the allocatively inefficient arrangement in the isolated market.[75]

Frontline antitrust theorists acknowledge the fundamental basis for the general equilibrium approach. For example, Bork acknowledged that "an expansion of output through increased efficiency would appear as pure gain in the consumer welfare model but might impose other welfare losses upon the society."[76] However, they are quick to discount its relevance by arguing that the problem which one might seek to solve through antitrust should better be left for legislatures and reflected upon in specialised legislation. The reasoning is that the approach would require us to trade-off values which cannot properly form the stuff of antitrust litigation.[77] Hovenkamp stated unequivocally that the "[p]roblems of second-best may be so overwhelming and so hypothetical that the antitrust policymaker is well off to avoid them."[78] One could disagree with the general equilibrium theory but one thing that remains is that its foundation is far from completely flawed. As such, rather than concerning ourselves with the perspectival positions of peculiar theories, the person-centred approach to antitrust simply requires us to assess the theory in light of the broadness requirement.

---

[71] Lipsey and Lancaster (1955–1956), pp. 11–32.

[72] Townley gives an example of liner-shipping conferences who engage in horizontal price-fixing. See Townley (2009), p. 186.

[73] This is regarded as highly controversial. However, Hammer favours this form of reasoning particularly for intra-market second-best trade-off. To him, this trade-off analysis is geared towards ascertaining whether "competition" is either workable or desirable.

[74] OJ 2000 L187/47.

[75] Note Guidelines on Article 81(3).

[76] Bork (1978), pp. 114–115.

[77] Bork (1978), p. 115.

[78] Hovenkamp (1985), pp. 213 and 241.

Set against the broadness requirement of the person-centred approach, the general equilibrium theory fails on similar grounds as the other welfare standards; despite the fact that it makes considerable progress by broadening the markets that could be considered in a single antitrust issue by internalising externalities in other markets, it does not escape one particular shortcoming of the above-explained theories. The fundamental flaw which is still transferred to this theory is that antitrust issues are addressed through narrow proxies such as price and consumer choice.[79]

Regarding the non-economic arguments, antitrust institutions are meant to consider public policy issues. It is possible that a standard welfare approach has public policy implications such as the increase of competitiveness and consequently, substantial growth and development.[80] It could also stimulate the growth of technological capabilities and exports.[81] These likely public policy effects notwithstanding, proponents of public policy are making bolder claims. One of such claims is that it is not enough that these welfare standards can be used to promote different public policy objectives[82] as there are many other public policy objectives that these standards ignore.[83]

Attempting to showcase the need for the inclusion of public policy considerations in antitrust, Townley weighs the pros and cons of a regime that, on the one hand, excludes public policy considerations and another which forges a compromise between whatever welfare standard that is chosen and public policy objectives.[84] He shows preference for the regime that considers public policy goals as long as such goals are rational, transparent and open and are determined in advance.[85] Also, Monti argues that competition policy can never be isolated completely from other public policy choices relevant to democratic societies by making due references to EU provisions and cases.[86]

The general idea that public policy concerns should be considered on their own terms (as a non-economic objective) rather than strictly perceiving public policy benefits through economic indicators such as price and choice seem laudable.[87] It is however difficult to assess it against the requirement of broadness primarily

---

[79] For example the *CECED* case. See below text surrounding note 26 above.

[80] UNCTAD's submission to OECD (2003); Townley (2009), p. 21.

[81] UNCTAD document TD/B/COM.2.EM/10/Rev 14.

[82] Either by internalising the policy area which would otherwise be external or by incorporating external considerations based on public policy such as the promotion of small and medium-sized enterprises.

[83] Townley (2009), p. 23; Pearson (2000), ch 2 and 3; Nadeaus (2003).

[84] Townley (2009), pp. 30–41.

[85] Townley (2009), p. 42.

[86] Monti (2002), p. 1065.

[87] Townley gives an interesting example. He queried that when evaluating the concept of "better off" under the total welfare standard, would one encourage an agreement between manufacturers that would increase their total surplus by 1 million Euros, if this were to immediately lead to an irreparable poisoning of all drinking water?

because open-textured, non-economic indicators of public policy lack conceptual foundation. The lack of theoretical underpinning for public policy in antitrust cases has over the years been the point of attack by the economic welfare scholars. Thus, even though some of the outcome deriving from the application of public policy goals may be the same as outcomes that derive from the person-centred analysis, we may still struggle to justify reasoning based on public policy as it fails to give a substantial theoretical reason as to why we should consider such non-economic concerns through antitrust rules and not through something else. On the other hand, the person-centred approach would argue for any such public policy consideration primarily because antitrust subjects who are interested in a peculiar public policy outcome should be included alongside others in our antitrust analysis on the account of "justice as inclusiveness".

4.3.6 Economic Freedom

Quite different from the theories on antitrust law and policy discussed above, the theory of economic freedom, which is built on the ordoliberal ideology, takes as fundamental, the political choices of individuals which create the basic structures of an economic system.[88] This thought was fostered during the Nazi era by some scholars at the University of Freiburg. The ordoliberals developed this concept as a wholesome political and economic philosophy aimed at preventing the accumulation of power which, if unrestricted, is often misused.[89]

To the ordoliberals, the idea of choice is reflected through an economic constitution which contains "a comprehensive decision concerning the nature and form of the process of socio-economic cooperation."[90] For the choice of an economic constitution to be effective, the legal system should be structured to implement the constitutional choice. Thus, where the economic constitution calls for a transaction economy, the policy framework[91] demands that the legal system should be configured so as to create and maintain the conditions of complete competition which would allow that type of economic system to function most effectively. According to this ideology, it is thus required that the economic knowledge behind the constitution should be translated into normative language.[92] For instance, if an ordoliberal framework is to be effective, it must be built on the legal conception of economic freedom—that is, the members of the community must have willingly supported it and actively co-operated in implementing it.

---

[88] Gerber (1998), p. 246.

[89] Gerber (1994), pp. 25–84 and 29.

[90] Bohm, referred to in Gerber (1998), p. 246.

[91] Ordungspolitik (order-based policy).

[92] Bohm, in Gerber (1998), p. 247.

Since the policy framework requires that there should be a complete state of competition in order to reflect choices and also to ensure that the right of individuals are protected, the goal of competition law, according to this school, should be the fostering of economic freedom. This is achieved by focusing on the problem of economic power[93] because such power threatens the competitive process and thus individual rights. The elimination or prevention of this harmful effect, proponents argue, should be the primary function of competition law. In other words, so as to prevent this economic power from turning into political power, it is essential to protect individual economic freedom. Hence, competition is necessary for economic wellbeing and economic freedom is necessary for political freedom.[94] In effect, competition law is meant to enhance and promote economic freedom of the individual[95] in the interest of a free and fair political and social order[96] which will ultimately ensure that the society remains humane.[97]

It is noteworthy that ordoliberals accept the use of economics as they seek to combine open market and individual freedom with social justice.[98] Even though it is clearly linked to the open market, the theory is based on humanist rather than efficiency considerations such that efficiency thoughts are to take a mere subordinated role in developing a free order.[99]

There is an obvious similarity between the economic freedom theory and the person-centred approach to antitrust, to wit, its conceptual bottom-up nature. It however appears that this seeming connecting point is inconsequential especially after one analyses the concept in the light of the broadness requirements. On requirement i(a) which calls for a plural understanding of the concept of welfare, it is pertinent to assess whether the interests conceived under the economic freedom theory evinces adequate plurality. According to this theory, save for limited cases,[100] wellbeing (that is, political and economic freedom) is achieved only if the competitive process is maintained. There is no gainsaying that this is too narrow to be accepted. For example, it can be clearly noted from the *Glaxo* case that even though an export ban could be said to be injurious to the competitive structure, the finding of anti-competitive practices in specific cases need not be limited to this market structure. It is quite possible thus that the denting of the competitive structure could be acceptable where, for instance, we consider the well-being of the alleged infringer (in this case, the pharmaceuticals). Thus, as was identified in

[93] Bohm, in Gerber (1998), p. 251.

[94] Möschel (1989), p. 142.

[95] Friedman and Friedman (1980). See also Hayek (1978), pp. 179–190.

[96] Möschel (1989), p. 146.

[97] Euchen (1952), p. 290 referred to in Gormsen (2007), p. 333, n 22.

[98] See Gormsen (2007), p. 334.

[99] See Gormsen (2007), p. 333.

[100] Such as cases where natural monopolies are expected because the market could not sustain more than one enterprise, i.e. utilities. See Gerber (1998), pp. 251–252.

Glaxo, it would not be out of place to consider other factors such as: distortive effect on competition brought about by the existence of national price regulation; the importance of innovation as a driver of competition; the very high cost of innovation; and the need to recover R&D costs.[101] Hence, we might find that it is important to give detailed attention to the efficiency gains.

On requirement i(b) which is about the broadness of the term "persons", economic freedom theory does consider the idea of "person" to be relatively wide—it looks beyond a section such as consumer and focuses on individuals in general. Nonetheless, it is not adequate for the person-centred approach because it does not include every form of persons that are generally referred to as antitrust subjects under the person-centred approach.[102] Further, this school of thought does not particularly fulfil other broadness requirements as well. For instance, contrary to requirement iv which is that focus should be placed on the real interests held by persons rather than the idea of interest which specific schools of thought seem to attribute to person, ordoliberal ideology tends to make assumptions of what individuals would prefer and choose to include in their economic constitution (that is, a competitive structure) rather than focusing on their real interests which might, in a particular instance, be strictly price-based.

4.4 Eclectic Platform for Antitrust

At this point, it is evident that the theories on antitrust addressed so far do not individually fulfil the person-centred approach's requirement of broadness. It appears thus that a broad enough platform for antitrust must "combine elements of the different theories in a way that avoids the objection to each."[103] The eclecticism required, Black notes, is no embarrassment. This is because the act of combining theories "reflects the fact that we have disparate intuitions about welfare". Hence, since interests and intuitions may not only be disparate but mutually contradictory, each theory will be inadequate as competing interests "cannot all be accommodated in a single acceptable theory."[104] With an eclectic approach however, we can adequately address interests by maintaining those interests as choices where in individual cases, "[t]he choice is between pursuit of a reflective equilibrium between intuition and theory, with some intuitions being rejected in the interest of meeting theoretical [and practical] constraints, and admission of more than one concept or conception of welfare"[105]

[101] As recognised by the Court of Justice in *Glaxo*.

[102] In the interest of brevity, it is not necessary to address the remaining requirement since it already fails the first two.

[103] Black (2005), p. 47.

[104] Black (2005), p. 47.

[105] Black (2005), p. 47.

In search for this reflective equilibrium and eclecticism, three approaches are tested against the broadness required in the person-centred approach. First are the philosophical theories on welfare, second is the differentiated normative approach while the third is the capability approach.

4.4.1 Philosophy

It is possible to conceive a philosophical definition of welfare/wellbeing that should be sought in antitrust. A definition that appears to be sufficiently broad is provided by Black. He says that an intuitive understanding of a person's welfare is simply what makes his life go well for him.[106] However, we are never really able to ascertain the broadness of this abstractive definition until we assess philosophical positions on the intuitive meaning of wellbeing. Black identifies two theoretical positions on what is meant by wellbeing: the subjective/positive and the objective/normative.[107]

Theories based on the subjective/positive idea of welfare identify welfare with one or more mental states. These theories are usually hedonistic[108] and are also based on proxies such as satisfaction, choice, preference or desire.[109] Satisfaction theories have their value. For instance, it is widely believed that they allow empirical tests of welfare and avoid paternalism.[110] More particularly as it might impact on antitrust, this perspective is favoured by those economists who view allocative efficiency as a test rather than as a definition of the maximisation of welfare.[111] However, in terms of broadness, these satisfaction theories can be faulted; they either do not fully represent what amounts to wellbeing, or they might even consider things that do not necessarily impact on wellbeing. As such, subjective/positive theories have been criticised as inadequate in substantiating welfare.[112] Thus, a possible conclusion is that this perspective cannot provide the eclecticism required by the person-centred approach. For instance, it is often strongly argued that welfare depends not only on one's mental state but on whether they are veridical[113]; satisfaction theories are built solely on mental state and as such their outcomes do not really reflect the plurality of interests. For example, it is

---

[106] Black (2005), p. 34.

[107] Black (2005), p. 40. For a classification of welfare, see Qizilbash (1997), pp. 227–240; Scanlon (1993), p. 186; Sen (1982), pp. 29–30.

[108] They are usually identified with states such as happiness, pleasure, comfort, contentment, enjoyments etc. See Black (2005), p. 40. For the downsides to this approach see Black (2005), p. 41.

[109] It is hereinafter referred to as satisfaction theories.

[110] See Black (2005), p. 42; Boadway and Bruce (1984), pp. 8, 11, 31–32, and 39; Scitovsky (1992), pp. 4–5.

[111] See Pigou (2002), pp. 10ff.

[112] For details, see Black (2005), p. 42.

[113] Gibbard (1989), p. 169; Nozick (1974), pp. 42–45.

argued that such theories give counter-intuitive results which make such theories hard to reconcile with theories of distributive justice.[114] In the same vein, satisfaction theories are said to produce odd results which are difficult to reconcile with distributive justice in the case of adaptive, unduly demanding or anti-social desires.[115]

The difficulty of developing a general theory of welfare through the subjective/positive philosophical approach makes it imperative that we consider the objective/normative. In this context, the satisfaction theory is refined so that a person's welfare consists in the satisfaction not of any desires he happens to have, but of the desires he would have under certain favourable conditions. This condition could, for example, be that he is perfectly rational and fully informed. Also, the desire could be set against the threshold of an idealised subject. It has been said that this philosophical approach avoids some of the objections of the subjective/positive approach.[116] There are however credible objections which suggest that the revised theory is equally inappropriate for expounding on welfare.[117] The major drawback of this arrangement in the light of the broadness requirement is that it directly contravenes the requirement that account should be taken of the interests held by persons rather than the idea of persons. Thus, by limiting its focus to the idealised subject, it fails to take into account the perspectival character of welfare[118] (such as actual desire) as against the idealised desires. Also like the theories based on the rational choice, the account of an idealised subject unduly limits the scope and nature of "wellbeing". For instance, a criticism which is similar (but distinct) to that often stressed by behavioural law and economics theorists, is that no matter how clear-headed and well informed people are, they often times want things that makes their lives go badly for them.[119]

One can think of a third perspective as suggested by Black who argues that the "best account of welfare" will be a qualified form of the objective theory which emphasises participation in various forms of the good. This, he says, could be achieved by gerrymandering the conditions or the specifications of the idealised subject so as to ensure that the revised theory applies only to those desires unaffected by objections that have been raised against the objective theory.[120] It is however difficult to appreciate this advantage in terms of broadness particularly

---

[114] See Elster (1993), p. 8. He explains that the implication would be that we would have to move resources from the happy "have-nots" to the discontented "haves" until their hedonistic levels are the same.

[115] Sen (1985), p. 191.

[116] Black (2005), p. 45.

[117] For example there are objections concerning the specification of the favourable conditions or the idealised subject and their relation to a person's actual circumstance. Another is that the concept of desire under the revised theory is idle which makes the theory unstable. See Black (2005), pp. 46–47.

[118] Raz (1986), p. 289; Black (2005), p. 47.

[119] Black (2005), p. 45; Harsanyi (1982), pp. 39–62.

[120] Black (2005).

with regards to the person-centred approach to antitrust because the revised theory does not state the extent to which the objective theory is to be altered to accommodate subjective considerations such as "satisfaction".

Conclusively, one is at pains to say that the philosophical approaches so far stated do not provide an adequate foundation for the mixed blend of attributes that fits the requirement of broadness herein sought.

4.4.2 Differentiated Normative Approach

In an attempt to build a bottom-up framework for antitrust, Kerber faulted the prevailing economic and legal approaches on the ground that they fail to focus on normative questions.[121] He argues that rather than limiting the normative inquiry to debates between economic welfare standards, antitrust could recognise normative approaches in economics which offer much broader arguments that might allow for a more differentiated discussion about the goals of competition law. His position thus was that a bottom-up normative framework, which is based on principles of constitutional economics, be applied in antitrust. His reason is that this might allow for more consideration of normative issues that are often emphasised by legal scholars. Examples of such issues include the protection of right of market participants or concepts like competition on merit.

Kerber sought to build a broader framework for antitrust based on normative individualism, constitutional economics, and the rules of the market. Constitutional economics is premised on the idea that all relevant values and goals in a society have to be derived from the preferences and values of individual members of that society. Of note under Kerber's approach is the requirement of voluntary individual consent.[122] It is argued that by consenting to transactions or to mandatory rules of society, individuals reveal their preferences and legitimise contracts and mandatory rules.[123] Built on the idea of social contract, the theory of constitutional economics describes the state as the result of a constitutional contract on which all members of society might agree under a "veil of uncertainty".[124]

Aside from its broad scope, the normative approach is also flexible as it by-passes the condition of unanimity which might be a problem in a regime that requires that individual consents be sought. It forges a transition from the *unanimity principle* (which is one of the most important constitutional rules) to a more pragmatic *decisions rule* which is based on the post-constitutional level of normal legislation.[125] The consequence is that there might be realms in which consent is deemed to be given to the state once a simple majority has been established.

---

121 Kerber (2008), p. 94.

122 Buchanan (1986), p. 243.

123 Kerber (2008), p. 109.

124 Kerber (2008), p. 109.

125 Kerber (2008), p. 109.

Likewise there might be other realms whereby basic right and freedom are considered sacrosanct and as such should not be tampered with even if it means that we lose some positive welfare effect that could have accrued to other persons or to the society as a whole.[126]

Kerber's perspective of the normative approach is said to be different from the welfare economics approach because it emphasises the preference of citizens as the ultimate normative criterion.[127] He argues that the citizens should decide:

> to what extent allocative efficiency and/or dynamic efficiency should be strived for, to what extent competition law should protect consumers from exploitation or competitors from being hurt through predatory strategies, and to what extent society is willing to sacrifice some "total welfare" in order to prevent redistribution through market power[128]

Though he states that the task of economics is simply to analyse the effect of legal rules with regards to the goals as identified by citizens, the approach is based purely on economics and not politics. He then explains the focus on citizens in economic terms by stating that market rules are "optimal" if they correspond with citizens' preferences.[129] Kerber iterates that citizens' preferences should decide the kind of competition that prevails in the market. Putting it in EU context, he states that:

> [W]hat 'effective competition' means in EU competition law is a normative question. If the European Commission defines 'effective competition' as competition that 'brings benefit to consumers, such as low prices, high quality products, a wide selection of goods and services, and innovation', then this is a normative decision, and the relevant question is whether this corresponds to the preferences of the EU citizens.[130]

This perspective of the normative approach attempts to pre-empt the citizens on how they, for instances, would value allocative efficiency or dynamic efficiency. It is presumed that citizens would like both because these efficiencies increase their wealth. There is also an unsubstantiated analysis which suggests that citizens would hardly consent to a total welfare standard. In addition, the approach considers the likely response of citizens to a pure consumer welfare standard which Kerber reckons is unlikely to be positive. Thus he concludes that the standard which most likely will represent the preference of citizens' is the weighted-surplus standard as it is considered to be an intermediate solution between pure total welfare standard and pure consumer welfare standard.

It is clear that Kerber's approach is much broader than the prevailing welfare-based approaches. Just like the person-centred approach, the broadness in Kerber's approach derives from his bottom-up perspective to antitrust analysis. It is relatively eclectic as, for instance regarding requirement i(a) which calls for a plural

[126] Kerber (2008), p. 109.
[127] Kerber (2008), p. 110.
[128] Kerber (2008), p. 110.
[129] Kerber (2008), p. 111.
[130] Kerber (2008), p. 111.

understanding of the concept of welfare, the approach defines interest from the plural perspective. In particular, it shows that the definition of interests (and consequently welfare) should not be narrowed down to either of the consumer welfare or total welfare standard. Moreover, the preferred weighted surplus standard combines some element of both total and consumer welfare. The approach sets a plural platform through which our definition of economic welfare can "take into account the effect of restrictive agreements, mergers and business behaviours not only on consumer welfare but also on a set of protected rights of competitors and up- and downstream firms which might suffer losses through the infringement of these rights."[131]

Kerber's differentiated approach fulfils requirement i(b) which is that "persons" must relate to a wide range of persons and not a section or group such as consumers. Arguing against the application of pure consumer welfare standard, this approach suggests that focus should be on citizens. This means that "persons" cannot be limited to consumers "but also owners of production factors such as, in particular, capital and labour, and are therefore interested in income from interest, wages and profits."[132] Thus, in line with this requirement, the differentiated approach does not accept a narrow conception of persons. It states that "the normative asymmetry which holds that competition law is only about the protection of consumers' interests and that the interests of all other firms on the upstream markets are irrelevant is hard to justify".[133] This differentiated perspective is particularly strong on this requirement as it also vividly analyses why a narrow focus on consumers is far from ideal. By analysing the role of competition law in protecting businesses on the supply side of a market from the buying power of other firms (a kind of collective monopsony), it is argued under this approach that a strict focus on consumers does not give a credible explanation as to why buying power that lead to a reduction of input prices (and therefore consequently to lower prices for consumers) should be assessed negative especially where such reduction does not lead to negative effect on consumers.[134]

However, though this approach is broad in its own right, it is arguable whether it affords a wide-enough interpretation of interests especially when one considers its likely position concerning other ideals that could be sought through antitrust.[135] One could also fault the contractarian foundation as it may deal with the idea of the person rather than real persons.[136] This might lead to outcomes which are not truly

---

[131] Kerber (2008), p. 117.

[132] Kerber (2008), p. 113.

[133] Kerber (2008), p. 113.

[134] Note the opinion of Thomas Rosch who argues that the US Sherman Act protects consumers in the strict sense of the word. See Rosch (2007).

[135] For example, competition law goals such as international competitiveness and economic integration.

[136] For example, see Sen's criticism of Rawls' *Theory of Justice* in Sen (2009), pp. 87–113.

reflective of what individuals consider to be of value to them. On these bases, this approach does not seem ideal for the person-centred analysis.

4.4.3 Sen's Capability Approach

Considering that a broad account would "combine elements of the different theories in a way that avoids the objection to each",[137] our task will be to identify the approach which is accommodating enough to combine elements of different antitrust theories while at the same time maintains its intelligibility. This is clearly a hard task considering the fact that quite often, different theories would conflict. Indeed it has been shown in the preceding chapter that out of the various welfare/freedom based jurisprudential thoughts, it is the capability approach that affords the best chance of conducting a person-centred analysis of antitrust right as it accommodates different interests—this approach is able to accommodate the element of different theories because it steers a middle course between mental-state and satisfaction theories on the one hand and objective theories on the other.[138]

In the specific context, capability approach can accommodate elements of the antitrust theories that have been discussed so far. It sustains it intelligibility and thus deals sufficiently even with potentially conflicting effects because the approach, by focusing solely on opportunities, only serve as a platform and nothing more: it does not propose a theory that could help us decide within and between the multitude of theories whose elements have been recognised; it cannot tell us what exactly should be the goal of antitrust and what the mode of analysing antitrust should be. The strength of the capability approach lies in the fact that it concedes that the approach "cannot pay adequate attention to fairness and equity involved in procedures that have relevance to the idea of justice."[139] Thus, when applied to antitrust, it means we have to desist from specifying one goal as against the other.

This thesis thus proposes the capability approach as the ideal platform upon which the broadness sought by the person-centred approach can be achieved. The next part is dedicated to detailing the content of the approach. It also contains the justification for choosing this approach.

137 Black (2005), p. 47.

138 Black (2005), p. 47.

139 Sen (2009), p. 295.

4.5 Capability Approach as the Platform for Antitrust Analysis

To reiterate the point, capability approach is able to maintain the value of all relevant theories primarily because it desists from judging between them. The broadness it achieves is through a bottom-up analysis. To establish its suitability, I give greater details on the approach itself. An attempt is also made to set it clear of the theories that have been discussed so far especially those that are right/freedom based. Thereafter, the approach is tested against the broadness requirements.

4.5.1 Capability Approach Detailed

The capability approach is a broad normative framework for the evaluation of individual well-being and social arrangements, the design of policies and proposals about social change in society.[140] One of its strengths lies in the fact that it can be applied in a wide range of fields. As such, the proposition that it should be applied to antitrust is by no means inconceivable. It can be used to evaluate a variety of aspects of people's wellbeing, such as individual well-being, inequality and poverty. The diverse instances or fields in which the approach can be applied implies that the contours of the approach which are considered relevant in particular cases will derive directly from the disciplinary perspective from which the approach is applied or the nature of the task or purpose for which it is applied. For instance, the aspect of the capability approach that might interest a philosopher might be different from that which a mainstream economist or heterodox economist might express interest.[141] For the purpose of this thesis, the aspect of the capability approach that is emphasised is the idea of broadness. In line with the very nature of antitrust, it is the wellbeing/welfare aspect that will be the focal point of our analysis.

The capability approach is concerned with evaluating a person's advantage by focusing on what people are effectively able to do and to be. As it would be shown, it places primary focus on individuals. This approach is substantially different from those wherein wellbeing is addressed strictly through happiness, desire, price, income, preferences and so on. Expounding on the need to place individuals at the centre of policy analysis and evaluations, Sen states that by focusing on what people are able to do and be and on the quality of their lives, we ensure for them more freedom to live the kind of life which, upon reflection, they find valuable. He states that:

[140] Robeyns (2005), p. 94.

[141] Sen said that the capability approach can be used for a wide range of purposes. See Sen (1993), p. 49.

> [T]he capability approach to a person's advantage is concerned with evaluating it in terms of his or her ability to achieve various valuable functionings as a part of living. The corresponding approach to social advantage – for aggregative appraisal as well as for the choice of institutions and policy – takes the set of individual capabilities as constituting an indispensable and central part of the relevant informational base of such evaluation[142]

Wellbeing is thus to be assessed in terms of people's capabilities to function. Assessing people's "achieved functionings" requires that we focus our evaluative exercise on their effective opportunities to undertake the actions and activities that they want to engage in, and to be the person they want to be. This approach concerns individual's ability to achieve different combination of functionings that they can compare and judge against each other in terms of what they have reasons to value. While functionings refer to those beings and doings that have been realised, capabilities refer to those that are effectively possible. To put it differently, the former relates to achievement while the latter relates to freedom. The important thing is that people have the freedom (capabilities) to lead the kind of lives they want to lead, to do what they want to do, and be the person they want to be. Once they effectively have these freedoms, they can choose to act on those freedoms in line with their own idea of the kind of life they want to live.

We extend our focus to opportunities under the capability approach because it affords versatility; it is more general and more informationally inclusive than merely relying on achieved functionings. Sen argues that there is no loss in looking at the broader informational base of capabilities, which allows that we simply rely on the valuation of achieved functionings and also allows the use of other priorities in evaluation, thereby attaching importance to opportunity and choice.[143]

Capability approach operates at three different levels. It operates: as a framework of thought for the evaluation of individual advantage and social arrangement; as a critique of other approaches to the evaluation of well-being and justice; and as a formula or algorithm to make interpersonal comparisons of welfare or well-being.[144] In the context of this research, while the first and second levels are of primary relevance in this chapter, the third level of application will be addressed in the next chapter. At the first level wherein the approach serves as a framework of thought for the evaluation of individual advantage and social arrangement, the focus on functionings and capabilities is the springboard upon which broadness is achieved. At the second level, whereby it serves as a critique, it helps to separate the capability approach from prominent theories in antitrust.

To identify the scope of this approach, it is pertinent that functionings and capabilities are addressed in greater detail. As already noted, while a person's functionings are his "being and doings", his capability is the various combinations

[142] Sen (1993), p. 30.

[143] Sen (2009), p. 236.

[144] Robeyns (2000), p. 3.

of functions that a person can achieve. Hence, capability is "a set of vectors of functionings reflecting the person's freedom to lead one type of life or another".[145] To put the difference between the two in context, we could proceed on the assumption that in a specific market, our functioning as antitrust subjects (either individually or collectively) might be that we are able to benefit from competitive prices and greater quality or simply to have a healthy competitive process in the relevant market. The relationship between that state of competition and the perceived functionings to achieve such state is influenced by three conversion factors.[146] The first factor is the personal characteristics of the individual or group. Put into perspective, whether or not a "functioning" is considered to be "achieved" will depend on our understanding of the antitrust subject. For example, if it is to be analysed whether persons in a relevant market have achieved functionings, one might come to different conclusions depending on the antitrust theory they aligned to; our finding where neo-classical economics is applied will differ from that which will be arrived at where behavioural law and economics or economic freedom are applied because the metric for assessing functioning differ from one theory to another.

The second factor is regarding social characteristics. This means that our finding on whether relevant persons have achieved functionings may depend on our understanding of the social state which they value. For example, aside from price, are consumers equally concerned about environmental factors or industrial policy to such an extent that they would readily factor them into competition law cases? The third factor relates to the environmental characteristics.[147] With regards to this conversion factor, it is meant that whether a functioning is achieved will depend on the extent to which the relevant antitrust institution thinks it needs to formulate and implements its antitrust policy.

It must be noted that it is not enough to know the functioning which persons' *can* achieve by merely forming an idea of *the beings and doings* of persons' in a market through the dictates of the conversion factors. Thus, in addition, there is need to know more about the person and the circumstances in which he is living. This is where the capability approach extends beyond mere functionings. Sen's Capability approach does not consider the functionings that a person has achieved as the ultimate normative measure. Rather, it focuses on people's real freedom. In sum, while the functioning of a person are the set of thing that they do in life, the capability of that person is the alternative combination of functionings that they can achieve and from which they can choose one vector of functioning.

It should be observed that, as a result of our theoretical inclination which is manifested through the conversion factors, a single competition scenario might

---

[145] Robeyns (2000), p. 3.

[146] The conversion factors are explained by Robeyns (2000), p. 3.

[147] "Environmental characteristics" in the context of the capability approach is different from the specific public policy issue of environmental protection that can be debated in competition law. Note that the environmental protection concern comes up under the second conversion factor, which is termed "social characteristics".

require conflicting state of competition with each of those states positing on what amounts to achieved functioning. In effect, since the conversion factors might differ, even where two people have identical capability set, they are likely to end up with different types and levels of achieved functionings since different theories imbue each set with different choices. This is because they have varied ideas on what constitute a good life from their effective options. With regards to the need to respect the difference in opinion on what constitutes a good life, Sen argues that it is capabilities, not achieved functioning which should be the appropriate political goal of institutions.

Because capability could accommodate alternative functionings, it allows a much broader meaning of wellbeing if applied to antitrust. To fully appreciate why capability accommodates different functionings even if they conflict, it is imperative that we understand the connection between well-being and individual freedom. The idea of individual freedom under the capability approach contains two aspects: the opportunity aspect and process aspect. The opportunity aspect of freedom means that individuals should have more opportunities to pursue their objectives so that they can live as they would like and to promote the ends that they may want to advance. The process aspect requires that individuals should be able to achieve what they value while also paying due regard to the process through which that achievement comes about. Capability approach focuses on substantive opportunities of antitrust subject. The modest nature of the approach makes it possible for it to accommodate even conflicting functionings.

All aspects of the approach have their relevance. Take for instance that, based on a particular conversion factor, particular individual values efficiency as the metric for antitrust assessment because of some perceived welfare benefits. If a particular market condition is efficient, we can say convincingly that the process aspect of the relevant antitrust subject's freedom is respected. However, we have to be able to conceive that the same antitrust subject might be influenced by different conversion factors such that he might prefer the pursuit of economic freedom. If an antitrust regime limits the meaning of achieved functioning to efficiency, the fact that in a particular instance, a person supports efficiency does not mean that his freedom has not been impinged. Thus, even though the process aspect of his freedom is fulfilled, the opportunity aspect of such person's freedom is bruised. Hence, the elimination of choice in the opportunity aspect should not be tolerated even where we feel convinced that the antitrust subject is unlikely to make the alternative choice.

4.5.2 Capability Approach and the Requirements of the Person-Centred Approach

From the preceding explanation, there should be no doubt that the capability approach contemplates a broad scope for social analysis. Nonetheless, it is important to put it in the antitrust context and specifically assess it in light of the person-centred approach. It has been noted that the capability approach seeks a good life which we can only say we have where the institutions are not only concerned with what a persons has achieved, but also the opportunity to achieve what he might want to achieve. This ensures that the institution takes note of the different interests held by people by paying attention to the circumstances in which people live. Put in context of antitrust, it means that even if, at one point, an antitrust subject desires a near perfect competitive state in a market, we should still take into account why such market condition might be justifiably undesirable to some other antitrust subjects (for instance, firms in an oligopolistic market). In sum, when these different interests are combined, we end up with the capability framework. Being a mere procedural framework, the capability approach herein deployed is completely agnostic of the normative appeal of the different interests. As such, it will be the responsibility of individual regimes to define the width and breadth of claims that might surface within the framework.[148]

More specifically on the person-centred approach, it behoves that since it has been shown that some relatively broad theories do not fulfil the broadness required in this thesis, it is pertinent that before the capability approach is firmly placed as the framework upon which the person-centred antitrust analysis is to be conducted, its realms have to be tested in light of the broadness requirement.

Starting with requirement i(a) which calls for a plural understanding of the concept of welfare, the capability approach evinces plurality in the meaning of wellbeing. By focusing on quality of life, this approach allows us to move away from the narrower understanding of interest which is that people primarily pursue their own wellbeing. Applied to antitrust, the idea of "good life" sought by the capability approach is a sum of the interests held by different persons and groups. A "good life" is only attained where we ensure that every antitrust subject who holds a stake in any antitrust issue must not be denied the opportunity to have their interest protected. In essence, we do not define good life or wellbeing by strictly focusing on interest of a type of person. In other words, a "good life" is not to be defined by reference to the self-interested individual. Where an antitrust framework gives one or more persons the opportunity to fulfil their interests at the expense of others, it could imply that the framework fails to ensure a good life for the whole market and even for those who were opportune to have their interest included in it. The reason for defining good life from both an aggregative and individual standpoint becomes apparent when one considers Sen's attempt to distinguish between agency[149] and wellbeing on the one hand and freedom and achievement on the other.

On the first set (that is, agency and wellbeing), Sen argues that the distinction is between the promotion of the person's wellbeing in the strict sense and the pursuit of the person's overall agency goals. Agency is broader in that it includes all the

[148] For example, it is for individual regimes to decide whether or not naked cartelist behaviour should or should not be included within the capability framework.

[149] "Agency encompasses all goals that a person has reason to adopt which can inter alia include goals other than the advancement of his or her own well-being" Sen (2009), p. 287.

goals that a person has reason to adopt, which can, inter alia, include goals other than the advancement of self-interested wellbeing. Thus, agency achievement will require that we achieve both our wellbeing and non-wellbeing objectives. As a result, one could argue that failure to achieve non-wellbeing objectives may cause dissatisfaction, which may lead to a reduction of wellbeing.

The distinction between *achievement* (functionings) and the *freedom* to achieve (capability) on the one hand, and *wellbeing* and *agency* on the other hand, yields four different concepts of advantage as it relates to a person. They are: wellbeing achievement; agency achievement; wellbeing freedom; and agency freedom. These possibilities are reflective of how broad our idea of wellbeing can be under the capability approach even though we would have to choose between these possibilities at a later stage. It is of value to the person-centred approach that the idea of a person's interest (his wellbeing) could be either one of or a combination of his achieved self-interested wellbeing, his achieved non self-interested objectives, the freedom to achieve his self-interested wellbeing, the freedom to achieve his non self-interested objectives. From the foregoing, it is apparent that the capability approach satisfies requirement i(b) (which is on the meaning of "persons") as well since the meaning of persons cannot be narrowed down to a self-interested group but rather to a wide range of persons. Moreover, this is a natural interpretation of the capability approach since no one or group of persons can possibly have a good life in isolation.

Put in context of European competition law, an example that can be given to establish this broader concept of advantage is the Court of Justice's decision in *Asnef-Equifax*.[150] This case was about Spanish banks setting up an information sharing facility which was to allow any bank to access the credit history of a borrower. Applying Article 101(3) in order to ascertain the benefits that this scheme could bring, the Court held that "registers such as the one at issue in the main proceedings are capable of helping to prevent situations of over-indebtedness for consumers of credit as well as, in principle, of leading to a greater overall availability of credit". In light of the capability approach, it could be argued that though the banks' ultimate aim was to maximise their profit, they could also be said to have had an intermediate goal which is partly motivated by their agency objectives. Thus, even if this case is to be addressed from the perspective of the banks as a group of persons (antitrust subjects) whose interests count, it was open to the court to consider whether their interests (wellbeing) are limited to their self-interested wellbeing achievement (in this case, their self-centred gain from collusion). Though not strictly apt on the fact of the case, one could possibly construe the finding in this case to be that the banks had an agency objective which is to prevent situation of over-indebtedness for consumers and also afford greater availability of credit. Hence, in assessing the case, it is for the court to realise that the wellbeing of the banks may incorporate both their wellbeing freedom and agency freedom.

[150] Case C-238/05 *Asnef-Equifax v Asociation de. Usuarios de Servicios Bancarios* (*Ausbanc*), (2006) ECR I-11125, para 67.

When assessed from the position of another set of antitrust subjects such as consumers, one could relate with how the capability approach ensures that their wellbeing is given a broad enough meaning. Take for example the *Microsoft v Commission* case.[151] In that case, the General Court came to the conclusion that Microsoft's tying arrangement amounted to a breach of competition law. This conclusion would have remained even if the Court was convinced by Microsoft's argument that it did not charge anything extra from consumers for using their Media Player, which was the tied product. The Court's allusion to the necessity of consumer choice would have been an adequate ground for the finding. One could analyse this reasoning through the broad idea of wellbeing as conceived by the capability approach. There are a number of achieved wellbeing effects that could be attributed to Microsoft's conduct. First, the consumers got a valuable product for free. Second, it saves them from searching costs. Third, by tying those products, the less tech-savvy consumers are saved from the stress and confusion they could face if they had to source these products separately. However, all these advantages relate only to a part of wellbeing, that is, achieved wellbeing. The court recognised another form of wellbeing that was implicated in this case. By addressing the issue of choice, the court flagged up the consumer's wellbeing freedom.[152]

In relation to requirement ii which is that "plural interests" should be understood as different interests held by different persons, the capability approach addresses "interests" as different interests held by different person all of which are worthy of consideration. Each person or a group of persons have a unique capability set. This approach maintains plurality of interests by recognising the different capability sets on the understanding that different persons could premise their interests on competing principles each of which may pass the test of non-rejectability.[153] Regarding *requirement iii* which is that plural interests should mean different interests held by a single antitrust subject or those held by a group of antitrust subjects, the capability approach attains the requisite broadness by assessing the quality of life of persons. It is argued that in non-utilitarian philosophy, public policy and everyday life, wellbeing (which is the product of a person's interests) is judged not only by preference fulfilment,[154] or the attainment of satisfaction. It also includes other factors such as their positive freedom or capability, that is, the range of attainable valuable functionings they face. It can be easily inferred (from explanation and distinction between a person's wellbeing freedom and agency freedom) that a single antitrust subject or a group of them may have multiple interests some or all of which are worth considering.

---

[151] Case T-201/04 [2007] ECR II-3601. See generally Ayal (2012), pp. 627–662; Lambert and Wright (2007–2008), p. 219.

[152] In this case, the court considered wellbeing-freedom to be of more importance. Note though that it is not the concern of the capability approach to decide between both. The decisional process of a regime will be addressed in Chap. 5.

[153] Note though that this does not mean we can demand equality of capability for everyone. Again, it must be noted that this decision is not of primary concern under the capability approach.

[154] Since preferences may be poorly informed.

In satisfaction of *requirement iv* which is that we should focus on the real interests held by persons rather than the idea of interest which specific schools of thought tend to attribute to person, the capability approach focuses on the real interests held by people by stressing the need to give them the opportunity to achieve what they value. Thus, rather than theorising their interest either through rationality, constitutional economics or through other contractarian approaches such as Rawls' indifference principle or Kerber's "veil of uncertainty", the capability approach gives no principled account of interests. This makes it suitable as a comparative assessment tool as it would aid in ascertaining the genuine interest of one or some of the antitrust subjects. This approach escapes the ills of idealised interests because, while the former could become relatively inflexible because of their transcendental stance, the framework based on the latter only calls on relevant interests on a case-by-case basis.

Take for example that an agreement is to be assessed. If we proceed from self-interest (rationality) as the idealised conception of interest, our framework might recognise only a state that primarily favours businesses (total welfare) or one that primarily favours consumer either in terms of price (wealth transfer) or one that includes non-price considerations (consumer interest and consumer choice). There is no gainsaying that the real interest that could be held by antitrust subject either individually or collectively cannot be summed up under either of these idealised interests. What capability approach does in order to keep the real interests that different persons have is to leave open the possibility, that is, give antitrust subjects (either individually or as a group) the opportunity to achieve the interest (including one or a combination of the idealised sets) that they may value as the case may require.

The capability approach passes *requirement v* which is that interests of a person cannot be predetermined through a universal preferential ranking, because it desists from making judgments about the principles underlying individual interests. This ensures that the approach accommodates interests on an equal footing at an *ex ante* stage.

4.5.3 Capability and Traditional Antitrust Theories

It needs to be reiterated that the person-centred approach to antitrust is not just proposed for iconoclastic reasons. As it has been shown in Chap. 1, the traditional ways of analysing antitrust can be faulted on the ground that they are not broad enough where antitrust is addressed from a bottom-up perspective. On the other hand, it has been shown that the capability approach meets the requisite conditions of broadness. Logically therefore, there must be substantial (theoretical and also practical) differences between the capability approach and the other theories. A basic expectation would thus be that the capability approach requires processes and outcomes different from those under the prevailing antitrust theories. Hence, it is pertinent to identify its distinct nature through a comparative analysis with the other theories. The comparison will be undertaken at the very foundational level. This means that accounts such as total welfare, consumer choice and consumer interest will all be placed under the umbrella of the revealed preference approach. The other groups that will be compared against the capability approach are the public policy accounts (general equilibrium and public policy) and the freedom-based (economic freedom and differentiated normative) approaches.

4.5.3.i Capability and Revealed Preference

The prevailing antitrust theories modelled on total surplus, consumer surplus and consumer choice[155] accounts derive from the revealed preference theory.[156] Regardless of the standard used, both static and dynamic effect[157] of competition can be normatively measured with the criterion of the consumer or society's net preference fulfilment. The link between these theories and preference fulfilment can be seen as a consequence of normative individualism, which is that all normatively relevant values in society derive from preferences of individual members of such society.[158] In basic terms, it means that what we value (which primarily maximises our utility) is revealed through our actions. In this context, individual preferences play two parts: first, they determine individual choices; and second, they represent individual welfares used in the evaluations of market equilibra.[159]

Before I detail the dividing line between the capability and the theories based on revealed preference, it is important to state what they share in common. Primarily, the two categories are motivated by preference of individuals—the revealed preference theories are motivated by preferences which they explain through the idea of rationality. In similar vein, the capability approach fit into the fundamental theorem of welfare economics in terms of preference fulfilment by taking preference as the binary basis of choice regardless of what the underlying motivation for choice are.[160] This is however where the similarity ends. While the capability approach seeks to represent all possible functionings in the framework because they invariably represent the preference of some antitrust subject, the latter seeks to achieve a set universal preference either for the society as a whole or for a group such as consumers. Hence, it must be understood that even where we use peculiar terms such as preferences or efficiency within either of the peculiar areas, the meaning of

[155] Averitt and Lande (2007) state that the options that consumers' accord with are identified by their preferences as expressed in the marketplace. See pp. 183–184.

[156] Consumer surplus refer to the perceived welfare of buyers in a particular market while total surplus refers to the perceived welfare of buyers and sellers in a particular market. See Orbach (2010), p. 5.

[157] Note though that dynamic efficiency is less geared on existing preferences.

[158] Kerber (2008), p. 99.

[159] Sen (2002), p. 520.

[160] Sen (1993), pp. 533–534.

those terms are bound to be very different. For example, if reference is made to the term "efficiency" when addressing an antitrust issue in the context of either total welfare or the consumer-based approaches, one is unequivocally referring to allocative, productive or dynamic efficiencies. However, if we seek to assess the efficiency of the person-centred approach and the capability framework in particular, we are simply assessing how well we have achieved or are likely to achieve our ultimate quest of having every relevant preference represented. Institutions must pay particular attention to every capability framework as it is their duty to ensure that "the basic analytical result relate directly to the fulfilment of preferences (in choice sense)".[161]

Thus, in relation to specific antitrust concerns, we are to seek the efficiency of the capability framework not through the narrow self-interested conceptions of allocative, productive and dynamic efficiencies. Rather, we are to seek *efficiency of preference fulfilment* as the theory of competitive market equilibrium indicates.[162] This state of well-being is achieved where it is impossible to move any one to a more preferred position (for instance, a position that the person would choose given the opportunity), keeping everyone in an equally preferred situation.[163] It would be impossible to achieve this unless we give adequate opportunity to all possible preferences and interests. Hence, the capability framework is efficient where it contains complete capability sets of each and every relevant antitrust subject.

Having noted the difference, it is pertinent to indicate why antitrust should be addressed through the capability framework rather than narrowing our analysis to the revealed preference theories. Primarily, there is a fundamental flaw in the revealed preference approaches which the capability framework is immune to—by narrowing the basis upon which antitrust subjects express preferences, these accounts fail to take note of peculiar circumstances and, as such, they fail to fully reflect preferences or to enhance welfare.[164] With the example of consumer-based approaches, it has been convincingly argued that there are a good number of cases in which revealed preferences are likely to lead to welfare losses.[165] The first category of cases in which these theories fail is where it is presumed that consumers are so attuned to prefer low prices that they would seek low prices for "bads".[166] Where the focus is narrowed to revealed preferences, we are likely to believe that a competitive state

[161] Sen (1993), pp. 533–534.

[162] Sen (1993), p. 521. Under this approach to antitrust, the process is efficient where there is a clear structure that allows for us to keep every interest in an equally preferred position up till the point when we are no longer able to avoid making firm decisions.

[163] Sen (1993), p. 521.

[164] This follows from the explanation that these specific theories are incomplete and mistaken as discussed in Chap. 1.

[165] Here, welfare is defined in the broader context.

[166] We can possibly categorise "bads" as legal "bads" or undesirable "bads". An example of legal bad is tobacco. On the other hand, many other legal products and services are arguably undesirable. Examples include abortions, alcohol, firearms, gambling, pornography, and sex services. See Orbach (2010), p. 18.

which ends up in low prices for consumers must be preferred in all conceivable cases[167] when in fact, one cannot rule out the likelihood that there would be a certain antitrust subject or a category of them who will consider low prices for particular products such as tobacco and alcohol to be particularly disadvantageous to their welfare.[168] The same narrow reasoning fails when we consider status goods and innovation in durables and fashion.[169]

4.5.3.ii Capability and Public Policy

At the conceptual level, the primary difference between the capability framework and public policy approach is that while the nature and purpose of the former can be effectively analysed (that is, based on the need for justice as inclusiveness), the latter does not furnish substantial justification for broadening the scope of antitrust beyond the fact that certain end-states must be preserved. It means in essence that while the public policy argument may be defeated where a solid counter-argument indicates that there are set mechanisms outside the realms of antitrust that can achieve such end-state, the capability-based approach will not be so affected because broadness is sought on the basis of justice—that is, the freedom to have one's interest considered in social and judicial evaluations. In this regard, even though actual analysis of individual cases might go in the same line, it is the justificatory basis of the capability approach that makes it superior to a mere public policy argument. This is because while public policy arguments are presented as a strategic issue which could consequently thus be shown to be inappropriate in particular instances through the identification of alternative strategies, the capability approach is presented as an atomistic account which is conceptually independent from institutional idiosyncrasies. As such, it could not be defeated by counter-examples of how a regime applies or could apply an alternative approach to antitrust.[170]

Further, the capability approach is able to pay greater attention to all the interests of persons since it concedes its inability to relate adequately with the diverging interests. This makes capability approach escape deconstruction as it merely paves the way for a comparative assessment of interests. On the other hand however, public policy accounts are likely to take a transcendental position which opens them to the scrutiny of the deconstruction ideology. For example, Townley's attempt to build a balancing framework can be deconstructed on the grounds that it attaches

---

[167] The US Supreme Court gave this impression in *Atlantic Richfield* where it stressed that "low prices benefit consumers regardless of how those prices are set, and ... they cannot give rise to antitrust injury" 495 US 328, 340.

[168] Orbach (2010), p. 354.

[169] Orbach (2010), pp. 20–24.

[170] As noted above, it is however open to individual regimes to ascertain the width and breadth of interests which they seek to accommodate within the capability framework.

relative weight to different interests. Analysing the text of the EC Treaty (now TFEU) in order to build a principled account for EU competition law, Townley establishes a qualitative weight where he divides different interests into two categories—High and Not High. Interests within each of these categories are further sub-categorised as "light" or "heavy".[171] This categorisation is susceptible to the deconstruction exercise. Moreover, an attempt to build a principled framework that balances welfare and public policy will likely impugn on the interest of persons and sets it far apart from the capability framework: while capability approach pays greater attention to interests because it merely accommodates every relevant interest without strengthening the value of one at the expense of the other, Townley's balancing framework tends to rank public policy concerns thereby promoting some interests and relegating others at an *ex ante* stage.

4.5.3.iii Capability and the Freedom-Based Antitrust Theories

The theory of economic freedom and Kerber's differentiated approach are theorised through the idea of the collectiveness of wills which interestingly has always been argued to be an integral part of European competition law.[172] These theories reflect different brands of normative individualism which brings in both economic and political implications. Though to differing degrees, both theories can be addressed in terms of individual right. However, while the differentiated approach may lead to case-specific (and consequently broad outcomes), the scope of the outcome deriving from the theory of economic freedom might be more restricted. The difference notwithstanding, one could either trace both theories to the foundational theory of constitutional economics.[173]

---

[171] For instance, in his qualitative assessment, Townley divides the relevance of public policy consideration to "High" and "Not-High". While the "High" group contains employment, public health, consumer protection, environment and competition, the "Not-High" group contains public policy concerns relating to culture, economic and social cohesion, R&D and development co-operation. See Townley (2009), p. 295.

[172] See e.g. Commission Report on Competition Policy 1979, paras 9 and 10; Commission Report on Competition Policy 1985 para 11.

[173] One of the prominent accounts under the theory of constitutional economics is Buchanan's common agreement theory. It provides that the network of rules constituting an institution are justified because they are freely consented to and that particular institutional events, in the form of actions, policies and decisions, are justified because they are required by rules that are consented to. It is believed within this theory that policies, market transactions or political decisions and so on can be given content or meaning only within an institutional framework. In the justificatory exercise, one should not address a rule in isolation. Rather, the network of rules should be considered since it is what "gives it life and substance". Even though desirable end-states such as utility and welfare have a role to play in this consent theory, they are merely derivative of the main measure which is the level of acceptance that the set of rules enjoy within a given community. As such, welfare or utility will only be relevant to the extent that they figure in the evaluation of institutions. See generally Buchanan (1991).

Unlike the capability approach, the freedom-based thoughts (be it the ordoliberals' *ordungpolitik* or Kerber's "veil of uncertainty") are based on a narrower understanding of wellbeing. Thus, an individual is expected to consent to a specific mode of analysing antitrust where it serves his interest whereas under the capability approach, "interests" and "choice" are beyond the actual interests or choice made or expected to be made. It also includes the opportunity to hold different interests and make other choices. The more practical difference between these accounts however lies in the fact that while the freedom-based thoughts are largely contractarian which means that processes and outcomes for antitrust are arrived at in advance through an ex ante recognition of a firm theory of antitrust, the capability approach on the other hand makes no grand statement on peculiar antitrust ideals, theories, policies or methodologies.

The effect of the freedom-based approaches is that their transcendental outlay (which gives a tone of finality on what antitrust should pursue) is likely to render the theories incapable of noting some imminent interests that are unique to specific cases. The capability approach on the other hand is able to escape this problem primarily because it is not a theory; it is simply a perspective for identifying interests irrespective of their theoretical undertone. Put in perspective, when one considers the assumptions of ordoliberals and Kerber, one can, without much effort, see some loopholes when we assess these theories through Smithian impartial spectator.[174] It becomes clear that these theories are predisposed to the demands of institutional rules and thus fail to take note of some important social factors. Also, it appears that these theories might fail to take note of some voices and interests.[175] The capability approach on the other hand accommodates all relevant functionings/interest as it particularly stays clear of decision-making.

4.6 Illustrating Capability as the Ideal Broad Framework Vis a Vis Other Theories

To illustrate the role of capability approach in the analysis of antitrust right as against other theories, I will give examples of price and non-price competition issues. The examples will relate with both anti-competitive agreements/ concertation and abuse of dominance. So as to observe the differences within them and most importantly how the capability approach absolves their (sometimes conflicting) implications, I apply the major theories underlying antitrust and the capability approach to a set of fact. Noting that certain anti-competitive behaviours such as cartelisation (even though for substantially different reasons) would in

[174] See generally Raphael (2007).

[175] Note though that Kerber's account might substantially reduce this weakness since it allows for a differentiation of the outcome of the deliberative process such that minority voices might be protected in specific instances through the grant of liberal rights.

principle be found wanting under most of the dominant antitrust theories, this illustrative exercise will particularly not focus on such conducts. Rather, the assumed facts will be based on the conducts of tying[176] and a host of other specific antitrust issues.[177] It will also include dimensions based on integration and the environment/health.

4.6.1 Capability Approach and Tying

It is trite to assert that anti-competitive behaviours ought to be prevented. We are however likely to disagree regarding what is meant by competition and what amounts to anti-competition. Different theories which have been stated above could shape our reasoning when we address competition issues. To showcase this difference and the role of the capability approach, I build an issue around contract franchise tying and tying as an exclusionary abuse. However, before I delve into those specific areas, it is pertinent to give a brief analysis of tying.

4.6.1.i Tying in Brief

Tying can be defined as the selling or licensing of a product or service made conditional on the sale or licensing of another related product.[178] This conduct can be categorised into three main types namely bundling, tying and metering.[179] The reasons why firms could choose to tie products has been categorised into two: efficiency and strategic reasons.[180] Concerning the welfare enhancing aspect, tying can be used by a firm to reduce cost. Such reduction can arise as a result of reduction in production, distribution and so on. Economies of scale can also be achieved such that a firm may benefit from producing two products together rather than selling them individually. Consumers could also benefit from a tying arrangement through a reduction in transaction cost.[181] In the same vein however, tying could possibly prejudice consumers in terms of price[182] and may lead to anti-

---

[176] I choose tying because it can be applied under both anti-competitive agreement and abuse of dominance. Also, it allows for more diverse interpretation between competing theories.

[177] Predation is chosen because of the diverse interpretation we could have between competing theories particularly since consumers may be (even if it is merely in the short term) better off with low prices.

[178] Schmidt (2009), p. 3.

[179] Nalebuff (2003).

[180] Nalebuff (2003), p. 18.

[181] See Evans et al. (2004), p. 320.

[182] Guidelines on Vertical Restraints, para 217.

competitive foreclosure effects on the tied market which affects consumer choice.[183]

4.6.1.ii Franchise Contract Tying Assessed as a Restrictive Agreement

The meaning, the motivations and some of the impacts of tying have been noted. It should thus be further noted that the extent to which these observations might impact on antitrust analyses depend on the facts of individual cases as well as the theory we align to. It would therefore be helpful to illustrate how tying arrangement might be assessed under the different theories through an assumed fact based on franchise contract tying. However, before the fact is set out, the nature of the restrictive concerns in both franchising and tying are summarised.

Franchise agreements contain license of intellectual property rights and also the provision of commercial and technical assistance. Amongst other things, a franchise agreement usually contains a combination of different vertical restraints concerning the products being distributed, in particular selective distribution and/or non-compete and/or exclusive distribution.[184] Tying on the other hand may constitute a vertical restraint falling under Article 101 where it results in a single branding[185] type of obligation.[186] The possible competition concerns arising from single branding are foreclosure of market to competing suppliers, softening of competition and facilitation of collusion between suppliers and, where the buyer is a retailer selling to final consumers, a loss of in-store inter-brand competition.[187] However, franchise contract tying arrangements do not automatically generate anti-competitive effects. Single branding through, for instance, non-compete obligations may be justified in a franchise agreement where there has been a transfer of substantial know-how from the franchisor to the franchisee.[188] The more important the know-how, the more likely it is that the restraints create efficiencies and/or are

[183] Guidelines on Vertical Restraints, para 216.

[184] Guidelines on Vertical Restraints, para 189.

[185] See Guidelines on Vertical Restraints, para 129.

[186] "Single branding" comprises those agreements which have as their main element the fact that the buyer is obliged or induced to concentrate its orders for a particular type of product with one supplier. See Guidelines on Vertical Restraints, para 214.

[187] See Guidelines on Vertical Restraints, para 130.

[188] "Single branding" comprises those agreements which have as their main element the fact that the buyer is obliged or induced to concentrate its orders for a particular type of product with one supplier. See Guidelines on Vertical Restraints, para 148. See also para 190(b) which provides that "[a] non-compete obligation on the goods or services purchased by the franchisee falls outside the scope of Article 101(1) where the obligation is necessary to maintain the common identity and reputation of the franchised network. In such cases, the duration of the non-compete obligation is also irrelevant under Article 101(1), as long as it does not exceed the duration of the franchise agreement itself."

indispensable to protect the know-how and that the vertical restraints fulfil the conditions of Article 101(3).[189]

Following from the broad explanation, let us assume that firm A franchises the Pizza service delivery of its quality brand to firm B. Some of the conditions in the franchise agreement is that firm B should source some related products from firm A. To put into perspective, we could say that the agreement requires firm B to buy dough, tomato sauce and paper cups exclusively from firm A or from approved suppliers.[190] Based on the foregoing, should the conduct be considered anti-competitive? Should our opinion depend on certain effects? What can the capability approach add to antitrust analysis in the context of the resulting issues?

Let us assume further that firm A's franchising practice seeks to divide the market in order to block the loophole that exist for arbitrage trading as a result of the price differentials in another geographical market.[191] If we also assume that firm A mandates franchisees to purchase dough and tomato sauce from its sales department for quality assurance purpose not solely for its image but because of its concern for the health of consumers, how should these added facts impact on our assessment in the context of the prevailing theories and the capability approach?

In Europe for instance, this issue could be addressed under both Article 101(1)(e) and Article 102(2)(d) TFEU.[192] In order to showcase the role of the capability approach under both price-based and non-price based infringement, the facts stated above would be applied as a restrictive agreement with price implication after which it will be applied as a non-price exclusionary conduct.

Article 101(1)(e) of the TFEU provides that any agreement which has as its object or effect the prevention, restriction or distortion of competition within the internal market, and in particular those which make the conclusion of contracts subject to acceptance by the other parties of supplementary obligations which, by their nature or according to commercial usage, have no connection with the subject of such contracts.

Applying the idea of economic freedom to these facts, we would be most concerned with the maintenance of the competitive process so as to ensure that the freedom of choice of firm B is not trampled upon. If we apply this approach strictly, we would come to the conclusion that the condition in the pizza franchise

---

[189] Para 190(a). Guidelines on Vertical Restraints.

[190] This is what happened in *Queen City Pizza v Domino's Pizza*, 124 F.3d 430, 433 & 438 (3rd Cir. Pa. 1997).

[191] For example, let us assume a well-known pizza company grants a franchise of its service to different franchisees located in different countries. Let us say further that the franchisees are bound by contract to buy certain commodities from the franchisor in order to maintain brand quality. It is quite possible that the franchisor might charge less for the product in country A as opposed to country B. The franchisor's pricing might reflect the economic conditions within both countries. In order to avoid arbitrage trading between the franchisees, the franchisor might seek to divide the market through its packaging. For instance, it might package the product under different names in the two countries.

[192] It could also be brought under mergers. See Carboja et al. (1990), pp. 283–298 and 285.

agreement is anti-competitive and as such should be voided regardless of the justifications (efficiency, health and so on) given by firm A. For as long as firm B can show that the condition is supplementary and has no connection with the subject of the contract, the condition will be regarded as illegal per se. Under this approach, the burden of proving that the tie-in condition has no connection with the franchising contract could be discharged by severing the need for quality delivery and adherence to brand standard from the direct condition on product purchase especially where such product could be sourced elsewhere without prejudicing the franchised brand. Moreover, since there is a clear link between market integration and economic freedom,[193] firm B could strengthen its claim that the agreement is "anti-competitive by object" by also referring to the clause in the agreement as an attempt to prevent inter-state trading of the supplementary products.[194]

Where we apply the welfare approaches, it is often required that we put the agreement in greater economic context. This may require that we take one of two opinions—it is either that we assess the fact and seek more detailed explanation as to whether or not the condition is, by its nature, not connected with the subject of the contract or simply that we should be able to rely on the provisions of Article 101 (3).[195] For the purpose of the exercise, let us assume that the relevant clause in the franchise agreement is not anti-competitive by object. Our conclusion whether the agreement has anti-competitive effect depends on the welfare standard we align to. Under the total welfare standard, we are to assess whether the condition has anti-competitive effect and/or whether it should be individually exempted by ascertaining: if the franchisee incurs additional costs which could have been avoided but for the condition; and if there are clear efficiencies that make the tie-in condition increase net welfare. For instance, it could be argued that the tie-in might solve the free-rider problem[196] and also address the possibility that the franchisee may reduce product quality.[197] Another efficiency gain that could be argued is that the tying arrangement reduces the franchisor's monitoring cost.[198] To the total welfare proponents, it does not matter that the efficiency gains are not shared by both firms A and B. Thus, even though the efficiency gains go to firm A,

[193] See Monti (2002), p. 1065.

[194] There are a lot of cases regarding distributors and suppliers where the Court of Justice decided against such restrictive practice. See e.g. case 19/77 *Miller International Schallplatten GmbH v Commission* [1978] ECR 131.

[195] Firms have to self-assess in order to determine whether their conduct can be exempted under Article 101(3) TFEU.

[196] This is considered to be very likely, as franchisees might seek to unduly cut cost and hence reduce the quality of products. See Brickley (1999), pp. 745 and 748. Also Klien and Saft (1985), pp. 345 and 349.

[197] Meese (1996), pp. 111 and 119.

[198] Klien (1999), p. 748.

the fact that the franchisee (who is the consumer/customer) incurs additional cost is immaterial as long as it leads to net welfare.[199]

If the wealth transfer standard is applied, it would be important to show efficiency gains to both the customer (firm B) and/or the final consumers. For instance, we might have to consider whether despite the additional cost incurred, the franchisee also benefits as a result of the reduction in searching cost and delivery cost. It would also be important to show how the franchisee's efficiency gains affect the final consumers. For instance, in *Queen City Pizza v Domino's Pizza*,[200] it was alleged that the franchisor, Domino's Pizza Inc., prohibited stores that produced dough from selling their dough to franchisees, even though the stores were willing to sell dough (which was of comparable quality) at a price 25–40 % below Domino's Pizza's price.

The two welfare standards assessed are unlikely to take seriously the issue on market integration as long as efficiencies are gained on the one hand and there are no deficits in consumer surplus or that the gains are passed to the consumers. However, while we might fail to appreciate the health gains in the tying arrangement where we apply either of these two standards as they do not translate to cost benefits, a public policy-friendly welfare approach might, even in the absence of cost savings (either for the franchisor, franchisee or final consumer), hold that the tie-in of dough and tomatoes does not constitute a breach of competition law.

If the assumed fact is addressed in the light of the normative differentiated approach, it means that we cannot rely solely on account of economic freedom. We also cannot rely solely on account of welfare. Rather, our conclusion whether the franchise contract tying is anti-competitive and hence amounts to a breach would depend on the specific antitrust regime. Thus, with focus on citizen's preference, it should be inferred whether the citizens in general would value quality delivery and uniformity in franchised products or services such that they are willing to dispense with the cost effect that is incurred by any of the parties or that they consider the freedom of the franchisee to source supplementary products (as long as it complies with the standard franchising criteria) to be strong enough to merit the status of a liberal right. The same reasoning applies to the issue on integration and health.

In line with the behavioural law and economics theory, we will be more concerned about avoiding errors based on theoretical assumptions on welfare. In this specific context, it has been stated under the welfare theories that tie-in could lead to efficiency benefits such as reduction of franchisor's monitoring cost and/or reduction of franchisee's searching cost. Without necessarily denying these possible benefits, the behavioural law and economics school will put to our attention more considerations which are not visible to the traditional welfare accounts. We

[199] For instance: that the franchisor can maintain the quality of its brand; that the franchisor can benefit from the brand; and that the final consumers can receive the quality expected from the brand.

[200] Above note 189.

may, for instance, note greater efficiency losses once we are prepared to move beyond the idea of unbounded rationality and realise that such tie-in might generate strong resentment and hence motivate franchisee to cheat. As noted by Benoliel, tying contracts increase centralisation: it leads to an increased tendency that the franchisor has a tight grip through direct involvement in franchisee's decision making.[201] As an aftermath of the concentration of powers in the franchisor, there is a constant deprivation of franchisee's managerial autonomy. This by itself could be a source of dissatisfaction given that franchisees are largely autonomy-oriented entrepreneurs.[202] From this perspective of antitrust analysis, welfare considerations should include the fact that the dissatisfaction that might arise from franchisor's effort to centralise might lead to inefficiencies such as an increase in franchisee's opportunism.[203] The ability to identify the tendency of the franchisee to lie, steal, cheat and engage in calculated efforts to mislead, distort, disguise, obfuscate, or otherwise confuse the franchisor[204] as a result of its dissatisfaction[205] sets this approach apart from the traditional welfare assumption.[206] Further, the extent to which the behavioural account will accommodate both the goal of integration and health will depend on the psychological effect arising from the surrounding circumstances.

We could relate the finding of the behavioural approach to the objective/normative philosophical account of welfare as both accounts, in this particular context, place a premium on franchisee/consumer satisfaction.

It is at this juncture that we assess how capability approach will deal with the stated fact. First, it is important to restate that one cannot apply the capability approach as the tool for choosing between antitrust theories and standards. This is because the approach itself makes no pretence of its capacity. Its strength and inherent broadness lies in the fact that it concedes that it cannot pay adequate attention to fairness and equity involved in procedures that have relevance to the exercise of "choosing". This observation makes the application of capability approach to antitrust straightforward indeed. If the Capability approach is placed as the platform for analysing the fact surrounding this contract franchise tying analogy, we must be willing to accommodate all possible functionings which, when joined together, forms our capability framework upon which concrete decision are to be made subsequently.[207] In particular, we must be willing to accommodate:

---

[201] See Benoliel (2010), p. 10. Also Provan and Skinner (1989), pp. 202 and 207.

[202] Benoliel (2010), p. 12; John (1984), p. 280.

[203] This is defined as behaviour by the franchisee towards the franchisor that involves self-interest seeking with guile. See Wiliamson (1975).

[204] See the context in which the term "guile" is used in Williamsom (1985), p. 47.

[205] There are a number of empirical studies linking decreased dissatisfaction and opportunism. See John (1984); Dwyer and Oh (1987), p. 347; Kidwell et al. (2007), p. 522.

[206] Benoliel (2010), p. 15.

[207] The decision stage is addressed in Chap. 5.

- The possibility that antitrust subjects may prefer to secure the competitive process and regardless of any benefit that could be derived from an otherwise restrictive tying arrangement;
- The possibility of inferring that citizens value the franchisee's independence as a matter of right;
- Depending on the welfare standard we align to, the weighing of pros and cons of the alleged tying;
- The possibility that the requisite weighing could also take into account public policy consideration, as in this case, the health concern;
- A more in-depth analysis of welfare which might require the alterations of theoretical assumptions and the inclusion of psychological effects on the nature of franchise contract tying;
- The possibility that the subjective/positive or the objective/normative philosophical account of welfare could impact on functionings;
- The possibility that the franchisor's interest might be to divide the market and maximise profit;
- And so on.

4.6.1.iii Franchise Contract Tying Assessed as an Abuse of Dominance

If we apply the same facts in ii above in the context of abuse of dominance, our first task will be to ascertain when a tying arrangement might be abusive. For the act of tying to be found to be anti-competitive, certain elements have to be satisfied. They are that: the alleged infringer must have market power; there must be two separate products; there must be finding of anticompetitive effect or a likelihood of such effect and; the alleged infringer must have no objective justification for the tying arrangement.

It is basic to state that dominant firms could engage in tying arrangement for clandestine purposes. In order to identify such clandestine purposes, the "leverage theory" was propounded. As applied in the US case of *Eastman Kodak*,[208] the theory provides that a tie-in agreement would amount to an abuse of monopoly power where: there are two separate products involved; the defendant had required the tied product to be purchased with the tying product; a substantial amount of commerce had been affected; and finally that the defendant had market power in the tying product. In other words, this means that dominant firms are in breach of competition law when they tie products so as to extend their market power from one market to another. This theory has however been heavily criticised as it has been shown that leveraging does not necessarily generate anti-competitive effects.[209] From this position, the leverage theory is a flawed theory of abuse as it could well be pro-competitive for a company to leverage its position by typing products which

[208] *Eastman Kodak Co. v Image Tech. Service*, 504 U.S 1 451 (1992).

[209] See Bowman (1967), pp. 19–36; Bork (1978), ch 19.

ultimately results in efficiency gains. It means thus that the finding of abuse in a tying arrangement cannot be based on a set method which divides cases into two mutually exclusive categories of "leverage" or "no leverage".[210] As such, effect analysis which takes into account the price of both the tied and tying product may be necessary to justify the finding of abuse.[211]

With regards to arguments that tying arrangements could have efficiency benefits, it can be argued that a dominant firm could be engaged in tying in order to improve quality. Tying could also be used for quality assurance purposes and to protect trademarks or trade secrets in franchising and leasing agreements. A lucid example of the tying of photocopier and cartridge has been given to illustrate this point.[212] It is also possible that a tied package is more valuable than the sum of the individual products.[213] Further, tying could reduce price inefficiencies. One way to achieve this is through price "discrimination by tying". This arrangement can be used to recover fixed cost in market where it is high.[214] There could be overall welfare effect arising from price discrimination by tying where a market is characterised by a combination of high fixed cost, network effects or economies of scale.[215] It could also help reduce the price inflation that arises as a result of the double marginalisation problem; where there exist two monopolists at both the upstream and downstream market of interrelated products, welfare may be better enhanced if the products are tied in order to eliminate one of the mark-ups.[216]

Further, there could even be greater efficiency benefits for tying or bundling especially in dynamic industries such as: the potential for price discrimination to lead to efficient recovery of fixed cost; the need for firms selling complex systems to protect their reputation; the ability of bundling to reduce prices and increase sales; the potential for cost savings from bundling; and rational product integration.[217] These benefits must however be weighed against the risk of market foreclosure, the discouragement to potential competitors and the stifling of innovation.[218]

In the same vein, tying arrangement could also lead to inefficiencies. Though, for such anti-competitive effect to be present, there must be; imperfect competition in the tied market; a commitment to tie; an inability on the part of the competitor to match the tie; the likelihood of competitor's exit; barriers to entry; and absence of

[210] Bowman (1967), p. 34.

[211] Bowman (1967), p. 34.

[212] For details on the example of photocopier and cartridges, see Hovenkamp et al. (2007), pp. 21–29.

[213] See Schmidt (2009), pp. 18–19.

[214] Charles River Associates (2002), pp. 82–83.

[215] Charles River Associates (2002), pp. 82–83.

[216] See Cournot (1897) and Nalebuff (2003), pp. 37–38.

[217] Lind and Muysert (2003), pp. 87 and 90.

[218] Lind and Muysert (2003), pp. 87 and 90.

buyer power.[219] Tie-in arrangements could affect both competitors and consumers: competitors may be excluded from such market[220] while consumer choice may be severely limited. On its possible foreclosure effect, tying could impede or deter a potential competitor from entering a tied product market[221] and also limit consumers' choice on downstream product.[222] It could also be used to protect the tying product market[223] and to undercut rivals' price.[224] Tying could be used to make prices of products obscure which may impact on consumer choice. Also, a dominant firm can tie products in an attempt to mitigate the competition that has arisen as a result of a market entry by a competitor.[225]

The European Commission, through its *Article 82 Guidance*, sets out circumstances which are likely to prompt intervention when assessing tying and bundling by dominant firms. The Commission states that a firm is dominant in the tying market where they tying products are distinct and where the tying practice is likely to lead to anti-competitive foreclosure.[226] With regards to the latter requirement, the Commission has identified certain tying practices that might foreclose the market. For example, it of the view that the risk of anti-competitive foreclosure is greater where the dominant firm makes its tying or bundling strategy a lasting one.[227] It also contends that by tying two products, a dominant firm may seek to chill the price elasticity that exists between its distinct products by tying them which then allows the firm to raise price.[228] The Commission however recognises that tying arrangements could lead to savings in production and distribution that would benefit customers.[229]

Proceeding from this observation to the particular context of the assumed facts on franchise contract tying, we should assume further that firm A has substantial market power in the pizza market. We can then assess whether there will be a finding of abuse under the different theories and hence showcase how the capability approach accommodates these theories.

From the economic freedom perspective, we would be concerned solely about the anticompetitive object. Though heavily criticised, this appears to be more in line with EU practice as there are clear signs that Article 102 has strong links with

---

219 See Ahlborn et al. (2004), pp. 331–333.
220 Whinston (1990), p. 837.
221 Schmidt (2009), p. 30.
222 Hovenkamp et al. (2007), pp. 21–23.
223 Ridyard (2005), pp. 316 and 371.
224 Baldwin and McFarland (1963), p. 743.
225 Baldwin and McFarland (1963), p. 743.
226 Article 82 Guidance, para 50.
227 Article 82 Guidance, para 52.
228 Article 82 Guidance, para 56.
229 Article 82 Guidance, para 62.

ordoliberal thinking.[230] Thus, in assessing the propriety of tying arrangements, economic freedom theory requires that we take into account the following steps[231]:

1. Defining the relevant market and the existence of a tied product separate from the tying product;
2. The firm concerned is dominant (normally in the tying product market, but can also be found dominant in the tied product market[232]);
3. There is an element of coercion as the customer is forced to purchase the bundle
4. There is no objective justification for the coercion.

In the *Microsoft* case, the European Commission was concerned that tying Windows Media Player (WMP) and Windows Operating System would foreclose competition and stifle innovation in the Media Software Encoding and Management market because WMP would become the preferred choice for complimentary content and application provider. Economic freedom regimes, on the one hand, would have given more relevance to consumer choice instead of focusing on efficiency. On the other hand, they are concerned simply about the exclusionary potential of tying rather than adding the requirement of consumer harm.[233]

Where we apply the traditional economic approaches (that is total welfare and wealth transfer), limitation of franchisee's choice will not in itself be indicative of a competition concern. The focus will be on the pros and cons of tying (in terms of efficiency and/or distribution) as it could be deduced from the specific franchise arrangement. All consumer-based theories might take into consideration, the likelihood of market foreclosure. However, they might address it only to the extent that it affects consumers. Above all, any of these standards represent the "more economic approach".

In all, these accounts require that closer attention is paid to the efficiency justification if we are to conduct a proper analysis of abuse cases (including tying). When applied, the outcome arrived at after balancing efficiency gains with possible negative effects will depend strongly on the welfare standard we align to.

Applying the normative differentiated approach, "a more economic approach" in Article 102 (and consequently, the case at hand) does not require that only the effects on consumer (or total) welfare be taken into account. In addition the effects on a certain set of protected rights, which can be derived from the preferences of citizens, can be considered. For instance, we might have to ask if tie-in will conveniently foreclose the market against the producers of dough and tomatoes. If so, do citizens consider the competitor's to be rights holders? This might involve us weighing not only the efficiency arguments but also to ascertain the risk of

[230] Gerber (1998), p. 241.

[231] See Schmidt (2009), p. 60.

[232] Commission's Decision *IBM Undertaking* [1984] OJ L118/24.

[233] This is said to be the position in Europe. In support of this conclusion, Monti referred to Case T-83/91, *Tetra Pak Rausing SA v Commission* (Tetra Pak II) [1990] ECR II-3092 see Monti (2007), p. 191.

market foreclosure and the likes. Though Kerber concedes that the weighing suggested in his theory can lead to additional trade-off problems, he still contended that such a more general approach is still entirely compatible with economic theory.

So as to make the weighing of pros and cons more in line with reality, proponents of the behavioural law and economics could argue that firm A might take into account possible inertia on the part of franchisees. We might, as such, have to take note that even where it appears that the franchisor is tying its products in order to reduce price inefficiency, it could in fact be that it is enhancing its market share especially where franchisees are unable to differentiate between the total price of the tied package and the price and cost of individual products. Such observations might lead to a change in the nature or outcome of our analysis.

Just as we noted under restrictive agreements, the capability approach will accommodate different possibilities within its framework. Individual theories, it has been shown, have their areas of strength but are all generally weak in that they cannot individually accommodate all reasoning and outcomes that antitrust subjects could possibly value.

4.6.2 Capability Approach and Other Issues Under Article 101 and 102

Since the capability approach simply accommodates the various theories that reflect different functionings of different persons, it is unnecessary to undergo the laboured exercise of assessing the adaptability of the approach to other antitrust issues. The simple message is that regardless of the antitrust issue, broadness should be ensured through the pursuit of inclusiveness. However, notwithstanding the fact that we do not envision that there might be any antitrust behaviour (outside of tying arrangement) which will be incompatible with the capability framework, it is still a good idea to relate with a few more examples; we could assess horizontal agreements and other Article 102 concerns such as selective low pricing.

When analysing horizontal agreements, one has to recognise that most welfare-based and freedom-based accounts would consider such agreements to be anti-competitive by object. The finding of breach is rife where parties agree to fix price or divide the market. It is important for us to ascertain how the person-centred approach will address such issue in the light of the capability framework. The need to be inclusive means that we should incorporate different possibilities that could arise from such horizontal agreement within the capability framework. Thus we cannot afford to decide *ex ante* that such agreement i.e. price fixing is anti-competitive. We should also take note of interests of antitrust subjects who, based on the application of a different theoretical insight such as transaction economics, are able to tease out the value that such cooperation brings to the market.

Perhaps the European Commission took note of such reasoning in the *Visa International-Multilateral Interchange Fee* case,[234] where, rather than merely seeing it as a price-fixing arrangement, it considered that an agreement containing a provision to fix the "Multilateral Interchange Fee" (MIF) paid by acquiring banks to issuing banks within the Visa system did not have as its object the restriction of competition since the MIF agreement in this instance, had "as its objective to increase the stability and efficiency of operation of that system ... and indirectly to strengthen competition between payment systems."[235] This decision was made despite the prima facie assumption on the collusive nature of information exchange by competitors.[236] If the Commission's reasoning was narrowed to economic freedom, it might not have taken time to identify the efficiency justification of such arrangement. The same level of broad reasoning is expected if we are dealing with vertical agreements such as retail price maintenance, agreements granting absolute territorial protection[237] and so on. These issues are to be analysed as object-based infringements and effect based infringements.

With regards to object-based infringements, there is need to understand the justification given by specific antitrust theories in designating specific behaviour as being anti-competitive by object. For example, if the competing capability sets/functionings present in the framework for deciding a pure cartel case lead to the conclusion that such cartelist activity is anti-competitive by object, we have to understand why the specific theory underlying each capability set/functioning (be it economic freedom, efficiency or any other) would come to that conclusion—is it simply because such behaviour overtly impugns on the inalienable aspect of antitrust subjects' freedom or because there is empirical evidence to show that such pure cartelist behaviour is bound to result in more efficiency loss than gain which thereby renders a full scale effect-based analysis unnecessary? When analysing their effect, we have to assess, on the basis of specific theories, whether they impact on inter-brand competition, intra-brand competition or they merely amount to ancillary restraints.

Concerning Article 102, reference can be made to the issue of selective low pricing. Some theories might find anti-competitive "intent" where even though low prices charged by dominant firms are not below cost as long as it can be shown that the pricing practice is part of a deliberate plan to eliminate competitors through selective price-cutting. Conclusions deriving from a rational choice analysis or a freedom-based theory may differ from the one reached under a behavioural law and economic analysis. Where for instance, we are concerned about economic freedom and hence the protection of the competitive structure, anti-competitive "intent" as

---

[234] [2002] OJ L318/17, [2003] 4 *CMLR* 283.

[235] [2002] OJ L318/17, [2003] 4 *CMLR* 283, para 69.

[236] On information exchange, see generally OECD Competition Committee Policy Roundtables on Information Exchanges between Competitors under Competition Law 2010.

[237] Example of this is given in the decisional context in Chap. 5.

shown by the Commission in *Eurofix-Bauco*[238] and *CEWAL*,[239] indicate that it would constitute abuse if it is shown that a dominant firm had exclusionary "intent" regardless of the fact that its pricing was not below cost. On the other hand, an account based on rational choice may lead to the conclusion that antitrust should not recognise any claim of above-cost predatory pricing regardless of the intent of the dominant firm since short-term threat or pricing strategies that exceed short-term cost should not be able to deter long-term investments or entry.[240] A behavioural law and economic account might take exception to this rational choice analysis by, for instance, stating how a new entrant might be psychologically discouraged from such market as a result of the dominant firm's exclusionary intent.

It is for us to consider all these possibilities within the capability framework. The same conflicting reasoning could be made of other abuse of dominance issues such as refusal to supply and so on.

4.7 Conclusion

The analyses of antitrust issues through the person-centred approach proceed from Coleman's questions on right. It was stated in Chap. 3 that when answering the question about the goal(s) of antitrust right, we should avoid choosing between normative propositions at an *ex ante* stage. In this chapter, we were preoccupied with the task of building a framework that would guide us to achieve inclusiveness by conveniently helping us resist the temptation to make categorical statements *a priori*. At the end of our analysis, it becomes clear that the capability approach is most appropriate for the person-centred approach as it maintains the broadness required.

However, as it will be observed in the next chapter, the capability approach does not practically answer the remaining questions of antitrust right which concern the proper way of analysing such right and how antitrust right should be enforced. It is impossible to go any further with the capability approach because its impact is limited to the recognition of opportunities. It is therefore imperative that we make conscious effort to build a decisional framework.

---

[238] Commission decision *Eurofix-Bauco v. Hilti* 88/138/EEC, [1988] OJ L 65.

[239] Commission decision Cewal, Cowac and Ukwal [1993] L34/20.

[240] Elhauge (2003), pp. 681 and 826–827.

References

Ahlborn C, Evans D, Padilla A (2004) The antitrust economics of tying: a farewell to per se illegality. Antitrust Bull 49(1/2):287

Ahn S (2002) Competition, innovation and productivity growth: a review of theory and evidence (January 17, 2002). OECD Economics Working Paper No. 317

Areeda P, Hovenkamp H (2000) Antitrust law. Aspen, New York, pp 106–107

Arezzo E (2008) Is there a role for market definition and dominance in an effect-based approach? In: Mackenrodt M-O, Gallego BC, Enchelmaier S (eds) Abuse of dominant position: new interpretation, new enforcement mechanisms? Springer, London, p 43

Averitt N, Lande R (2007) Using the '*Consumer Choice*' approach to antitrust law. Antitrust Law J 74:175

Ayal A (2012) Counter-intuitive fairness in antitrust: protecting the monopolists and balancing among competing claims. J Competition Law Econ 8(3):627–662

Baker J (2005) Competition policy as a political bargain. American Antitrust Institute Working Paper No. 05-02 (16 January 2005), p 2

Baldwin W, McFarland D (1963) Tying arrangement in law and economics. Antitrust Bull 8:743

Benoliel U (2010) The behavioural law and economics of franchise tying contracts. Rutgers Law J 41:10

Berlin I (1997) In: Hardy H, Hausheer R (eds) The proper study of mankind. Chatto & Windus, London

Bishop S, Walker M (2002) The economics of EC competition law: concept, application, and measurement, 2nd edn. Sweet & Maxwell, London, p 25

Black O (2005) Conceptual foundations of antitrust. Cambridge University Press, Cambridge

Boadway R, Bruce N (1984) Welfare economics. Blackwell, Oxford, p 62

Bork R (1967) The goals of antitrust policy. Am Econ Rev 57:251

Bork R (1978) The antitrust paradox. Free Press, New York

Bowman W (1967) Tying arrangements and the leverage problem. Yale Law J 67:19–36

Brickley J (1999) Incentive conflict and contractual restraints: evidence from franchising. J Law Econ 42:745, 748

Brodley J (1987) The economic goals of antitrust: efficiency, consumer welfare, and technological progress. N Y Univ Law Rev 62:1020, 1027

Buchanan A (1985) Ethics, efficiency and the market. Rowman & Allanheld, Totowa, p 9

Buchanan J (1986) The constitution of economic policy. Am Econ Rev 77:243

Buchanan J (1991) Constitutional economics. Basil Blackwell, Cambridge

Buttigieg E (2009) Competition law: safeguarding the consumer interest. Kluwer Law International, Alphen aan den Rijn, p 1

Carboja J, De Meza D, Seidman D (1990) A strategic motivation for commodity bundling. J Ind Econ 38:283–298, 285

Charles River Associates (2002) Innovation and competition policy, part 1 – conceptual issues. Economic Discussion Paper 3, March 2002, report prepared for the Office of Fair Trading, pp 82–83. www.oft.gov.uk/shared_oft/report/comp_policy/oft377part1.pdf

Clark J (1961) Competition as a dynamic process. The Brookings Institution, Washington

Cournot A (1897) Research into the mathematical principle of the theory of wealth (trans: Bacon N). Macmillan, New York

Cseres K (2006) Controversies of the consumer welfare model. Competition Law Rev 3:121, 127–128

Doern B (1996) Comparative competition policy: boundaries and level of political analysis. In: Doern B, Wilks S (eds) Comparative competition policy: national institution in a global market. Clarendon, Oxford, p 23

Dwyer R, Oh S (1987) Output sector munificence effect on the internal political economy of marketing channels. J Mark Res 24:347

Elhauge E (2003) Why above-cost price cuts to drive out entrants are not predatory-and the implication for defining cost and market power. Yale Law J 112:681, 826–827
Elster J (1993) Introduction. In: Elster J, Roemer J (eds) Interpersonal comparison of wellbeing. Cambridge University Press, Cambridge, p 8
Euchen W (1952) Grundsatz der Wirtschaftspolitik. Mohr/Seibeck, Tubingen, p 290
Evans D, Padilla J, Ahlborn C (2004) The antitrust economics of tying: a farewell to per se illegality. Antitrust Bull 49:320
Fox E (2008) An antitrust fable – a tale of predation. Concurrence No. 3, p 1
Friedman M, Friedman R (1980) Free to choose: a personal statement. Harcourt Brace Jovanovich, New York
Gerber D (1994) Constitutionalizing the economy: German neo-liberalism competition law and the 'New' Europe. Am J Comp Law 42:25–84, 29
Gerber D (1998) Law and competition in twentieth-century Europe: protecting Prometheus. Oxford University Press, Oxford
Gibbard A (1989) Interpersonal comparisons: preference, good and the intrinsic reward of a life. In: Elster J, Hylland A (eds) Foundation of social choice theory. Cambridge University Press, Cambridge, p 169
Gormsen L (2007) The conflict between economic freedom and consumer welfare in the modernisation of article 82 EC. Euro Competition J 3:333
Harsanyi J (1982) Morality and the theory of rational behaviour. In: Sen A, William B (eds) Utilitarianism and beyond. Cambridge University Press, Cambridge, pp 39–62
Hay D, Morris D (1979) Industrial economic: theory and evidence. Oxford University Press, Oxford, p 37
Hayek F (1978) Competition as a discovery procedure. In: Hayek F (ed) New studies in philosophy, politics, economics and the history of ideas. University of Chicago Press, Chicago, p 179
Hovenkamp H (1985) Antitrust policy after Chicago. Mich Law Rev 84:213, 241
Hovenkamp H, Janis M, Lemley M (2007) IP and antitrust: an analysis of antitrust principles applied to intellectual property law. Aspen Law & Business, New York, pp 21–29
John G (1984) An empirical investigation of some antecedents of opportunism in marketing channels. Mark Res 21:280
Kaplow L (2012) On the choice of welfare standard in competition law. In: Zimmer D (ed) Goals of competition law. Edward Elgar, Cheltenham, pp 3–26
Kaplow L, Shavell S (1994) Why the legal system is less efficient than the income tax in redistributing income. J Legal Stud 23:667–681
Kerber W (2008) Should competition law promote efficiency? Some reflections of an economist on the normative foundations of competition law. In: Drexl J, Idot L, Moneger J (eds) Economic theory and competition law. Edward Elgar, Cheltenham, p 105
Kidwell RE, Nygaard A, Silkoset R (2007) Antecedents and effect of free riding in the franchisor–franchisee relationship. J Bus Venturing 22:522
Klien B (1999) Market power in franchise cases in the Wake of Kodak: applying post-contract hold up analysis to vertical relationships. Antitrust Law J 67(2):283
Klien B, Saft L (1985) The law and economics of franchise tying contracts. J Law Econ 28:345, 349
Lambert T, Wright J (2007–2008) Response to the antitrust marathon: antitrust (over-?) confidence. Loyola Consum Law Rev 20:219
Lande R (1989) Chicago's false foundation: wealth transfer (not just efficiency) should guide antitrust. Antitrust Law J 58:631
Lind R, Muysert P (2003) Innovation and competition policy: challenges for the new millennium. Eur Competition Law Rev 24:87, 90
Lipsey R, Lancaster K (1955–1956) The general theory of second best. Rev Econ Stud 24:11–32
Mankiw G (2008) Principles of economics, 5th edn. South-Western College Publishing, Cincinnati, p 142

Meese A (1996) Antitrust balancing in a (near) Coasean world: the case of franchise tying contract. Mich Law Rev 95:111, 119
Mitchell G (2002) Why law and economics' perfect rationality should not be traded for the behavioural law and economics equal incompetence. FSU College of Law, Public Law Research Paper No. 49
Monti G (2002) Article 81 EC and public policy. Common Market Law Rev 39:1065
Monti G (2007) EC competition law. Cambridge University Press, Cambridge
Möschel W (1989) Competition policy from an Ordo point of view. In: Willgerodt H, Peacock A (eds) German neo-liberals and the social market economy. Macmillan, London, p 142
Nadeaus R (2003) The wealth of nature. Columbia University Press, New York
Nalebuff B (2003) Bundling, tying and portfolio effect, part 1 – conceptual issues. DTI Economics Paper No. 1
Nozick R (1974) Anarchy, state and Utopia. Blackwell, Oxford, pp 42–45
Orbach B (2010) The antitrust consumer welfare paradox. Arizona Legal Studies Discussion Paper No. 10-07 July 2010
Pearson C (2000) Economics and the global environment. Cambridge University Press, Cambridge
Pigou A (2002) The economics of welfare. Transaction Publishers, New Brunswick, pp 10ff
Porter M (2001) Competition and antitrust: towards a productivity-based approach to evaluating mergers and joint ventures. Antitrust Bull 46:919, 958
Posner R (1979) Utilitarianism, economics and legal theory. J Legal Stud 8:103–140
Posner R (1980) The value of wealth: a comment on Dworkin and Kronman. J Legal Stud 9(2):243
Provan K, Skinner S (1989) Interorganizational dependence and control as predictors of opportunism in dealer–supplier relationship. Acad Manag J 32:202, 207
Qizilbash M (1997) Wellbeing and despair: Dante's Ugolino. Utilitas 9:227–240
Raphael D (2007) The impartial spectator: Adam Smith's moral philosophy. Clarendon, Oxford
Raz J (1986) The morality of freedom. Clarendon, Oxford, p 166
Ridyard D (2005) Tying and bundling – cause for complaint? Eur Competition Law Rev 26:316, 371
Robeyns I (2000) An unworkable idea or a promising alternative? Sen's capability approach re-examined. Discussion Paper 00.30, Centre for Economic Studies, Katholieke Universiteit Leuven, p 3
Robeyns I (2005) Capability approach: a theoretical survey. J Hum Dev 6:94
Rosch T (2007) Monopsony and the meaning of 'Consumer Welfare': a closer look at Weyerhaeuser. Colum Bus Law Rev 353
Scanlon T (1993) Value desire and quality of life. In: Nussbaum M, Sen A (eds) Quality of life. Clarendon, Oxford, p 186
Schmidt H (2009) Competition law, innovation and antitrust: an analysis of tying and technological integration. Edward Elgar, Cheltenham, p 3
Scitovsky T (1941) A note on welfare propositions in economics. Rev Econ Stud 9:77
Scitovsky T (1992) The joyless economy: the psychology of human satisfaction (revised edn). Oxford University Press, New York, pp 4–5
Sen A (1970) The impossibility of the Paretian liberal. J Polit Econ 78:152
Sen A (1980–1981) Plural utility. Proc Aristotelian Soc 81:193–215
Sen A (1982) Choice, welfare and measurement. Harvard University Press, Cambridge, pp 29–30
Sen A (1985) Wellbeing, agency and freedom: the Dewey lectures 1984. J Philos 82:191
Sen A (1993) Market and freedom: achievement and limitations of the market mechanism in promoting individual freedom. Oxf Econ Pap 45:533–534
Sen A (2002) Rationality and freedom. Belknap, Cambridge, p 520
Sen A (2009) The idea of Justice Belknap. Harvard University Press, Cambridge
Sibnony A-L (2009) How are consumers' interests taken into account when applying competition law? Paper presented at the EU Commission event Competition and Consumers in the 21st century on 21 October 2009

Stucke M (2012) What is competition? In: Zimmer D (ed) The goals of competition law. Edward Elgar, Cheltenham, pp 27–52
Tor A (2004) A behavioural approach to antitrust law and economics. Consum Policy Rev 14:18
Townley C (2009) Article 81 and public policy. Hart, Oxford, p 186
UNCTAD (2003) The objectives of competition law and policy and the optimal design of competition agency. OECD Global Competition Forum CCNM/GF/COMP/WD(2003)31
Whinston M (1990) Tying, foreclosure and exclusion. Am Econ Rev 80:837
Wiliamson O (1975) Market and hierarchies, analysis and antitrust implications. Free Press, New York
Williams B (1973) A critique of utilitarianism. In: Smart J, Williams B (eds) Utilitarianism: for and against. Cambridge University Press, Cambridge
Williams B (1985) Ethics and the limits of philosophy. Harvard University Press, Cambridge
Williamsom O (1985) The economics of institutions of capitalism. Free Press, New York, p 47

Chapter 5
Antitrust Pluralism and Justice

5.1 Introduction

So far, this thesis has sought to establish the person-centred approach as an account that can truly strive towards *justice as inclusiveness*. It is hoped that this account will escape the ills of the prevailing approaches as revealed through the deconstruction analysis in Chap. 1. So far, the construction exercise seem to be taking due account of the position of the "Other". It is however yet to be seen how the approach will hold up when concrete decisions are to be made. It is indeed very crucial that the person-centred approach is able to live up to its promise of inclusiveness at this decision-making stage; it would live up to its promise if the procedure is able to avoid subjectivity inherent in the deconstructed traditional approaches as well as the discourse ethics.

As shown in the preceding chapter, capability approach provides the conceptual foundation for accommodating various antitrust interests. However, while it could guide policy-makers to be prudent when formulating policies, it does not go as far as guiding competition authorities and courts in their decision-making. This is because while the framework gives antitrust subjects adequate opportunity to achieve/protect their interest or wellbeing, it cannot possibly deal with the process of reaching a state of wellbeing. In other words, the capability approach cannot, by itself choose amongst the lots, the interest which should be vindicated in specific cases. The reasoning, as identified by Sen, is that:

> Capabilities are characteristics of individual advantages and while they may incorporate some features of the process involved . . ., they fall short of telling us enough about the freedom of citizens to invoke and utilize procedures that are equitable[1]

The task here is to build a less fallible decisional framework as it would be outright unrealistic to aim at building an absolutely watertight framework. This is

[1] Sen (2009), p. 296.

A. Al-Ameen, *Antitrust: The Person-centred Approach*,

DOI 10.1007/978-3-319-01724-2_5,

because every position is, as a matter of fact, deconstructible.[2] To build a less frail account, it is required that we maintain a broad framework even as we proceed to making concrete decisions. There is need to maintain impartiality when choosing between the set of interests within the capability framework. If we simply try to picture a decisional regime that promotes broadness all through, it becomes evident that it is quite impossible to ignore the enormity of the task—how do we combine the need to get concrete results with the need to accommodate all relevant interests?

In an attempt to build up an acceptable process, I divide the remainder of this chapter into four sections. First, I define the broadness that we should seek at the decisional stage. This is where the capability approach is still relevant. I argue that though it cannot help us build a process, we could make progress by following the capability approach's concept of "broadness as inclusiveness". In Sect. 5.2.1, I explain the nature of the process aspect wherein substantive decisions are made. In Sect. 5.3, I assess the possibility of reaching concrete decisions without falling short of *justice as inclusiveness*. Sect. 5.4 details the conclusions.

5.2 Broadness and the Informational Focus for Antitrust

Over and above theoretical discourse, when it comes to concrete cases, stakeholders are often primarily concerned about the outcomes, and consequently, the impact those outcomes have on the field of antitrust in general. The outcome arrived at in a specific case would invariably be the "state of affair" that is determined by relevant vectors and decisional variables (be it action of the parties, modes of argumentation, applicable rules or disposition) through which the case is decided.[3]

When we address issues from an idealised position, what we consider to be the appropriate constituent of the "state of affair" will largely depend on our school of thought. Our school of thought will shape the perspective (that is, the informational focus) from which we assess the antitrust issue. Our choice of the informational focus will be influenced by the outcome we desire. For instance, we might ask ourselves if the peculiar method of analysing the antitrust issues in any given instance results in the enhancement of *consumer welfare*. It is also possible that we take into account factors other than the desired outcome when deciding on the informational focus: we might take into account the process of choice and the agency information that may be relevant and all the personal and impersonal relations that may be seen as important to our decisional task.[4] Where our focus is influenced by narrowly defined ultimate results, we are concerned with what is called "culmination outcomes". On the other hand, where we take into account

[2] Derrida (1990).

[3] Sen (2009), pp. 215–221.

[4] Sen (2009), pp. 215–221.

other factors such as the process of choice and the agency, we are concerned about "comprehensive outcomes".[5]

A capability platform requires that we broaden our informational focus by taking note of and demanding comprehensive outcomes since the end does not always justify the means. To put this into perspective, what it means is that as opposed to individual theories that seek strictly to achieve specific goals, the capability approach will also take into consideration the need to have a procedure that gives due regard to different goals as this ensures that choices are presented before concrete decisions are made.

In line with the person-centred framework, we should be concerned with persons' opportunities to achieve. In assessing such opportunity, we might follow a culmination perspective. For instance, we might assess a consumer's opportunity in line with what he ends up with (e.g., competitive prices and brand choices) under the narrowly defined consumer welfare goal. We could also assess the outcomes from a comprehensive perspective. Here, we can assess the way the person *reaches* the culmination situation—it means that we should not only be interested in the opportunity to get competitive prices and brand choices, but also whether the consumers had the choice to wish for something else even if we assume that they would most likely have chosen the advantages of competitive prices and choices.

The capability approach requires us to reach this idea of comprehensive outcome. It means thus that our analysis and evaluation need to take note of both the opportunity and the process aspect. The framework based on this approach sets the ground for us to achieve this comprehensive state by accommodating every relevant interests or outcomes that could be teased out of any antitrust issue. However, as it has been continuously iterated, the capability-based framework in itself cannot possibly deal with the process aspect.[6]

Consequently, in order to ensure that our person-centred approach meets the requisite comprehensive outcome, authorities and courts must not only desire that the process aspect is considered. It is imperative that we build a person-centred/capability compliant decisional process.

5.2.1 The Process Aspect

As stated above, the process aspect of capability approach simply focuses on the process of choice-making and the degree of agency information considered in particular instances. This is very much in line with the strictly procedural nature of the person-centred approach. For instance, one might assess whether a functioning has been achieved by assessing a peculiar end-state against relatively narrow agency information. Alternatively, one could assess such end-state against broader agency information.[7]

---

[5] Sen (2009), pp. 215–221.

[6] Sen (2009), pp. 225–230.

[7] See explanation about culmination and comprehensive outcomes in Sect. 5.2 above.

As earlier mentioned, the capability framework sets its focus on comprehensive outcomes. However, the framework in itself cannot be relied on by antitrust regimes in their decisional activities. In essence, we have to build a decisional process outside the capability framework. It must be further noted that the process aspect (that is, our decisional activities) and the opportunity aspect (the capability framework) are not independent of each other. We cannot thus be unconcerned with the process aspect especially as the overall theme of the person-centred approach centres around broadness. Our decisional process must not undo the steady and elaborate effort of the capability framework by failing to be inclusive.

As an indication of how a decisional process might fail to be inclusive and hence undo the capability approach, one could illustrate with *Michelin II*[8] on rebates. The usage of rebate could spring up serious competition issues.[9] Hence the Commission stated in *Michelin II* that by "providing an advantage not based on any economic service justifying it, [a] rebate system tends to remove or restrict the buyer's freedom to choose his sources of supply and thus bar competitors from access to the market".[10] Contrary to the Commission's statement, if we are to be in compliance with the broadness requirement at the process aspect, we cannot afford to exclude other reasoning in our decision.[11] In *Michelin II*, the Commission failed to be inclusive as it did not substantiate alternative efficiency justifications and other potential positions. For a decisional framework to comply with the requirement of justice as inclusiveness, it would be expected that alternative normative justifications are, at least, taken into account. For instance, it is quite possible that if we reason in the line of behavioural law and economics, buyers may well be willing to forego brand choices for the pecuniary benefit. We might also find, as part of that capability set that the firm was unlikely to have had anti-competitive "intent".

Another example can be made out of predation cases. Europe's tendency towards "culmination outcomes" can be inferred from the strictly form-based assessment in *Wanadoo Interactive* [12] and also the fact that in *France Télécom,*[13]

[8] See *Michelin II*, COMP/E-2/36.041-PO/Michelin.

[9] See generally OECD Competition Committee Policy Roundtables on Fidelity and Bundled Rebates and Discounts 2008. http://www.oecd.org/dataoecd/41/22/41772877.pdf.

[10] See generally OECD Competition Committee Policy Roundtables on Fidelity and Bundled Rebates and Discounts 2008. http://www.oecd.org/dataoecd/41/22/41772877.pdf, para 227. See also Monti (2007), 24, n 17.

[11] The quest for broadness would however have to be done within reason. Cost burden and other relevant factors would have to be taken into account in determining the width and breadth of the informational focus.

[12] COMP/38.233- *Wanadoo Interactive*. COMP/38.233 Wanadoo Interactive, Commission Decision of 16 July 2003. Note that we do not make judgment about the propriety of applying a form-based approach. The problem is that in arriving at the decision, it does not appear that the Commission addressed other options.

[13] Case T-340/03, *France Télécom* [2007] E.C.R. II-107; C-202/07 P, *France Télécom* [2009] 4 CMLR 25 para 333. Note that analysis of recoupment in para 336 was merely subsidiary. This position was confirmed by both the General Court and the Court of Justice.

the Court of Justice refused to acknowledge the possibility of assessing through a consumer welfare approach which requires that the alleged infringer is able to recoup the cost of the predatory strategy. The failure to accommodate interests of the antitrust subjects as expressed through other theories (such as consumer welfare standard) weakens the decisional framework even if the form-based approach would have been chosen anyway.

However, even if we leave open the room for different consequences, the inevitability of making concrete decisions provides another challenge. To make concrete decisions between the duly recognised and substantiated theories, it is simply impossible for us to accommodate all conceivable interests till the very end. For instance, where there is no chance of recoupment in a predation case, how are we to satisfy the interest held by the defendant (which is that, since there is no chance of recoupment, there cannot be predation) and also those held by another antitrust subject (perhaps a competitor who initiated the claim) who claims that predatory intent is enough to prove anti-competition.

At this point, it is important for us to draw a distinction between accommodating various interests and vindicating each of them all the way. We cannot make concrete decisions and at the same time vindicate all (particularly conflicting) interests equally till the very end of our decisional activity—it is simply impossible. As such, though it is ideal for us to apply a high threshold of equality in our assessments, it is imperative that if substantive decisions are to be made, the chain of strict equality might have to be broken at some point. Moreover, we cannot base our exercise on a strict threshold of equality as we have to realise that "a number of very well-known proposals cannot [all] be retained".[14] Hence, we might have to reject some proposals in the interest of meeting practical justice. This is in line with the deconstructionist reasoning of transcendental deconstruction. We can therefore see the inevitability of choice-making as deriving from the insatiable part of the people's yearning for *justice as inclusiveness*.

Hence, our inability to treat various interests equally till the end does not mean they cannot be accommodated within the decisional process. If we strive towards inclusiveness, we would have desisted from ranking these interests *ex ante* thereby ensuring equality up until the operational stage whereby the chain of equality has to be broken. One thing we can be sure of is that even though some interests may be rejected, it is of value that they were included in the process of choice making as such interests could well have been vindicated had the circumstances that impacted on the decisional framework been different. Hence, comprehensive outcomes will be achieved in our antitrust analysis where we have accommodated all interests (within practical limits)[15] into the capability framework (opportunity aspect) and

[14] Kolm (1996), p. 4.

[15] The practical limitations will likely differ from jurisdiction to jurisdiction.

also duly considered all those interests on our way to reaching concrete decisions (process aspect).

It is noteworthy that not even the capability framework will require equality of capabilities/functionings. Freedom is not akin to equality. When we apply the capability approach, we make no promises or state no *a priori* position on how these interests are to be subsequently addressed. It is thus pertinent to restate that the capability approach is no more than a perspective in which the advantages and disadvantages of a person can be reasonably assessed. Though this perspective plays a significant role particularly for theories of justice and of moral and political evaluation, the concerns of justice cannot be limited to the overall opportunities and advantages of individuals in society.[16] As long as the capability sets/functionings are accommodated and even if we attach significance to the equality within and between these functionings, there is no need to define equality in one way or the other especially if a firm definition will conflict with other important considerations.[17]

Hence, required from our decisional process is that it must accommodate varying theories and ideals and as such, varying interests in order to reach a comprehensive outcome. We have to proceed on the ground that plural values are distinct and incommensurable and as such it is impossible to reduce all things we have reason to value into one homogenous magnitude. It is also required that we go about our decisional activities with persons as the main subject. Hence, whether implicitly or explicitly referred to, all analysis, evaluations and argumentations should be seen as firmly nested on the need to harness the best of the opportunities of antitrust subjects.

These germane requirements placed on the decisional process come with their own unique sets of concerns. There are debates as to whether accommodating plural interests in our decisional process will work. We are however also faced with real concerns that require compliance with the rule of law. Regarding the effectiveness of a *plurivalued*[18] regime, Schaub for instance, states that we may debate whether competition rules could be an instrument to serve pluralism and democracy, and whether the provisions should be limited to protecting the efficient functioning of the markets or extended to controlling economic power.[19] Also, as components of rule of law, legal certainty[20] and the avoidance of arbitrariness are infinitely important to our decisional process; certainty, it has been said, should be given due consideration, otherwise the value of antitrust policy will be seriously

[16] Sen (2009), p. 297.

[17] For example wealth transfer and allocative efficiency can both be seen as means of achieving equality. The problem therefore is that there is no principled reason to follow one interpretation and not the other.

[18] Word borrowed from Kőlm (1996).

[19] See Schuad (1998), p. 121.

[20] Bertea (2007), p. 69; Bańkowski (2001), pp. 39–42.

impaired.[21] In Europe, the importance attached to predictability and certainty is reflected by the Union's religious pursuit of uniformity.[22]

It would not be far-fetched to say that a pluralistic regime increases our concerns for the attainment of the rule of law. In fact, it has been argued by some that by incorporating plural values to antitrust, we will be applying certain social criteria into antitrust enforcement and that such social, political and moral criteria are likely to be applied arbitrarily and subjectively because we have to define vague terms such as fairness and social justice.[23] The potency of these concerns will be assessed as the decisional framework is further developed. However, short of dismissing these concerns, it is pertinent to note the unique position of the person-centred approach especially when compared with the traditional monist and pluralist ideals. The person-centred approach is unique because it avoids the two major problems that are respectively attributed to the monist and pluralist antitrust ideologies. Monists want a pre-determined sole goal for antitrust as they think this will curb arbitrariness and uncertainty. The pluralists think differently. They think that allowing plural values will lead to optimal balance of objectives.[24] The person-centred approach however requires comprehensive outcomes. Monist ideologies fail to address substantive opportunities as they focus too narrowly on a set outcome (culmination outcome). Inductively therefore, since the capability approach requires that the decisional process does not merely lead to culmination outcome, it is clear that the person-centred approach is not affected by the shortcomings of monist thoughts.

On the other hand, pluralists consider it necessary that we take a broader view in our analysis as no theory is prescriptive enough to provide sufficient empirical guidelines for policy-makers.[25] As such, any theory that lays absolute claim to a regime "will be ill-suited both to the extent of social heterogeneity and to the plurality of the relevant values at stake."[26] The monists however kick against the idea of plurality on the account that it is prone to arbitrariness as a result of the uncertainty involved. The person-centred approach seeks to be differentiated from other pluralist accounts as it aims at developing a firm procedure that will avoid arbitrariness while also focusing on comprehensive outcomes. It is important that this ambitious exercise is reasonable and practicable. Of course,

---

[21] Van den Bergh (2002), p. 35. Legal certainty is particularly a strong requirement in Europe. Though its necessity cannot be doubted, claims based on the idea of legal certainty can be linked to the bounded rationality problem of "availability heuristic". As such, it must be noted that whatever the position of the law may be, there will always be criticisms based on legal uncertainty.

[22] This is, for example, the motivation behind the provision of section 267 TFEU which grants the Court of Justice the power to grant preliminary rulings. See also Case C-63/93 *Fintan Duff v Ministry of Agriculture and Food and Attorney General,* [1996] ECR I-569.

[23] Schuab (1998), p. 126.

[24] For example see generally Townley (2009).

[25] Andriychuk (2010), p. 163.

[26] Sunstein (1996), p. 99.

comprehensive outcomes require that we consider a broad range of interests, but inherent in this requirement is that the decisional process itself must be intelligible. This naturally implicates the need to avoid arbitrariness—typically, an arbitrary decisional process will most likely generate self-contradictory outcomes and as a matter of logic, what is self-contradictory is unintelligible and incoherent.[27] The person-centred approach thus recognises that an unsubstantiated pluralistic antitrust regime is as bad, if not worse than a myopic one. Hence, it is required that to achieve comprehensive outcome through our decisional process, institutions must not act arbitrarily for how can we say that we have given due consideration to all relevant interests at both the opportunity and process aspect if our process rests absolutely on whims? Where we fail to structure our pluralistic regime, our efforts might end up to be nothing more than "mere assertions of a different set of personal preferences"[28] which will definitely run afoul of the spirit of the person-centred approach.

Thus in sum, our decisional framework seeks to move away from the unrealistic specificity inherent in monist thought by seeking broadness. It is however yet to be seen whether it can reduce the likelihood of arbitrariness that attends a pluralistic regime.

Summing up these requirements, what it means for the decisional aspect of antitrust is that the decisional process must stay plural but "follow a course" if it is to achieve comprehensive outcomes. This condition limits the relevant institution's discretion in deciding on antitrust issues by making it necessary to mark the line so that "however discretional decision-making activities may be, they are never wholly arbitrary or irrational". Consequently, "with the aid of tools, even forms of reasoning which are not completely rule bound can be made to follow a course" in a way that "legal decisions will not rest entirely on acts of will."[29]

To achieve comprehensive outcomes, we have to develop a decisional process that "follows a course". The primary ingredient for achieving this aim is to substantiate an ordering or structure for the person-centred analysis of the decisional aspect of antitrust. Without a structure, a pluralistic regime might be trapped into arbitrariness. To check this potential snag, the ordering herein proposed is called *antitrust pluralism*. Above all, we have to test the decisional process in order to ascertain whether the reality of decision-making is compatible with the overall idea of *justice as inclusiveness*.

---

[27] See Raz (1994), p. 261. Raz emphasises that "[c]oherence conveys a specific good, the value of which is undeniable. What is incoherent is unintelligible, because it is self-contradictory, fragmented, disjointed."

[28] Bork (1978), p. 72.

[29] Bertea (2005), pp 370–391, p. 371.

5.3 Antitrust Pluralism

As it has been shown in the preceding part, a legal regime should be reasonably accommodating if it is to solve complex and controversial issues (such as those prevalent in competition law) mainly because social life is too rich in complicated details to permit resort to monistic overriding abstractions.[30] A narrow focus will not be ideal as "[e]very general principle will confront cases in which its application will run at cross purposes with its aspirations".[31] As such, antitrust law and policy should be pluralistic in nature.

Upon closer look, it appears that the call for plurality is after all not revolutionary especially when one considers that the major antitrust institutions' accommodate plural goals and that even those who make claims to sole goal/limited goals such as consumer welfare are often times merely "philosophical".[32] For instance, one could sense Europe's unspoken avoidance of monism in antitrust cases as its institutions have avoided abstracting relevant terms. For example, with regards to Article 101 TFEU, Advocate General Tesauro in *Gøttrup-Klim* stated that the protection of competition pursued by the Court cannot be defined in abstract terms but must rather be seen in the specific context in which the conduct of the firm came about.[33] Even within the academia, there are some who not only accept plurality but promote it. Rodger, for instance, states that "[c]ompetition law or policy has no fixed content ... It can therefore be justifiably stated that in applying the core economic thesis which informs competition law, any set of principles and policies may play a part in a coherent competition law system"[34]

What we can infer is that, much more than it appears when addressed on surface level, there is a greater likelihood that plurality is/will be accepted by stakeholders. But the person-centred approach requires more. It must meet the requirement of *justice as inclusiveness*.

Antitrust pluralism is the process of expounding the ordering of antitrust. It is the primary vessel through which stakes of substantive antitrust rights are assessed. The end result of such process is unknown but would be considered *correct* (regardless of its normative content) as long as such outcome derives from a pure procedure. This procedure, it is hoped, will also balance the need for legal certainty and the flexibility required for governing an economy in a state of constant flux.

The process of antitrust pluralism has been set into two stages; *ascertaining* and *choosing*. There are many factors that find their way into antitrust policy, some at the centre and others at the peripheral level. A single measure might be explicable

---

[30] Bertea (2005), pp 370–391, p. 371.

[31] Christie (1995), p. 115.

[32] Schuab (1998), p. 125. Hawk also observed the consensus among stakeholders from different enforcement regimes. He reveals that there is a considerable gap between the rhetoric of competition law objectives and the reality of their actual implementation. See Hawk (1998), p. 353.

[33] Case C-250/92 *Gøttrup-Klim v Dansk Landbrugs*, para (1994) I ECR 5641, 5654.

[34] Rodger (2000), pp. 303–304.

through different theoretical groundings. In such cases, face value evaluation may lead us to conclude that it is not of much importance to identify the theoretical basis of an antitrust issue but in fact, the importance of such an exercise cannot be overemphasised. This is because failure to *ascertain* all conceivable interests, corresponding theories and their consequences on the case in hand means that we might fall short of the broadness requirement. Afterwards, the next task is the *choosing*; here, we have to choose between competing functionings/capability sets.

The two stages in the process are treated in turn:

5.3.1 Ascertaining

In general, the task of ascertaining competition issues require that we take into account the actual context in which competition would occur in the absence of the behaviours under review.[35] Here, our primary aim is to put the person-centred description of antitrust into more practical context. From the person-centred approach, the structure to be employed when attempting to ascertain the conduct in question is likely to differ from the structure under specific theories. First, the person-centred approach would require that we engage in ascertaining a broad range of legal conclusions that could be drawn from the behaviour under consideration. Each conclusion, backed by a theoretical insight and/or peculiar antitrust goal, represents a functioning/capability set. Second, depending on the way each functioning is to be ascertained, the person-centred approach might obscure the neat differentiation between traditional assessment methods. For instance, the task of ascertaining does not require us to make concrete judgment about how and whether Article 101(1) and Article 101(3) should be assessed. The ascertaining task does not limit the reach of any of the functionings. In other words, the relevant authorities should be able to fully describe a singular antitrust issue through each of the applicable antitrust theories. For example, while the functioning attached to the economic freedom theory may require that our ascertaining task ends with our assessment of Article 101(1), the consumer welfare or total welfare-based functionings might require a full scale analysis of both Article 101(1) and (3) TFEU in order to reach substantive conclusions which are thereafter set against themselves at the *choosing* stage.[36]

[35] Case 56/65, *Société Technique Minière*, [1966] ECR 337.

[36] The reader might feel a sense of déjà vu with this ascertaining task as the reasoning here is similar to that given for the semantics of right as well as the explanation under the capability approach. Rightly, the same thread of reasoning runs through these concepts. But rather than being mere repetitions, it is important that they are explained separately. This is because while the semantics of right addresses the issue of broadness through the position of the parties involved, the capability approach addresses it from the policy perspective while the ascertaining task addresses it from an adjudicative perspective. Also, the explanation under the ascertaining task gives greater details on the working of the whole system.

To clarify the impact of the person-centred approach on the ascertaining stage, the ascertaining task is divided into two—the general ascertaining task and the specific ascertaining. To effectively detail the nature of the general ascertaining task, closer attention is placed on effect-based infringement. The two tasks are treated in turn.

5.3.1.i General Ascertaining Task

The general ascertaining task is about addressing and teasing out issues in relation to shared antitrust queries that could result from specific issues. In other words, it is about identifying, designating and describing issues which competing antitrust theories are likely to raise. For instance, concerning Article 101, we would take into account factors such as the likely impact on inter-brand competition, intra-brand competition,[37] other markets or other policies. Regarding inter-brand competition, standard competition analysis would require that we ask if the agreement restricts actual or potential competition that would have existed without the agreement. To answer this question, account may be taken of competition between the parties and competition from third parties. For intra-brand competition, another question we would be expected to address is whether the agreement restricts actual or potential competition that would have existed in the absence of the contractual restraint. It is also imperative that we understand the divide between object and effect-based infringements.

At this stage, it is enough to merely address peripheral issues and to raise questions because we are only able to give thorough response to the antitrust issue when they are specifically ascertained through the lens of individual antitrust theories. It must however be noted that the demarcation between the general and the specific ascertaining tasks is not watertight. For instance, even though questions about the objects and effect of an agreement can be asked at the general ascertaining stage, the importance and meaning of the object based assessment and effect-based assessment is also implicated at the specific ascertaining stage. So while ascertaining common terms of this nature, we are invariably engaging in specific ascertaining tasks as well.[38]

We also have to bear in mind at the general ascertaining stage the germane issue of market definition. On the one hand, the society could be identified as the relevant market and on the other hand, a specific product market could be identified etc. Regarding the latter, the task in the market power analysis is, based on welfare analysis, to ascertain if businesses can profitably raise price above marginal cost.

[37] As it was stated in Joined Cases 56/64 and 58/66, *Consten and Grundig*, [1966] ECR 429.

[38] For example, we might be defining object-based infringement through revealed preference whereby restrictions of competition by object are seen as those with such high potential of negative effect on competition that it is unnecessary to demonstrate actual effect on the market. The freedom-based theories could hold that certain agreements are restricted by object because they breach a sacrosanct and inalienable market right.

From a liberal point of view however, market power analysis might be geared at simply preventing the accretion of private power.[39] As such, it is expected at this stage to identify the ways in which market power could be potentially defined. For instance, in light of the welfare-based analysis of market power, firms with such power can raise prices without losing sales to the extent that the rise in price becomes unprofitable. For example, in line with the Lerner index,[40] market power is expressed "as the setting of price in excess of marginal cost by measuring the proportional deviation of price at the firm's profit-maximising output from the firm's marginal cost at that output."[41]

Without drawing conclusions, we have to consider factors and approaches that could impact on our market power assessment. For instance, we should identify the possibility that market power may be exploited in the short term or long term. We should also recognise the possibility of measuring market power directly[42] or indirectly.[43] We could also ascertain the power of the firm or group of firms in the relevant market by focusing on the market share of the firms and/or by analysing barriers to entry in the relevant market.

What we should desist from doing at this stage is to make judgments about concepts such as market power. As it would be seen under the specific ascertaining task, we could attach different weight to the question of market power possession depending on the interpretative method we choose. Each of these methods represents an antitrust subject's functionings and/or capability set.

As a guide to the general ascertaining task, we could sum up the task by saying that an agreement could be regarded as anti-competitive either by object or effect. It is not for the relevant authorities to decide at this stage on whether the agreement under review amounts to an object-based or effect based infringement as this depends on the specific theory applied at the specific ascertaining stage. Both forms of analysis could however require substantiation here. For instance, in relation to the effect-based assessments, when ascertaining the nature of an agreement under this general stage, our thorough exposition of the idea of market power would serve as an ideal background for determining the normative anticompetitive effect of such issue.

Hence, to elucidate this task, efficiency and public policy claims are addressed. Regarding the efficiency analysis, it should be noted that this ascertaining task will not be undertaken within the narrow context of any of the economic theories of antitrust.

For efficiency assessment, there are three levels of analysis involved in the measurement exercise. First is identification, followed by substantiation and then

[39] Odudu (2009), p. 4.

[40] Lerner (1934), p. 157.

[41] Van den Bergh and Camesasca (2006), p. 110.

[42] That is by using econometric methods.

[43] That is through the use of structural approach.

quantification.[44] As the task implies, by identifying, we are to determine the identity of potential (anti) competitive effects. It should be noted that such effect could be on inter-brand competition, intra-brand competition, other markets or other policies. The nature of these effect-based assessments has to be noted. For example, in specific context of inter and intra-brand competition, the former is considered by the consumer welfare model to be generally more problematic than changes in intra-brand competition.[45] We simply have to be aware at this stage, for instance, that agreements can reduce inter-brand competition either through coordination, foreclosure or tacit collusion.[46] We should be aware that the next process is to substantiate by measuring the size of the effects from the agreement. It should be noted that while merely identifying the task here, actual substantiation will be undertaken in line with specific antitrust theories at the specific ascertaining stage.

Regarding the exercise of identification, we could be guided in our ascertaining task by a set of questions. We might identify an isolated issue by answering either in the positive or in the negative to whether: the agreement covers a significant part of the firms' activities and cost; the parties exchange information on marketing strategy or pricing; the parties distribute each other's products; the firms in the market become similar in terms of cost, technologies, or market share; price transparency increases; the parties cooperate on important Research and Development activities; it is not commercially justifiable to enter a new market without agreement; other suppliers cannot sell to particular buyers; other buyers cannot buy from particular distributors; buyers cannot switch easily and without significant cost to other suppliers; the agreement involves tying; distributors sell one brand only; the number of distributors decline; the agreement contains exclusive customer allocation; the agreement contains recommendation or maximum resale prices.[47] The relevance of these questions will depend on the specific theories applied at the specific ascertaining stage.

Afterwards, the relevant authorities should identify the need for substantiation of anti-competitive effects. Substantiation makes it possible to ascertain whether the anti-competitive effects of an agreement are small or large without engaging in actual quantification. The overall anti-competitive effect of an agreement depends on three factors which are (i) the latent effect of each of the individual anti-competitive effects pertaining to the agreement (ii) the market power of the parties to the agreement and (iii) the sensitivity of the market to anti-competitive effects.

In assessing the latent effect when substantiating the agreement, the scope of the agreement is of vital importance[48] as "knowing the scope of the agreement makes it

---

[44] Copenhagen (2006).

[45] See e.g. Baxter (1982) pp. 661, 693; Fox (1981) p. 1140; Liebeler (1982), p. 1; Pitofsky (1979), p. 1051.

[46] Copenhagen (2006), p. 29.

[47] Copenhagen (2006), p. 32.

[48] It is important as "the broader the scope, the higher the risk that coordination leads to significant anti-competitive effects per se." Copenhagen (2006).

possible to roughly calculate the share of the market affected by the agreement".[49] We are expected to be aware at this general stage that regarding, for instance, intra and inter-brand competition, "the smaller the share of the market affected by the agreement, the smaller is the anti-competitive effect."[50] This can be measured by looking at the product, cost strategy and duration. Of course, the determination of the scope of the market is dependent on our conceptual foundation of market which is itself influenced by the specific normative account employed at the specific ascertaining stage.

Detailed knowledge is a prerequisite at this stage. For instance, if we are to establish our awareness of the possible latent effects that could arise from agreements, we must have a clear idea of the steps that will lead us to establishing the presence or absence of such effect. For example, in substantiating foreclosure, we should be able to ascertain that anticompetitive effect may arise where agreements raise competitors' costs and where agreements reduce demand for competitors' products. Indicators available to measure the importance of foreclosure effect include the determination of the share of the relevant market open to competition, typical contract duration, churn in the market and countervailing power. Concerning the likelihood that tacit collusion would arise, we are expected to generally ascertain that such possibility is limited to specific market circumstances where: firms are homogeneous; there is potential for retaliation; the market is relatively stable; and there is absence of short term incentive to cheat. In addition, the agreement itself must increase the likelihood of tacit collusion.[51]

Where we substantiate intra-brand competition, we focus on the tendency of the agreement to limit the number of distributors and the attendant risk that such agreement might result in collusion. Also, when substantiating the likelihood of foreclosure effect of an agreement, due consideration is given to the duration of the agreement being reviewed.[52] Substantiation of market power affirms that an agreement is more likely to cause anti-competitive effect if the parties to the agreement have significant market power. For horizontal agreements, what is considered is the combined market share of the parties to the agreement, while, for vertical agreements, attention is placed on the buyer and the supplier's market share.[53]

---

[49] Copenhagen (2006), p. 34.

[50] Copenhagen (2006).

[51] Copenhagen (2006), p. 37.

[52] Copenhagen (2006), p. 36. In *Delimitis* for instance, the Court of Justice, deciding on the anti-competitive effect of beer supply agreements stated that: "the contribution of the individual contracts entered into by the [supplier] to the sealing-off of [a] market ... depends on their duration. If the duration is manifestly excessive in relation to the average duration of ... supply agreements generally entered into in the relevant market, the individual contract falls under the prohibition under Article [101(1)]."

[53] Article 3 of the Block Exemption Regulation provides that the market share in any particular Article 101 TFEU issue is constituted by an analysis of the supplier's market share on the market where it sells the contract goods or services and the buyer's market share on the market where it

Our ascertaining task requires that we engage in substantiation analysis on market power with the outcome that if contracting parties' combined market power is low, the agreement is not likely to have significant anti-competitive effect vice versa.

Likewise, it must be noted that the overall result of substantiation is largely dependent on either the presence of competitive restraints or the incidence of sensitive market condition that induces anti-competitive effect. Thus, in order to make appropriate decision, the assessor would consider competitors' market power, market concentration, market maturity, entry barriers and product characterisation.[54]

It is important that we engage in substantiation exercise under the general ascertaining task because, by so doing, we are able to assess the sensitivity of the market or the presence of competitive restraints regardless of conclusions that could be drawn under specific theories. Taking the substantiation of market concentration as example, we would find that substantiating the market condition at this stage plays a large role in determining the presence or absence of anti-competitive effect under specific theories. For instance, we might find under the specific ascertaining task that a small agreement actually causes major competition concerns as a result of the highly concentrated nature of the markets, while we might find that a large agreement actually raises limited concern because of the low concentration in the market.

Where substantiation of anti-competitive effect is not adequate, it becomes necessary to measure through quantification of anti-competitive effect. Thus, being a corollary to substantiation, this task does not add much substance to the overall task. However, it is still worth a mention. Quantification requires the use of complex economic tools. For example, for an analysis of coordination, the UK Competition Commission applied diversion ratio in the *Somerfield–Morrisons case*.[55] It was also used by the European Commission in the *Volvo–Renault case*.[56] Others are critical elasticity methodology and market simulation models. In quantifying foreclosure, the event study methodology and simulation models can be used. In relation to intra-brand competition, econometrics price studies and simulation models could be used.[57]

Amongst other factors which must at least be mentally noted at this stage, we are expected to have a clear idea of the types of agreements and the classifications of efficiencies. With specific example of efficiencies, it is imperative that we note the four issues in efficiency analysis. First, we have to note the need to identify the nature of the claimed efficiencies. Second, we have to note the need to assess the

---

purchases the contract goods or services. The Article provides further that in order for the block exemption to apply, the supplier's and the buyer's market share must each be 30 % or less. Also, para 88 and 89 of the Vertical Guidelines (2010) states how market share is to be calculated from both the buyer and supplier's perspective.

[54] See European Commission (2000), pp. 1–44.

[55] See http://www.competition-commission.org.uk/inquiries/ref2005/somerfield/.

[56] European Commission Decision Case No COMP/M.1980.

[57] Copenhagen (2006), pp. 53–55.

link between the agreement under review and the efficiencies claimed. Third, we have to note the need to assess the likelihood and magnitude of the each claimed efficiency and fourth, we have to note the need to determine how and when each of the efficiencies claimed would be achieved.[58] At this stage of the ascertaining exercise, we should focus on the identification exercise (which addresses both the first and second issues) and the quantification (the third issue). The fourth issue is not to be addressed here because our finding at the point of weighing would depend on the welfare theory underpinning the specific ascertaining task.

Still on the example of economic effects, it is imperative at this stage that we note, for instance, the three efficiency gains that could be potentially substantiated through specific normative accounts, namely: within-firm efficiency gains; between-firm efficiency gains; and innovative benefits.[59] It is expected that we are aware that within-firm efficiency gains could be one or a combination of economies of scale, economies of scope, bargaining power and duplication savings. Regarding between-firm efficiencies, we are meant to understand that the agreement could solve either or a combination of the free rider problem, hold-up problem and double marginalisation. Innovation benefits could be obtained through technology diffusion, creation of new products and the creation of new processes. It is worthy to note at this stage that different agreements give rise to different efficiency gains. For instance, while production agreements often give rise to within-firm efficiency gains in the form of economies of scale or scope and so on, single brand agreements (such as specific rebate schemes) typically lead to between-firm efficiencies.[60]

Understandably, antitrust institutions are expected to be aware of every factual detail and how they could be harnessed by specific theories at the specific ascertaining stage. Thus, still with the example of efficiencies, it is imperative that if we are to have a sophisticated specific ascertaining analysis of economic effect of an antitrust issue, we should ordinarily know how to identify efficiency gains at the general ascertaining stage. For instance, we should be aware that to identify such gains, it might be necessary to assess the agreement in question to ascertain whether: production volume increases in at least one production facility thereby generating economies of scale; other products will be produced at the same production facilities thus leading to economies of scope; purchasing is to be coordinated or rationalised so that bargaining power is enhanced; parties have parallel production facilities upon which they agree in order to avoid duplication; parties increase their sale effort as a result of the reduction in free-riding; parties increase their investment as they could side-step the hold-up problem; the agreement is vertical and pricing or production will be coordinated in a way that solves the double marginalisation problem; significant technology knowledge will be shared between parties which leads to technology diffusion; new products of higher

[58] European Commission (2004).

[59] See Copenhagen (2006), p. 56.

[60] See Copenhagen (2006), p. 56.

quality will be introduced into the market; or more cost efficient production techniques will be developed.[61]

At this stage, we are expected to clearly detail the conditions that have to be established for a specific claim to hold. For example, if we presume that the issue on ground is such that when specifically ascertaining efficiencies, we might have to show that the agreement in question is indispensable to the attainment of the efficiencies, then we should have clearly identified at this general stage, the conditions that have to be fulfilled. We could for instance identify the two tests that can be applied: first is that the restrictive agreement as such must be reasonably necessary in order to achieve the efficiencies; second, the individual restrictions of the competition that flows from the agreement must also be reasonably necessary for the attainment of the efficiencies.[62] In Europe for instance, what we need to ascertain concerning the indispensability of efficiency gains is whether or not the restrictive agreement and individual restrictions make it possible to perform the activity in question more efficiently than would likely have been the case in the absence of the agreement or the restriction concerned.[63] Once it is found that the agreement in question is necessary for the attainment of the efficiencies, it must be assessed whether individual restrictions are reasonably necessary to produce the efficiencies. In doing this, we would have to take into account both the nature of the restriction and its intensity.[64]

We should also be aware at this stage that claims are to be treated in their peculiar context. For instance, as different from between-firm efficiencies, we should know that where claims are made about within-firm efficiency gains deriving from an agreement, the party making such claims is expected to substantiate economies of scale by assessing one of the cost function, the cost structure, the degree of specialisation, the degree of indivisibility and so on. Further, taking the free-rider problem as example of the between-firm efficiency gains, we would expect the party making the claim to substantiate the likelihood that there will be such market failure in the absence of the agreement.[65]

If a claim is to succeed within its specific theoretical category or capability set, we must know what to look out for. For instance, regarding the free-rider problem, three market criteria must be fulfilled in order to establish the efficiency gain: First, pre- and after-sales services should be important in the industry; second, promotion activities should be generic in character and not brand specific; third, products must be of a reasonably high value. The free-rider problem could be demonstrated by comparing the level of sales services with that of other brands or other industries.

---

[61] See Copenhagen (2006), p. 60.

[62] Commission 2004, para 73.

[63] Commission 2004, para 74.

[64] Commission 2004, para 78.

[65] Commission 2004, para 78.

The general ascertaining task can be deployed to other antitrust related issues as well. Where for instance, an issue involves public policy consideration, the general ascertaining task should seek to identify the nature of the public policy concern—is it about integration or trade policy? Afterwards, the task will be to ascertain how the claim links to a competition issue—is it aimed at buttressing or substantiating an allegation of anti-competition? Is it raised as a defence or to mitigate the claim of anti-competition?

Conclusively, the general ascertaining task can be undertaken within the purview of the different interests and theories that are represented in the capability framework of any particular case.

5.3.1.ii Specific Ascertaining Task

On the specific ascertaining task, our primary task should be to ascertain what, within the confines of specific theories, competition law should protect. This stage of the process simply puts the abstracted capability framework into decisional perspective. For concrete assessment, decision-makers will have to give meaning to peculiar words—what is competition, restriction of competition, object, effect, exception, exemptions etc in light of the individual normative accounts. We strive to make meaning of antitrust as an institution. Academics and competition authorities continuously endeavour to find the meaning of competition law terms and for every attempt, the inadequacy of adopted concepts become ever more vivid. Most theories generally attempt to rationalise the limits of antitrust and depending on their ideological inclination, some believe that specific terms should be incapable of manipulation,[66] while others consider the obscurity of terms to be necessary since the market is prone to changes.[67] An intermediate ideology is that which seeks legal certainty but also wishes to maintain the flexibility required for governing an economy in a state of constant flux.[68]

Using as example the term "restriction" as applied in Europe, it has been noted that neither the Court of Justice nor the Commission have defined "restriction of competition" with sufficient clarity or consistency.[69] The lack of precision here has been regarded as a scandal for antitrust.[70] However, rather than viewing the obscurity of the term as a problem, the person-centred approach celebrates it because it gives us the latitude to specifically ascertain the term in its different ramifications. In other words, the fact that the meaning of the term remains obscure is of value to our task of attaining heterogeneity, broadness and inclusiveness in

[66] Marenco (1999) referred to in Townley (2009), p. 205, n 17.

[67] Möschel (1991), p. 7.

[68] Townley (2009).

[69] Townley (2009), p. 206.

[70] Richard Whish said that the failed attempts to define "restriction of competition" remain the central conundrum to EC competition law. See Ehlermann and Laudati (1998), p. 461. See also Odudu (2005), p. 97.

antitrust. Thus, in light of the capability framework, our specific ascertaining task requires that we address every conceivable meaning within the context of the agreement under review. This exercise should be encouraged because each meaning represents a functioning or capability set which is worthy of recognition.

Hence, as a result of the specificity of individual normative accounts, it is pertinent that we give meaning to the term "restriction of competition" in line with specific theories or goals. To the freedom-based theories (particularly the ordoliberals thought of economic freedom), "restriction of competition" means an undue restriction of the economic freedom of the parties or a restriction of other market participants.[71] Thus, we may engage in our specific ascertaining task by distilling the general terms such as inter/intra brand competition and object/effect through the goal of economic freedom. As stated in *Metropole*,[72] the ascertaining task may thus require that we take into account the actual condition in which an agreement functions, in particular the economic context and the actual structure of the market concerned.[73] Overall from the economic freedom point of view, we should only be concerned with undue restriction of economic freedom.[74]

In ascertaining the term "restriction of competition" through the theory of economic freedom, we could adopt either a strict or effect-based approach. If we apply economic freedom in the strict term, it may be difficult to vindicate any state that reduces competition regardless of its efficiency gains. The effect-based approach would however seek to challenge only "undue" restriction of economic freedom.[75] In this case, a restriction of economic freedom might be acceptable where there are overriding welfare/public policy gains. However, regardless of such gains, the restriction of economic freedom will be regarded as undue where effective competition is completely eliminated. Thus, it is essential to ascertain whether the firms involved hinder the remaining sources of (actual and potential) competition which then affects the proper functioning of the market. To establish this fact, we could check if the important barriers and drivers of effective competition have been significantly affected. The indicators can be alluded to by establishing the actual competition in the market against the ideal state of competition as recognised by specific antitrust theories.

In line with total welfare, "restriction of competition" would arise from allocative inefficiency. Our specific ascertaining task however requires more than abstractive definition. We must take note of the multiple implications that could arise from the application of this welfare standard as we could reach different outcomes depending on how we seek to address the market presumptions. Starting with total welfare analysis, it is explained how Williamson's trade-off model can be

[71] See generally Monti (2007).

[72] T-112/99 *Metropole Television (M6) v Commission* [2001] ECR II-2459.

[73] T-112/99 *Metropole Television (M6) v Commission* [2001] ECR II-2459, para 76.

[74] Monti (2007). This implies that behaviours that results in ancillary restraints do not fall foul of competition rules.

[75] See generally Monti (2007).

applied in our specific ascertaining exercise. Regarding his basic welfare function, he stated thus:

> The partial equilibrium apparatus that I would propose for purposes of examining the trade-off question is one in which the welfare function is expressed as W = (TR + S) - (TC - R), where TR refers to total revenue, S to consumer surplus, TC to total cost, and R to intramarginal rents. The terms in the first set of parentheses reflect the social benefits associated with the activity in question, while the terms in the second (under appropriate restrictions) reflect social costs. The allocative efficiency consequences of any merger that increases both efficiency and market power can be evaluated only by estimating net effects.[76]

The implications of the alleged restraint on allocative and productive efficiencies are simply sub-components in a broader welfare analysis. The ultimate focus is the impact of a proposed restriction on total welfare.[77]

The divergence that could arise from the different interpretation of the total welfare model is worth ascertaining. Over and above the requisite trade-off between allocative efficiency and productive efficiency, there are those who believe that market analysis should take note of second-best problems. If we assess restraint of competition strictly on the basis of Williamson's trade-off on the one hand[78] and combine the Williamson's trade-off with the second-best theory on the other hand,[79] we are likely to address wellbeing in different ways and consequently vindicate different interests even within this narrow capability set.

The ascertaining task here requires an in-depth understanding of the rationale behind this welfare standard. Competitive equilibria are Pareto-efficient where there exists no reallocation of resources that makes someone better off without making someone else worse off. Interpreted through the general equilibrium theory, this Pareto-state relates to the whole economy. As such, the idea of allocative efficiency is built on certain restrictive assumptions[80] which must all be fulfilled to have a perfectly competitive state. The impossibility of reaching a perfectly competitive state means that we should off-set gains in one market with loss in another. On the other hand, the partial equilibrium approach contends that where any of the conditions fail in a market, thereby resulting in allocative inefficiency, such failure should be addressed in isolation.

---

[76] Williamson (1989), p. 105, 107; Williamson (1977), p. 708, n 27.

[77] Hammer (2000), p. 878. Note however that the Borkean version of total welfare is even stricter as he expressed his reservation to Williamson's model. He believes that economic analysis would show that cost saving or social loss does not exist. He also argues that since all consumers are also owners of businesses and hence benefit from monopolistic price increases, efficiency with price increases would not hurt the average consumer. See Bork (1978), p. 110.

[78] For example Bork (1978) prefers this confined analysis on welfare.

[79] For example Hammers argues that analytically, second-best concerns are the flip side of the same coin as Williamson's productive efficiency defence, and both fit comfortably within a total welfare orientation. See Hammers (2000), p. 879.

[80] See generally Williamson (1989).

Regardless of the equilibrium theory we align with, we assess total welfare on the account of allocative efficiency. This cannot be the end of our analysis. Total welfare model states that a seeming market failure arising from an allocatively inefficient state might be counteracted by productive efficiency gains. As such, we should assess the Pareto state on net basis. Under this welfare standard, any productive efficiency gains (for example, the economics of scale or economic of scope) may be allowed and may trump the allocative inefficiency deficit regardless of whether such gain is transferred to the consumer. For instance, following from the explanation of the efficiency gains under the general ascertaining task, sufficient within-firm efficiencies may offset the allocative inefficiency even where such efficiencies are primarily internal to the firms and are in no way transferred to consumers.

The varying ideas of market definition mentioned under the general ascertaining task can impact on our total welfare analysis. In assessing allocative efficiency, the practical nature of the decisional aspect means that we might specifically find that the requirement of "net welfare" is established where, on the one hand, we balance second-best option with the allocative inefficiency in a specific market or on the other hand, we focus solely on the allocative (in)efficiency in the specific market. Where we apply the former, we might find a seeming allocatively inefficient state to be efficient. Assuming we find under both approaches that certain behaviour is allocatively inefficient, then we are to balance the allocative inefficiency with productive efficiency.

It is therefore possible that a total welfare model can be sub-divided into at least two forms of practical analysis. First is that, in line with the Williamson trade-off we might ascertain that an agreement is not unduly restrictive not because we challenge the claim that a state is allocatively inefficient but on the grounds that, on the net, the allocative inefficiency has been counteracted. This means thus that in our assessment of allocative inefficiency, we ascertain nature of "restriction of competition" by isolating the relevant market and assessing market power. On the other hand, a total welfare approach that accommodates the second best theory widens the functionings within a capability set. Thus, depending on the case in hand, we might, in regards to our ascertaining task, conceive of this broader scope of assessment by allowing for trade-offs at two different ends: first, in assessing whether the specific product market is allocatively inefficient; second, where the general market is considered allocatively inefficient.[81] Then we can assess whether such effect can be balanced with productive efficiency gains.

Under the wealth transfer (consumer welfare) standard and the consumer choice theories, we are to ascertain "restriction of competition" by analysing inter- or intra-brand competition in the relevant market through consumer harm. A state of allocative inefficiency would harm consumers. The correction of this market failure thus should form the initial aspect of this task.[82] Recognition of allocative

[81] Townley (2011a), pp. 490–499.

[82] See generally Odudu (2005) on the goal of Article 101(1).

efficiency nonetheless, we still have to take into account distributional issues. Where the focus on consumer is adhered to in ascertaining whether a firm's behaviour amounts to a "restriction of competition", the concept of market power would be at the very centre of antitrust analysis.[83] Thus, regardless of gains in other markets, there will be a restriction as long as market power impacts negatively on consumers in the relevant market.[84] The initial aspect of our ascertaining task will thus be limited to the assessment of whether there is a (likely) increase in market power which could occur directly through an arrangement that facilitates coordination and reduces competition among rivals, or indirectly, by foreclosing rivals from the market.[85]

To assess an agreement in a particular market, we are to ascertain whether the behaviour in question is restrictive and consequently anticompetitive by building a theory of harm that explains how the agreement leads to an increase in price, reduced output, reduced choice and/or reduced innovation compared with a counter-factual where there is no such agreement.[86] Its restrictive nature notwithstanding, an agreement might be accommodated if there are corresponding gains to consumers. It is at this stage that consumer-based approaches diverge. The two broad categories that should be acknowledged in our specific ascertaining task are (i) those limited to efficiency effects on consumers and (ii) those that take into account, public policy effect on consumers.[87] For the first category, the harm could be balanced against gains arising exclusively[88] from either or a combination of productive and dynamic efficiency. We must however have in mind in our ascertaining task that it is only objective and direct efficiency gains for consumers that would count rather than subjective and indirect gains. For instance, cost savings resulting from mere exercise of market power will be rejected as an efficiency gain.

After applying the theory of harm, our measurement exercise gives meaning to "restriction of competition" while the weighing addresses whether we can objectively validate a seeming anti-competitive agreement as a result of the (likely) improvement such agreement could have on the production or distribution of goods or to the promotion of technical or economic progress.

Unlike the total welfare model, the consumer approaches require that efficiency gains are narrowed to the actual consumers. This must be reflected in the pass-on and weighing. Here, we first have to be sure that the efficiency gain is passed-on directly to consumers. This means that we are more likely to be interested in

[83] This is evident from the General Court's assessment in *Glaxo* case.

[84] In contrast to the second-best theory addressed above.

[85] Reindl (2011), p. 5.

[86] Nazzini (2006), pp. 497, 514–517.

[87] See generally Townley (2009).

[88] For instance, it is believed that to allow a trade-off between allocative inefficiency and a range of efficiencies and gains (other than purely productive efficiency and dynamic efficiency) as well as the pursuit of multitude of non-efficiency goals is detrimental to consumer interest. See Buttigieg (2009), p. 133.

between-firm efficiencies and innovation benefits as they are more likely to be passed-on.[89] Afterwards, we have to ascertain the volume of the efficiency gains which are passed on to those consumers who experience the anti-competitive effect. There are various tests in this pass-on analysis. First, we have to ascertain who the consumers are. They could, for instance, include all direct or indirect users of the products which are covered by the agreement. Also, rather than focusing on the impact on individual consumers, it is the impact on the group of consumers of the relevant market that counts.

For within-firm efficiencies, the gains are usually internal cost savings which could lead to lower prices. We could ascertain the pass-on rate by analysing a number of indicators such as: type of cost saving, type of pass-on, state of competition, demand condition, and supply conditions.[90] We might for instance be concerned about the type of cost savings because of the distinction that exists between cost savings lowering marginal cost and cost savings lowering fixed cost.[91]

With regard to between-firm efficiencies, we could ascertain pass-on by, for example, assessing the willingness of consumers to pay for new products. Also, we could estimate the return on sales service or advertising services. Here, where the returns are high, it implies that consumers will receive additional value from the agreement, but where the returns are low it implies that consumers will not receive significant benefits from the agreement.[92]

The ascertaining task may be further illustrated by distilling necessary elements of, for instance, public policy in any single antitrust issue. Where the public policy issue relates to the environment, we should aim, through the specific ascertaining task, to establish the elements required for granting to grant an exemption for a seeming anti-competitive practice. In such a case, what would have to be ascertained is first, whether consumers individually and in general have a positive rate of return from the supposed environmental benefit within a reasonable payback period. With this in mind, one would have to ascertain the implication if such benefit is immediately obtainable and also consider claims which have a longer gestation period and, as such, would perhaps only benefit generations yet unborn.[93]

It should be noted that the manner in which antitrust laws are drafted might impact on our ability to engage in the ideal ascertaining task. Hence, though there is always scope to interpret the provisions of Article 101 and 102 TFEU more flexibly and to some extent more broadly, those provisions (particularly Article 101) are not suitable for the person-centred antitrust because they limit the applicability of certain principles and theories which should in principle be allowed into the capability framework. For instance, with regards to Article 101 TFEU as a whole,

---

[89] Guidelines on Article 81(3), para 83–104; Copenhagen (2006), p. 98.

[90] Guidelines on Article 81(3), para 83–104; Copenhagen (2006), p. 99.

[91] The distinction between these cost savings reflects the difference between short run and long run effects.

[92] Copenhagen (2006), p. 101.

[93] Townley (2011b), p. 580.

it might be difficult to engage in the ascertaining task strictly in line with specific theories. For example, it might be impossible to argue on the basis of strict efficiency considering the requirement that any restrictive practice must not have the effect of eliminating competition in the relevant market. Strict efficiency argument might also be excluded because of the requirement that consumers get a fair share of the resulting benefit.

Taking into account these impediments, if a regime is to apply the person-centred approach, it should endeavour to leave its antitrust provisions as wide as possible. A good example of an antitrust provision that might be able to adapt with the person-centred approach is the Section 2 of the Sherman Act which provides that "[e]very person who shall monopolize, or attempt to monopolize, or combine or conspire with any other person or persons, to monopolize any part of the trade or commerce among the several States, or with foreign nations, shall be deemed guilty of a felony."[94] This provision is broad and open-textured. As such, it gives us the room to engage in detailed ascertaining. Thus, if the person-centred approach is successfully established, antitrust law should simply be broad enough to accommodate different interpretations that could be drawn from different antitrust principles and theories.

5.3.2 Choosing

The ascertaining task represents the starting point of the practical aspect of the person-centred analysis. It has been shown that the ascertaining task simply offers a much more detailed analysis of the various functionings that can be abstracted in the capability framework and sets them up in an adjudicative context. After the different functionings and their underlying antitrust logic have been thoroughly identified, the more germane task would be to choose between them. Here, the *choosing* task addresses the more practical question as to how functionings are to be chosen while maintaining the primary aim of the person-centred approach, to wit, meeting the requirement of *justice as inclusiveness*. How can we practically choose between different interests whilst at the same time respect the idea of plurality that has so far been emphasised under this approach? This is indeed an important question. It must be kept in mind that our answer to this question is particularly crucial in determining the true value of the approach—the true value of the approach would have to be assessed on two criteria. First, it has to be shown that the alternative approach is practical. Second, the alternative approach has to be evaluated vis-à-vis the traditional accounts and even against the deconstructed discourse ethics.

Once we think of choosing, we are typically faced with genuine practical restraints that could jeopardise our desire to ensure "broadness as inclusiveness".

---

[94] Sherman Act, February 30, 1890, ch. 647, 26 Stat. 209, 15 U.S.C.

This is because we cannot make concrete decisions that suit all the relevant functionings. This concern notwithstanding, we have to choose. An apt statement about the inevitability of choosing is given by Isaiah Berlin who said that:

> [W]e are doomed to choose, and every choice may entail irreparable loss. The world we encounter in ordinary experience is one in which we are faced with choices between ends equally ultimate and claims equally absolute, the realization of some of which must inevitably involve the sacrifice of others.... If, as I believe the ends of men are many, and not all of them are in principle compatible with each other, then the possibility of conflict – and of tragedy – can never be wholly eliminated from human life, either personal or social. The necessity of choosing between absolute claims is then an inescapable characteristic of the human condition.[95]

To bring home Berlin's point, I use predation to illustrate. The total welfare, consumer welfare, and economic freedom theories abhor predation. However, the difference in the way they define anti-competition might consequently affect our finding on whether a particular behaviour is predatory. For instance, depending on whether we are reasoning through either consumer welfare or economic freedom, we would have to determine whether recoupment is a condition for establishing violation. Even though we might, as a matter of principle, regard predation to be anticompetitive, our different theoretical inclinations would impact on whether we consider a firm's behaviour to be predatory. In essence, we have to choose between the different interpretations. This is just one of numerous instances where *choosing* is ultimately inevitable. Another example can be derived from the *T-Mobile* case—is a concerted practice an infringement by object chiefly because it obstructs economic freedom or because of the likely negative welfare effect?[96] In this case, the Court of Justice stated that the distinction between 'infringements by object' and 'infringements by effect' arises from the fact that certain forms of collusion between firms can be regarded, by their very nature, as being injurious to the proper functioning of normal competition. Consequently, there is no need to consider the effects of a concerted practice where its anticompetitive object is established. Also, it is possible that we regard the same concerted practice to amount to an infringement by object but on a different ground—perhaps because its anti-competitive effect is so obvious that we need not go into any detailed analysis in individual cases.[97]

The inevitability of engaging in some form of choosing does not necessarily mean that the person-centred idea of inclusiveness should be dispensed with. However, if the *choosing* task is to be compliant with the ideals of the person-centred approach, it is essential that some basic conditions are complied with. First, we must not choose functionings *a priori*. As such, just as some scholars contend,[98]

---

[95] Berlin (1998), XLV.

[96] Case C-8/08 *T-Mobile Netherlands BV and Others Raad van bestuur van de Nederlandse Mededingingsautoriteit*. 2009 [ECR] I-4529.

[97] Note though that this second example is not as serious as the first one.

[98] See e.g. Hawk (1998), p. 353.

it would mean in practice that competition law provisions should not express objectives. In light of the alternative approach, the rationale for desisting from making a priori decisions is to resist the influence of normative accounts on fundamental antitrust conceptions. To illustrate the need to avoid normative subjectivity, reference can be made to the now commonplace assertions that antitrust laws should be strictly concerned about consumer welfare. From the person-centred point of view and in light of the condition herein addressed, the consumer welfare ideology could potentially restrict certain interests. As such, it offends the person-centred approach and would thus corrupt our choosing exercise.

The second condition is that the procedure for reaching concrete decisions must be appropriate since correct answers cannot be determined ex ante. The task here is to choose between the varied interests whilst at the same time give adequate consideration to various interests. To see if this can be achieved, a number of options would be substantiated and evaluated. First, I will consider the possibility of seeking *correct* outcomes by perusing the normative accounts objectively. It will be shown that this option is inappropriate as it fails on the same ground as the discourse ethics, which is that it is impossible to rule out subjectivity. Also, the social choice theory is considered. The result is equally pessimistic as it falls short of the requirement of justice as inclusiveness in general and more particularly of requirements (i)–(v) identified in Chap. 4.

5.3.2.i Procedural Objectivity and Correctness

Having developed the person-centred approach till this point, one is drawn back to the question as to whether we could reach concrete results by relying of our analytical strength to ascertain correct answers. The pursuit of correctness appears to run counter to the understanding that the person-centred approach is motivated by pure procedural justice since we do not know with certainty what is correct or what we should strive for. This is however not the case. Correctness is sought here, not on the basis of an idealised position or standard but as a consequence of a fair and objective procedure.

To substantiate the possibility of making substantive judgments objectively, the works of scholars such as Alexy, Finnis and Dworkin are worthy of mention. Alexy for instance, argues that law itself makes a claim to correctness. In principle, this means that we can achieve correctness. He states that law seeks correctness by linking the claim to those subjects who act for and in law by creating, interpreting, using and enforcing it. On the contrary, Finnis argues that a claim to correctness is completely based on subjectivism—it is based on "the disposition of the chooser".[99] Alexy recognises criticisms of this nature. He thus states that in raising a claim, the legal subject can be said to be correct only where he does so objectively. The claim is said to be objectively raised where everybody

[99] Finnis (1987), p. 357.

who decides, judges, or discusses the matter in a legal system must necessarily raise it.[100] Thus though the claim is raised by "person", he does not do so subjectively because he raises such claim on behalf of the law. It therefore could be said that "law raises this claim through persons who work for and in it."[101] Alexy contends that correctness implies justifiability. As such, in raising a claim to correctness, law also raises one to justifiability. He states further that in recognising the claim to correctness:

> law does not only accept a general obligation to justification on principles; it also maintains that this obligation is complied with or can be met. The claim to correctness therefore includes . . . three elements: (1) the assertion of correctness, (2) the guarantee of justifiability, and (3) the expectation of acceptance of correctness.[102]

The role of law as correctness can also be gleaned from Dworkin's *Law as Integrity*. He argues that the goal of the interpretative attitude constitutive of the practice we call law is to find in every situation of civil dispute, *the right* which the given society's law makes available in most difficult cases.[103] Specifically, in their task towards correctness, "[j]udges who accept the interpretative idea of integrity decide hard cases by trying to find, in some coherent set of principles about people's right and duties, the best constructive interpretation of the political structure and legal doctrine of their community."[104] To assess correctness, we can set a judge's decision against conviction of *fit* and *justification*. Conviction of fit will provide a rough threshold requirement that an interpretation of some part of the law must meet if it is to be eligible at all. This will limit subjectivism as it will eliminate interpretations that some judges would otherwise prefer. The second conviction comes in particularly in hard cases where a judge's threshold test does not discriminate between two or more interpretations. Here, he must choose based on inherent substantive moral soundness. In other words, he must choose between eligible interpretations by seeking the one that reflects the community's structure of institutions and decisions in a better light from the standpoint of political morality.[105]

Any claim to correctness, particularly as it pertains to hard cases, would have to contend with the objection provided by Finnis. He argues that no judge, no matter how superhuman, could justifiably claim unique correctness for his answer to a hard case "for in such a case, a claim to have found the right answer is senseless".[106] Finnis argues that hard cases can meet the threshold of not only the "fit" but also of "justifiability" such that "not only is there more than one answer which violates no

100 Alexy (1998), pp. 205, 206.

101 Alexy (1998), pp. 205, 206.

102 Alexy (1998), p. 208.

103 See generally Dworkin (1986).

104 See generally Dworkin (1986), p. 255.

105 See generally Dworkin (1986).

106 Finnis (1987), p. 372.

applicable rule, but the answer thus available are ranked in different orders along each of the available criteria of evaluation."[107]

If the idea of correctness proposed in the person-centred approach is considered to be theoretically sound, Finnis' objection must be taken seriously. Every relevant functioning is recognised because they have theoretical depth and do fit with past decisions. Further, owing to the exposition of the five requirements of broadness as they relate to specific theories,[108] it has been shown that all the contending theories have their strong and weak points meaning thus that they will be ranked differently from requirement to requirement. If we cannot substantiate a way through which law could attain correctness, it really would not matter that, as Alexy says, law *could* make claims to correctness.

This concern, as raised by Finnis, brings to fore the difficulty of applying this approach in our *choosing* exercise. The problem identified by Finnis is to the effect that values are incommensurable. Thus, there cannot be an objectively correct choice. This reasoning particularly flaws the utilitarian assumption of the commensurability of basic good. Even Dworkin, in his attempt to head off the problem of incommensurability, falls into the utilitarian trap. His propositions on a kind of lexical ordering[109] have been flawed.[110] It must thus be conceded for the purpose of this exercise that to seek absolute correctness either by deciding objectively or by comparing objectively inherent values in the competing functionings will be far-fetched.[111] This problem weakens the prospect of maintaining inclusiveness through correctness as it appears that every task aimed at correctness would, by itself, lead to inherent subjectivity.[112]

Notwithstanding the concerns raised, some scholars are convinced about the possibility of achieving correctness and objectivity. For instance, Nagel contends that the pressures towards objectivity and correctness (even on the basis of conflicting pluralistic values) are very strong wherever values come into practical conflict.[113] Further, Alexy states that "the law is an idea that is intrinsically connected with the idea of objectivity." He states further that "[o]bjectivity is an essential feature of law, a feature that is not compatible with complete subjectivity of the purposes at issue. . ."[114]

It is noteworthy that the constraints to objectivity might vary depending on the case at hand. The task of maintaining objectivity might be easier where different antitrust theories and models lead to the same result.[115] In such instance, one could afford not to make a categorical statement as to the underlying theory/model that is

---

107 Finnis (1987), pp. 372–373.

108 As dealt with in Chap. 4.

109 See Dworkin (1977), pp. 340–341; Dworkin (1986).

110 Finnis (1987), pp. 373–374.

111 Note however the argument in Da Silva (2011), pp. 273–301.

112 As expressed by Grisez (1978), pp. 21, 46–47.

113 Nagel (2001), pp. 110–111.

114 Alexy (2007), p. 49.

115 For example, naked cartelist behaviours.

ideal. Contrariwise, objectivity could prove difficult where more than one functioning (and outcome) seem well poised to underlie a specific antitrust issue. These are cases where there exist several distinct reasons of justice each of which survive scrutiny but leads to different results.[116]

From the foregoing, as much as one might admire the concept of objectivity especially with regards to its inherent relationship with law, the prospects of this concept is weakened by two pitfalls. First, if correctness implies the presence of right and wrong answers, it is practically difficult or perhaps impossible to set out a truly objective criterion for deciding between these interests. Secondly, even where the criteria of objectivity is not to be applied in determining the rightness or wrongness of particular theories or outcomes but rather in determining the inherent logic of the competing theories, one still has to take note of the plurality of robust and impartial reasons that can emerge from searching scrutiny. This means the choosing task as a whole cannot be practically achieved while maintaining the purely procedural nature of the person-centred approach.

Given that it is practically impossible to follow through with the choosing exercise while at the same time applying the broadness criteria of the person-centred approach in its pure form, one might be tempted to make a contrived attempt at defining objectivity in a way that suits the exercise. For instance, of the two types of objectivity—epistemic and metaphysical—one might be disposed to building the choosing exercise on the definition that accommodates the inherent subjectivity contained in the *choosing* exercise.

Epistemic objectivity requires that our decisions are free of bias (or other factors that distort our judgment) that prevent the things we are judging from presenting themselves clearly and accurately.[117] It thus demands that the cognitive process and mechanisms by which we form beliefs about the world be constituted in such a way that they, at least, tend towards the production of accurate representations of how things are. Epistemic objectivity does not require that the cognitive process in question yields an absolutely correct representation.[118] To be epistemically objective, our cognitive processes need not yield accurate representations. The standard test rather is that our cognitive processes are free of factors that we know to produce inaccurate representation. On the other hand, metaphysical objectivity requires an ability to deliver accurate representations of the way things truly or objectively are. Thus, we achieve metaphysical objectivity where we can see things as what they are independent of how we take them to be.

Applied to legal decisions and consequently to the task of choosing, we expect legal decisions to be objective in the sense that arbiters make decisions without letting bias or prejudice intervene. It is vivid that the idea of objectivity is inherently linked to the task of correctness. But it must be noted that this legal requirement says nothing about the meaning of objectivity in itself. In line with the above explanation about the types of claims to objectivity, it means that in metaphysical

---

[116] Sen (2009), p. 201.

[117] Leiter (2001), p. 2.

[118] Leiter (2001), p. 2.

terms, the law is objective insofar as there are correct answers as a matter of law. On the other hand, the law is epistemically objective insofar as the mechanisms for discovering correct answers (for instance, the adjudicatory process and legal reasoning) are free of distorting factors that would obscure correct answers.

Thus, based on the foregoing exposition, the idea of objectivity can still be conceivable if it is understood in the epistemic sense. Nevertheless, it does appear to be impossible to divorce metaphysical objectivity from the claim that the law is epistemically objective.[119] As we have seen, seeking metaphysical objectivity has been faulted on the grounds that our decisions are inherently value-based. If we cannot achieve epistemic objectivity without having to seek metaphysical objectivity, then our idea of objectivity and the whole attempt to achieve inclusiveness through the capability framework would appear to be a recipe for unbounded judicial discretion, subjectivism, inconsistencies and arbitrariness.

In theory, it is possible to seek epistemic objectivity between the relevant functionings within the capability framework when engaged in the *choosing* task. Postema has developed an account of objectivity that makes sense for law and adjudication and desists from combining the two types of objectivity.[120] To him, the role of political and moral values in adjudication is compatible with the objectivity of law. We can view objectivity in generic terms such that we say that our act of choosing is objective when we are open in the appropriate way to the subject matter of the judgment. Specifically, we would be objective if our judgment is independent of the interests of antitrust subjects in the appropriate way. That is, the judgment on each functioning must be truth-evaluable, and that its truth-value should be an objective matter. Thus, if every functioning detailed through the specific ascertaining task is truth evaluable in that they are backed by substantial theoretical or empirical evidence, one would suppose that all that need to be done in the pursuit of objectivity is to ensure that the adjudicatory process and legal reasoning are free of distorting factors that can obscure correct answers. This simply reinforces the idea of pure procedural justice.

The above contrived analysis notwithstanding, the objectivity account is still severely flawed on account of the *choosing* exercise for two major reasons; it is impossible to attain metaphysical objectivity. Secondly, even though the attainment of epistemic objectivity is theoretically conceivable, this idea of objectivity falls short of telling us how decisions are to be made through the person-centred approach.

Metaphysical objectivity contemplates the setting of objective criteria for deciphering right from wrong. This has been shown to be conceptually and practically impossible. Epistemic objectivity is concerned about the objectivity of the process and not necessarily in the substance. If one is to rephrase this idea of objectivity, it means that one can for instance, subjectively rank different interests

[119] Leiter (2001), p. 3. He states that "we can get no purchase on the notion of a 'distorting factor' without reference to the 'things' we are trying to know".

[120] Postema (2001), p. 99.

as long as the process through which ultimate results will be reached remains objective. Even if one is to accept that it is possible to attain objectivity in this sense, we must keep in sight that objectivity is not an end in itself but rather a vessel to ensure broadness and inclusiveness. The decisional framework loses its claim to broadness and inclusiveness the moment that we are able to rank and compare interests on the basis of their inherent subjective qualities.

Conclusively therefore, the idea of correctness and objectivity has proved unhelpful in moving us beyond the capability framework as it does not tell us how to make concrete decisions while at the same time respecting the idea of *justice as inclusiveness*.

5.3.2.ii Social Choice Option

The task of choosing correctly between normative accounts on the basis of objectivity has been rightly shown to be rather unrealistic. We need therefore to look into an account that recognises this impossibility but still seeks to reach concrete result on the basis of impartiality, hence, the need to consider the social choice theory.

Social choice is an evaluative discipline which is deeply concerned with the rational basis of social judgment and public decisions in choosing between social alternatives.[121] The outcomes of this procedure "take the form of ranking different states of affairs from a 'social point of view', in the light of the assessment of people involved."[122] Though its present mode of analysis is largely mathematical, it has been said to be of very general application.[123] This theory is concerned with arriving at overall judgments for social choice based on diversity of perspectives and priorities.[124] With this theory, judgments are arrived at by desisting from ranking interest on the basis of cardinal comparison of welfare. Rather, it only allows for ordinal non-comparable preferential rankings.[125] Justice is sought by converting preferences over all positions in all alternatives into justice statement about the alternatives.[126] In effect, interpersonal comparisons are made on the basis of individuals in society. This does not mean that an actual opinion poll is conducted. Rather, correctness is attained through practical reason. The impartial observer (i.e. competition authorities or the Court) could engage in a thought experiment[127] through which they are expected to choose by applying certain standards to the diverse perspectives and priorities. Recognising the impossibility of choosing objectively between normative accounts because of their ordinal

[121] Sen (2009), p. 95.

[122] Sen (2009), p. 95.

[123] Craven (1992), p. 1.

[124] Sen (2009), p. 109.

[125] It is otherwise called ordinal non-comparable preferences.

[126] Craven (1992), p. 126.

[127] Harsanyi (1953), p. 455

nature, some social choice scholars claim that the theory takes us beyond the intrinsic value of individual norms by comparing outcomes on the basis of utility, equity and efficiency etc deriving from each.[128]

According to Sen, social choice is based on comparative justice as against the idea of transcendental justice which, he claims, keeps "us engrossed in an imagined and implausible world of unbeatable magnificence."[129] He thus considers comparative justice to be better because it is more practical. He also contends that since justice is sought on relational basis, social choice is better because it helps us to avoid making firm statements for future cases particularly where in the light of the social welfare standard, the outcomes reached when we applying the competing theories will be the same. In this light, Sen argues that through "dominance" and "intersection",[130] there can be an overlap between interpersonally different orderings of principles of justice, leading to an overlapping consensus with respect to the particular point under consideration. In such cases, there will be no need to determine the relative priorities to be attached to the relevant criteria. This in other words means that high level meta-objectives might be unnecessary especially where different accounts of justice all reach the same outcome in any particular case.

The potential for prudent decision-making makes the social choice theory truly appealing. One does not expect antitrust enforcers or courts "to express broad views on great issues of the day, at least if those views do not contribute to the particular outcome"[131] because to do otherwise would amount to building a rule-based affirmative metric for assessing competing normative accounts. Thus, there are two ways that the prudence inherent in social choice helps the process of antitrust pluralism. First, the celebrated incompleteness of social choice theory saves us from subsequent absurdities that may derive from an *a priori* specification of a "correct and objective" social welfare standard. Secondly, it could foster general coherence of the system as it affords the relevant authorities to balance the need to vindicate the plurality of interest and also avoid arbitrariness. They can achieve this by maintaining their quiet in such cases and desisting from making high level theoretical statements.[132]

The above notwithstanding, most competition cases are characterised by hard questions which ultimately limits the possibility of overlapping consensus which means we might have to determine the priorities to be attached to relevant principles before we can make adequate judgments. This, it has been argued, renders social choice impotent because it reflects rather than resolves collectively

[128] Fleurbaey and Hammond (2004).

[129] Sen (2009), p. 106.

[130] Sen (1992), p. 54.

[131] Sunstein (1996), vii.

[132] In addition to Sen's *Overlapping Consensus*, other accounts that seem to favour prudence are in forging prudence are Rawls notion of *Reflective Equilibrium* and Sunstein's *Incompletely Theorised Agreements In Particular Cases*.

incomplete ranking of principles.[133] In particular, Sen's attempt to solve the social choice problem by making comparative judgment rather than transcendental judgment is considered inadequate because it is incapable of giving determinate and unambiguous answer to the question of how to avoid, resolve, or transcend the different intuitive ranking people make.[134]

Further, even if it is possible to overlook the intuitive rankings because of overlapping consensus, an adjudicatory system is unlikely to benefit from such procedure as judicial decisions require concrete reasoning. It has thus been stated in this regard that "[a]rticulating reasons play a much more essential role in legitimizing a judicial decision ... A decision that is not supported by reason may be ignored, distinguished into oblivion, or labelled as 'bad law' and simply overruled."[135] This means thus that whether there is overlapping consensus or not, a choice has to be made between different alternatives.[136]

Hence, notwithstanding the seeming advantage of the social choice theory in terms of its comparative value and its potential for prudence, it remains problematic because when we are faced with the bottom-line task of making concrete decisions, it appears that the theory is bedevilled by three fundamental pitfalls. First, social choice, as a tool, fails to produce any result at all. Secondly, it fails to produce consistent and transitive result. Thirdly, the system of precedents, vulnerability of procedures, and the fact that the preference ranking could take the form of a mental exercise within a single adjudicator increase the chance that a decisional approach modelled on social choice will be susceptible to "agenda influence" or "path dependence".

To flesh up these problems, I will illustrate with an assumed fact. However, a brief summary of Arrow's impossibility theorem is first detailed.

Kenneth Arrow in his seminal work *Social Choice and Individual Values*,[137] sought to prove that no reasonably consistent and fair voting system can result in sensible results. He proved this assertion by establishing the impossibility of formulating a social preference ordering that satisfies all of the following conditions:

(i) Unanimity: If all people entitled to a say in the decision prefer one option to another, that option prevails.

---

[133] Boot (2012), p. 2, 18.

[134] Boot (2012), p. 19.

[135] Chapman (1994), pp. 42–43.

[136] Reason may not play such as essential role in politics and in market transactions. In this regard, Chapman states that, in politics for instance, "while the final vote may be preceded by much discussion and exchange of reasons, the authority of the vote is not affected by the quality of this discussion ... [I]n market transacting, so long as one has the property right in question, one need only justify, or defend with reasons, one's willingness or reluctance to trade. What makes a political vote or market transaction ultimately authoritative is simply the fact that those different acts of choosing have occurred, not the cogency of the reasoning involved."

[137] Arrow (1977).

(ii) Nondictatorship: No one person's views can control the outcome in every case.
(iii) Range: The system must allow every ranking of admissible choices, and there must be at least three admissible choices with no other institution to declare choices or rankings out of bounds at the start.
(iv) Independence of Irrelevant Alternatives: The choice between options A and B depends solely on the comparison of those two.
(v) Transitivity: If the collective decision selects A over B and B over C, it also must select A over C. This is the requirement of logical consistency.

Arrow states that no voting system can satisfy the five conditions simultaneously. He showed that ideally a broad-based framework that recognises the impossibility of ordinal ranking but still seeks to impartially decide between plural alternatives would have to abide by a voting system built on the five conditions. He however shows the impossibility of meeting all these conditions as one of the five conditions must go unsatisfied in every collective decision-making body. For instance, he contends that any process for making collective choices that satisfies conditions (i)–(iv) cannot also satisfy condition (v) on transitivity. Analysing Arrow's account, Easterbrook recognised that it appears counterintuitive to assert that circular preferences, path dependence, and other problems are not only endemic to collective decision-making systems, they are produced by the very things we find desirable in such systems.[138] Nevertheless, he considers it a sound theory even for judicial application.[139]

Specifically on the concerns raised, the claim that social choice is likely to result in indeterminacy is explained through an illustration. Assuming there are three interests (efficiency (E), economic freedom (F) and market integration (M)) to be considered within the capability set in a single case and parties agree that the criteria to be assessed are consumer welfare, freedom and the public policy. In this case, two will represent the majority. If E and F rank freedom over market integration and E and M rank consumer welfare over economic freedom and F and M rank market integration over consumer welfare, the majority rule does not help us in making concrete decisions as it does not tell us the value that should be ranked first. This is because a majority rank freedom over market integration meaning that we cannot give priority to market integration; a majority rank market integration over consumer welfare so that we cannot give priority to consumer welfare; and a majority rank consumer welfare over economic freedom meaning that we cannot possibly give priority to economic freedom. This results in a voting paradox which according to Allingham, makes social choice susceptible to yielding vacuous results.[140]

Regarding the transitivity problem, Arrow stated that any decision-making process that satisfies condition (i)–(iv) cannot satisfy the transitivity condition.

[138] Easterbrook (1982), pp. 802, 814.
[139] Easterbrook (1982), pp. 802, 814.
[140] Allingham (2002), p. 94.

Assessing this contention in light of judicial decision-making, Easterbrook stated that the first two conditions appear to be essential parts of any method of judicial decision-making. Condition (i) means that a judge does not delegate his authority to someone else. Also, where issues are raised before an appellate court, it is important that the court does not allow a particular judge to always decide the cases. The idea of non-dictatorship can also imply that the court should not always decide strictly on the basis of one normative claim as opposed to others. Concerning condition (iii), Easterbrook referred particularly to antitrust as an area where there is potential for at least three choices which may be ranked in multi-peaked fashion. For example, he stated that Justices have been divided about the utility of bright line test and about the objectives of antitrust laws as some believe that the per se doctrine should be employed frequently while others conclude that the Rule of Reason is preferable. This basic divide springs up at least four admissible approaches which are; per se rule for political values, per se rule for efficiency, rule of reason for political values, rule of reason for efficiency. The multi-peaked ways in which this condition can be reflected reinforces the contention that social choice approach is bound to result in inconsistencies.

The problem of inconsistency raises a serious concern for the person-centred approach particularly in terms of the potential for legal uncertainty and arbitrariness. These concerns cannot be overlooked as there is no doubt that as a precondition a good competition law regime must accord with the rule of law since anything to the contrary will be illogical.[141] Stressing the requisite qualities of a competition regime, the OECD stated in its 2005 Roundtable that a standard antitrust regime would: strive towards accuracy; ensure that its standard should be easy to apply; strive towards consistency and predictability; ensure that decisions are reached objectively; ensure that the scope of the standard should be wide enough; and that the standard and its objectives should be understandable.[142] In general, legal certainty is important to competition law as it is considered essential that businesses are able to assess and determine in advance the likely impact and consequence of their conducts.[143]

The problem of intransitivity could perhaps be linked to Bork's concern when he said that where we pursue plural ideals, "horns of plenty make anything resembling a rule of law impossible."[144] In effect, there will be legitimate concern that the potential uncertainty that might result from the comparative decision-making framework might gravely affect business such that it "increases the risk that firms may be breaking [the] law when they have been trying in good faith to abide by it."[145]

---

[141] Stucke (2009); Marsden and Waller (2009), p. 16.

[142] *See* Organisation for Economic Co-operation and Development, Policy Roundtables: Competition on the Merit 23 (2005). http://www.oecd.org/dataoecd/7/13/35911017.pdf.

[143] It should be noted however that a regime such as Europe would still trade-off some level of certainty because of the peculiarity of the field. The present initiative of moving away from the more certain rule-based approach and towards the more economic approach is a good example.

[144] Bork (1978), p. 427.

[145] Neven et al. (1998), pp. 18, 19.

The spiral effect of such uncertainty on business is aptly reflected by Stucke who identifies the potential for rent-seeking behaviours in such instance. He stated thus:

> [s]uppose a competitor abides by competition rules (and incurs cost to do so), while its rivals cheat (and seek a competitive advantage). Failure to uniformly enforce the rules will invite others to cheat. Without rules yielding predictable legal outcomes, firms may refrain from welfare-enhancing activity and opt for less efficient forms of doing business. Alternatively, competitors may engage in socially harmful activity but rely on lawyers and lobbyists to try to clear them of legal difficulties.[146]

Some scholars have however attempted to challenge the claim that social choice theory facilitates inconsistency and arbitrariness in judicial decision-making. For instance they have taken great pains to differentiate between consistency and coherence.[147] More specifically, they have argued that inconsistency is unavoidable in judicial decision making, and that the important criterion for the judicial system is coherence, not consistency. Hence, inconsistencies in individual cases add to the overall reasonableness of the system.[148]

Concerning the problem of path dependence, Chapman identifies the vulnerability of legal decision-making particularly in relation to the practice of precedence. He stated that:

> [D]ifferent legal precedents have, as a matter of contingent historical fact, set different agendas for rationalising like cases. Private law adjudication is quite self-consciously and unabashedly, therefore, subject to what social choice theorists have come to refer to as 'agenda influence' or 'path dependence', a feature they claim is suspect within any theory of goal-directed rational choice[149]

Easterbrook points out that social choice could still be susceptible to path dependence because of the law's inherent respect for precedent which is needed to meet the transitivity requirement. Precedents, he argues, has the tendency to reinforce the problem of circular preferences.[150] Also, social choice has been shown to be susceptible to strategic procedural manipulation. To this effect, Levine and Plott contend that the final social choice ordering of a group can be highly influenced by the agenda or groupings in which alternatives are considered for adoption or elimination.[151] They contend that ethical and practical issues arise from the fact that participants in a decision-making or fact-finding exercise may be manipulated simply by conditioning the process in order to achieve a set preferential ordering. They state that:

> [p]rocesses seem to be accepted as legitimate in part because they are thought to allow decisions to be based impartially on the subjective preferences of the participants towards the alternative presented. Although 'intrinsic' qualities of procedures can probably be

[146] Stucke (2009), p. 16.

[147] Chapman (1994); Easterbrook (1982), p. 803.

[148] Chapman (1994); Easterbrook (1982), p. 803.

[149] Chapman (1994), pp. 42–43.

[150] Easterbrook (1982), p. 824.

[151] Levine and Plott (1977), pp. 561, 564.

> appraised normatively without reference to subject matter, it is ordinarily a serious objection to a candidate process that it systematically and predictably can be made to select certain outcomes even though other outcomes are thought to command 'more' support[152]

Levin and Plott state further that for any given set of individual preferences, groups can reach a variety of outcomes by majority processes that reflect the views of the individual members with respect to the alternatives presented. They therefore assert that if there is no outcome that the group "wants" independently of the procedure used to reach the decision, all one can do is to choose an acceptable agenda that dictates the final result. However, they contend that the true subversion becomes empty if there is no single reflection of a group's preferences, only a set of possible outcomes that depend on the agenda. Based on their empirical analysis, they are of the opinion that procedural deftness may be not so different from a rhetorical gift and charisma.

Conclusively, the social choice theory, just like the pursuit of analytical objectivity, fails to provide an acceptable framework for making concrete decisions. This is regardless of any advantage that has been attributed to theory or the wide ranging attempts to disprove or justify some of the above-mentioned pitfalls.

5.4 Conclusion

In the preceding chapter, the thesis identified the need to move beyond the opportunity aspect of the person-centred approach to the decisional aspect. This transition is important if the person-centred approach is to have a decisional perspective to it. Considering that the construction of this approach was motivated by the need to avoid exclusion of interests, it is essential that the person-centred framework is capable of producing concrete decisions whilst it at the same time maintains the pure procedural framework. Two alternative decisional routes were considered—procedural objectivity and social choice. However, unfortunately, the finding is that there is no principled way of remaining value-neutral while we, at the same time, make concrete decisions. The only way concrete results can be reached without recourse of normative positions will be to completely disregard reason in decision-making. This is not in fact an option because failure to accord with reason will severely hamper antitrust as arbitrariness and uncertainty would reign.

Conclusively, this chapter reveals that as much as the person-centred approach gives a unique and helpful perspective to policy discourse, it is less potent as a decision-making tool. The impossibility of making concrete decisions at the choosing stage means therefore that the elaborate ascertaining exercise may have to either be dispensed with altogether or scaled down dramatically. Even where it is scaled down, one would not expect that the ascertaining task will be undertaken in individual cases. However, as it would be shown in the concluding chapter, the

[152] Levine and Plott (1977), p. 588.

person-centred approach holds a lot of promise for policy discourse on antitrust at both national and international levels. The approach also holds practical relevance at the enforcement stage.

References

Alexy R (1998) Law and correctness. Curr Leg Probl 51(205):206

Alexy R (2007) An answer to Joseph Raz. In: Pavlakos G (ed) Law, rights and discourse. The legal philosophy of Robert Alexy. Hart, Oxford, p 49

Allingham M (2002) Social choice theory: a very short introduction. Oxford University Press, Oxford, p 94

Andriychuk O (2010) Dialectical antitrust: an alternative insight into the methodology of the EC competition law analysis in a period of economic downturn. Eur Competition Law Rev 4:163

Arrow K (1977) Social choice and individual values, 2nd edn. Yale University Press, New Haven

Bańkowski Z (2001) Living lawfully: love in law and law in love. Kluwer, Dordrecht, pp 39–42

Baxter W (1982) Separation of powers, prosecutorial discretion, and the 'common law' nature of antitrust law. Tex Law Rev 60(661):693

Berlin I (1998) On value pluralism. New York review of books, vol 8, XLV

Bertea S (2005) The arguments from coherence: analysis and evaluation. Oxf J Leg Stud 25(3):370–391

Bertea S (2007) How non-positivism can accommodate legal certainty. In: Pavlakos G (ed) Law rights and discourse: themes from the legal philosophy of Robert Alexy. Hart, Oxford, p 69

Boot M (2012) The aim of a theory of justice. Ethical Theory Moral Pract 15(2):18

Bork R (1978) The antitrust paradox. Free Press, New York

Buttigieg E (2009) Competition law: safeguarding the consumer interest. Kluwer Law International, Alphen aan den Rijn

Chapman B (1994) The rational and the reasonable: social choice theory and adjudication. Univ Chicago Law Rev 61:42–43

Christie G (1995) The uneasy place of principle in tort law. In: Owen D (ed) Philosophical foundation of tort law. Clarendon, Oxford, p 115

Copenhagen Economics (2006) Practical methods to assess efficiency gains in the context of article 81(3) of the EC treaty final report by Copenhagen Economics published on 21 April 2006 2208 DG Enterprise and Industry, p. 56

Craven J (1992) Social choice: a framework for collective decision and individual judgements. Cambridge University Press, New York, p 1

Da Silva V (2011) Comparing the incommensurable: constitutional principle, balancing and rational decision. Oxf J Leg Stud 31:273–301

Derrida J (1990) Force of law: the mystical foundation of authority. Cardozo Law Rev 11:919

Dworkin R (1977) Taking right seriously. Duckworth, London

Dworkin R (1986) Law's empire. Harvard University Press, Cambridge

Easterbrook F (1982) Ways of criticizing the court. Harv Law Rev 95:802, 814

Ehlermann CD, Laudati L (eds) (1998) European Competition Law Annual 1997: the objectives of competition policy. Hart, Oxford, p 121

European Commission (2000) Commission notice: guidelines on vertical restraints. OJ C 291:1–44 (13.10.2000)

European Commission (2004) Commission notice: guidelines on the application of Article 81 (3) of the treaty. OJ C 101 (27/4/2004)

Finnis J (1987) On reason and authority in law's empire. Law Philos 6:357

Fleurbaey M, Hammond P (2004) Interpersonally comparable utility. In: Barberà S, Hammond P, Seidl C (eds) Handbook of utility theory, vol 2. Kluwer, Dordrecht
Fox E (1981) The modernization of antitrust: a new equilibrium. Cornell Law Rev 66:1140
Grisez G (1978) Against consequentialism. Am J Jurisprud 23(21):46–47
Hammer P (2000) Antitrust beyond competition: market failures, total welfare, and the challenge of intra-market second-best tradeoffs. Mich Law Rev 98:878
Harsanyi J (1953) Cardinal utility in welfare economics and in the theory of risk-taking. J Polit Econ 61:455
Hawk B (1998) Competition law implementation at present. In: Ehlermann CD, Laudati L (eds), European Competition Law Annual 1997: the objectives of competition policy. Hart, Oxford, p 353
Kolm S-C (1996) Modern theories of justice. MIT, Massachusetts
Leiter B (2001) Introduction. In: Leiter B (ed) Objectivity in law and morals. Cambridge University Press, Cambridge, p 2
Lerner A (1934) The concept of monopoly and the measurement of monopoly power. Rev Econ Stud 1(3):157
Levine M, Plott C (1977) Agenda influence and its implications. VA Law Rev 63(561):564
Liebeler W (1982) Intrabrand "Cartels" under GTE Sylvania. UCLA Law Rev 30:1
Marenco G (1999) La notion de restriction de concurrence dans le cadre de l'interdiction des entenes'. In: Mélanges en homage á Michel Waelbroeck. Bruylant, Brussels
Marsden P, Waller S (2009) Antitrust marathon: antitrust and the rule of law. Loyola Consum Law Rev 22:21
Monti G (2007) EC competition law. Cambridge University Press, Cambridge
Möschel W (1991) The goals of antitrust revisited. J Int Theor Econ 147:7
Nagel T (2001) Pluralism and coherence. In: Dworkin R, Lilla M, Silvers R (eds) The legacy of Isaiah Berlin. New York Review Books, New York, pp 110–111
Nazzini R (2006) Article 81 EC between time present and time past: a normative critique of 'restriction of competition' in EU law. Common Mark Law Rev 43:514–517
Neven D, Papandropoulous P, Seabright P (1998) Trawling for minnows. Centre for Economic Policy Research, London, pp. 18, 19.
Odudu O (2005) The boundaries of EC competition law. Oxford University Press, New York, p 97
Odudu O (2009) Editorial - competition: efficiency and other things. Competition Law Rev 6:4
Pitofsky R (1979) The political content of antitrust. Univ PA Law Rev 127:1051
Postema G (2001) Objectivity fit for law. In: Leiter B (ed) Objectivity in law and morals. Cambridge University Press, Cambridge
Raz J (1994) Ethics in the public domain. Clarendon, Oxford
Reindl A (2011) Resale price maintenance and Article 101: developing a more sensible analytical approach. Fordham Int Law J 33(4):1300
Rodger B (2000) Competition policy, liberalism and globalization: a European perspective. Columbia J Eur Law 6:303–304
Schuad (1998) Competition policy goals. In: Ehlermann CD, Laudati L (eds) European Competition Law Annual 1997: the objectives of competition policy. Hart, Oxford, p 121
Sen A (1992) Inequality reexamined. Harvard University Press, Cambridge
Sen A (2009) The idea of Justice Belknap. Harvard University Press, Cambridge
Stucke M (2009) Does the rule of reason violate the rule of law. UC Davis Law Rev 42:1375
Sunstein C (1996) Legal reasoning and political conflict. Oxford University Press, New York
Townley C (2009) Article 81 and public policy. Hart, Oxford
Townley C (2011a) The relevant market: an acceptable limit to competition analysis? Eur Competition Law Rev 10:490–499
Townley C (2011b) Inter-generational impacts in competition analysis: remembering those not yet born. Eur Competition Law Rev 11:580

Van den Bergh R (2002) The difficult reception of economic analysis in European competition law. In: Cicinotta A, Pardolesi R, Van den Bergh R (eds) Post-Chicago development in antitrust law. Edward Elgar, Cheltenham, p 35
Van den Bergh R, Camesasca P (2006) European competition law and economics: a comparative perspective, 2nd edn. Sweet & Maxwell, London, p 110
Williamson O (1977) Economics as an antitrust defence revisited. Univ PA Law Rev 125:708
Williamson O (1989) Allocative efficiency and the limits of antitrust. American Economic Review Papers, p 105

Chapter 6
Person-Centred Approach and Antitrust Enforcement

6.1 Introduction

The attempt to construct a procedural framework for the substantive assessment of antitrust has proved abortive. Much effort was put into creating a broad account so as to avoid the deconstruction trap. It has however been shown in chapter five that the constructed person-centred approach is difficult if not impossible to apply without taking a firm normative stance. It thus creates a sort of "catch-22" problem: despite our attempt to avoid deconstruction through the detailed exposition of the account of right, the capability approach and the ascertaining task, the only way to proceed would be to take a position one way or another on the prevailing antitrust theories whose deconstructability in the first place warranted the introduction of the person-centred approach. It is however not all gloom for the proposed approach as it appears that the person-centred reasoning could still be of value at the enforcement stage.

In terms of enforcement, the person-centred approach seeks to (in response to Coleman's third question) ascertain how antitrust right might be enforced. In answering this question, it should be noted that motivation for enforcing antitrust right could differ from jurisdiction to jurisdiction. Possible differences notwithstanding, antitrust enforcers are generally expected to assess: the nature of an antitrust violation; the effect of such violation; and the degree of enforcement required to curb such anti-competitive behaviour. In line with the person-centred approach, there is an additional element to the question of how antitrust right is to be enforced. Thus added to the three elements stated above, antitrust enforcement procedures must be broad, flexible and adaptable.

To illustrate the need for flexibility and adaptability, examples can be made of areas of antitrust which have evolved over time. For instance, while an antitrust authority might feel or might have felt strongly against vertical integration or retail price mechanism, it became clear over time that the authorities should not disregard credible evidence to the effect that such behaviour is not in the particular instance, anti-competitive. Another example can be made of predation. We have found that it

A. Al-Ameen, *Antitrust: The Person-centred Approach*,

DOI 10.1007/978-3-319-01724-2_6, © Springer International Publishing Switzerland 2014 should not be enough to disregard an allegation of predation merely because the price charged by the dominant firm for its product is above cost. Authorities must take seriously and must be willing to follow necessary procedural channels where complainants allege a concealed abuse.

To put the proposition in this chapter in much graphical form and to effectively explore its whole components, I will focus on cartel enforcement. Cartelisation has been chosen because of the consensus in this area by antitrust institutions. It is therefore thought that if this proposition is to be effectively digested by a wide range of readers, cartel enforcement would be the ideal vehicle. Further, much in line with the other chapters, I focus on the EU regime in order to aid the fluidity of the thesis as a whole. I however make reference to UK and US under private enforcement.

The remainder of this chapter is divided into six sections. In Sect. 6.2, I analyse briefly the nature of cartels and state why enforcement actions against them are imperative regardless of the perspective from which we address antitrust. In Sect. 6.3, I briefly state peculiar efforts that have been made by public enforcers as well as the attempt to encourage private actions. In Sect. 6.4, I establish a potential enforcement deficit which is often overlooked—driven by their set objectives (such as the urge to discourage cartelist behaviours), the policies, mechanisms, procedures and remedies applied by institutions and courts may be structured too narrowly such that they overly disregard some interests. I argue that, from the person-centred perspective, this may result in an enforcement deficit which has to be corrected. To illustrate this problem, I explain generally how public enforcement activities of the European Commission (particularly against cartelist behaviours) might blind enforcers from appreciating other equally important aspects of enforcement. I also illustrate with private action initiatives. In Sect. 6.5, I argue that institutions and courts should follow an *incremental enforcement* method in order to balance the urge of achieving institutional goals with the need to address the interests of antitrust subjects. To show how this can work, I illustrate through the use of private remedies in antitrust cases. In Sect. 6.6, I analyse a recent EU case that warranted incremental enforcement. I conclude in 6.7.

6.2 Ills of Cartels

The words of Adam Smith[1] in his book, *The Wealth of Nations*, come to mind when we consider cartel cases. He stated that where businesses converge, there is a tendency that competitors regard themselves as friends while the consumer is seen as the enemy. A cartel is essentially an agreement to limit output with the

[1] Adams Smith (1776) said: "People of the same trade seldom meet together, even for merriment and diversion, but the conversation ends in a conspiracy against the public, or in some contrivance to raise prices."

objective of increasing prices and profit. The negative effect of cartelisation is that it generates overcharge and deadweight social loss to consumers.

That cartels have the potential to harm consumers[2] is a fact that can be taken for granted. There are in fact enormous body of theoretical and empirical literatures that reflect this possibility. For example, it has been shown that the publication of firm specific transaction price leads to an average increase in prices by almost 20 %.[3] As a result of the *Vitamins cartel* for instance, studies revealed monumental losses caused by this clandestine behaviour: on a worldwide scale, the size of the affected market was $31 billion.[4] The total worldwide direct overcharge incurred by buyers was estimated at $7 billion. The deadweight loss would have been between one-fifth and one-tenth of the overcharge.[5] In the US alone, the cartel was estimated to have generated economic waste of over $1 billion.[6] To mention but a few, enforcement institutions such as the Office of Fair Trading (OFT) have also made practical efforts to substantiate the dangers caused by cartels. It estimated that if the cartel activities of Harbros/Argos/Littlewoods have not been brought to an end, consumers would have been overcharged by over £40 million.[7] Also, it stated that price fixing for Replica Football Kit would have cost consumers over £50 million in overcharge.[8] Even more alarming is the bid-rigging in the construction industry estimated at the value of £3 billion.[9]

The pecuniary impact of cartels to the society as a whole has been well documented. A case against cartel could thus be substantiated on the basis of this evidence alone. In order to avoid the ills of cartels, antitrust regimes have fashioned various enforcement tools. Some of which will be addressed below.

6.3 Enforcement Efforts

If the war against harmful cartels is to be won, it is imperative to deploy functional enforcement tools. For example, in order to control the reign of cartels, antitrust institutions such as the European Commission and national antitrust authorities have employed different mechanisms with the main objective of deterring such

---

[2] Baker (2003), p. 27.

[3] Monti (2000).

[4] This estimate was based on the reflection of 2005 currency. See Connor (2006). See further Connor (2001).

[5] This is based on a general finding in most manufacturing industries. This estimate was based on the reflection of 2005 currency. See Connor (2006). See further Connor (2001).

[6] See OECD (2000).

[7] See OFT press release 149/06, dated 19 October 2006.

[8] See OFT press release 149/06, dated 19 October 2006.

[9] See OFT press release 49/07, dated 22 March 2007. Over 122 firms were said to be involved in the bid-rigging.

behaviour. Instruments often used include one or a combination of fines, economic tools, leniency, settlement procedure, criminalisation, private participation, reward schemes and so on. These instruments are summarised below:

6.3.1 Detection

Sophisticated investigative techniques are required if harmful cartels are to be uncovered. One of such tools which authorities utilise is dawn raid. Another effective and arguably more productive alternative is through use of the leniency programme. In Europe for instance, it can be argued that leniency has to a large extent been a great success as the Commission is more likely to uncover cartels which would otherwise have remained undetected.[10] Another tool is through the use of settlement procedures which fast-track proceedings. A typical cartel investigation can last up to 5 years. This length is often further increased up to an average of 10 years because the alleged infringer often appeal the Commission's decision. This snag necessitated the settlement procedure.[11] This procedure reduces the administrative burden through the introduction of simplified administrative process. In event, antitrust authorities will be able to utilise their resources more efficiently by redirecting their manpower to uncovering new cartels and consequently raise the probability of detection.[12]

Cartels can also be detected through forensic economic analysis. With this approach, one could imagine that the economic analysis will at least serve as an initial indicator of violation and hence increase the probability of cartel detection.[13] For example, it has been recorded that the Netherlands Competition Authority used the structural approach,[14] to uncover collusion in the Dutch shrimp industry.[15]

---

[10] Guidance on the present leniency procedure can be found in the Commission Notice on Immunity from Fines and Reduction of Fines in Cartel cases (2006/C 298/11). This has a great deterrence effect. See Motta and Polo (2003), p. 347.

[11] See Commission Notice on the Conduct of Settlement Procedures in Cartel Cases (OJ 2008 C167/1). Neelie Kroes had, at an earlier point, made unequivocal declaration that she aims at swift enforcement and timely punishment through direct settlement. See "Delivering on the Crackdown: Recent developments in the European Commission's Campaign Against Cartels" Speech delivered at the 10th Annual Competition Conference at the European University Institute, Fiesole, 13 October 2006.

[12] Motta (2008).

[13] See Harrington (2007), p. 51; Grout and Sonderegger (2007), p. 83; Rey (2007), p. 69.

[14] Structural approach to cartel detection considers the characteristics of an industry that increases the probability that a cartel will arise or be sustainable. Cartelisation is likely where: there are fewer firms; demand is stable; the market is characterised by frequent interaction and price adjustment; firms encounter each other in different markets; and the products are homogenous. See Grout and Sonderegger (2007).

[15] See Harrington (2007).

Further, antitrust institutions encourage private participation in order to increase the probability of detection. This could be achieved by encouraging whistle-blowing and/or encouraging the institution of private actions. Regarding reward schemes, a peculiar activity of the UK OFT is notable—It publicised a reward of £100,000 to informants who help to uncover cartels.[16] It is believed that such a scheme will be successful as it serves as a potent weapon against concealment[17] as the initiative gives monitoring task to those closest to the relevant information.[18] Concerning private enforcement, there has been efforts in Europe to encourage private parties to institute actions against cartelists either on a standalone basis or through follow-on actions. Attempts are thus being made to sensitise private participants about the remedies available to them and also to unclog the private enforcement procedure.

6.3.2 *Penalising*

Fines are a major tool for deterring cartel behaviours. It is thus believed that the fines that are to be imposed on cartel violations should be high enough to truly deter. Europe for example, has stepped up its fining policies and practice. For instance, in 2007 the total fine imposed on 41 firms in eight final decisions was €3,334 million. This was an improvement to the seven final decisions in 2006 wherein an aggregate fine of €1,846 million was imposed on 41 firms.[19]

Also, there is an increased use of criminal sanctions in order to deter cartels. Thus, rather than limiting enforcement to companies,[20] the individuals primarily involved are also sanctioned.[21] Only a few would doubt that individual criminal responsibility could be effective. For instance, the force of a possible jail term was obvious in the *Lysine* case as conspirator were clearly worried about the possibility of criminal prosecution if they were caught.[22] Thus, the threat of imprisonment has

---

[16] See http://business.timesonline.co.uk/tol/business/industry_sectors/industrials/article3458691.ece. Last assessed 14-08-2012.

[17] See Kovacic (2007), p. 578.

[18] There is no doubting the fact that it is more efficient to have an employee make copies of relevant cartel-revealing documents in the course of his employment than having a "squadron" of public enforcers effect a dawn raid in order to obtain impossible information.

[19] European Commission Report on Competition Policy 2007. COM (2008) 368 final.

[20] See generally Coffee (1981), p. 408.

[21] It is noteworthy that there is no one way to delineate enforcement procedures that are criminal in nature and those that are administrative. For example, The Danish Competition Authority use criminal sanctions but are only imposed on firms, while the Germans mainly impose fines on individual through an administrative enforcement mechanism (note exceptions in bid rigging cases). See Wils (2007).

[22] Baker (2003).

been said to be the most potent deterrence tool.[23] Furthermore, the possibility of imprisonment passes a strong moral message about the ills of cartels.[24] Also, the newsworthiness of jail terms would discourage businessmen because of its socially and morally demeaning effect.[25] At present, the United Kingdom, Ireland, Estonia and some other member-states[26] do provide for criminal sanctions. In the case of *Marine Hose Cartel*, three businessmen were sentenced to jail and disqualified as directors in the United Kingdom.[27]

All these enforcement efforts are laudable especially where they help to avoid, stop, or limit the negative effects of cartelisation. It is however still important especially from a person-centred perspective that activities of antitrust enforcers do not act rigidly. It sounds banal to state that antitrust enforcers should be cautious by maintaining a broad outlook to antitrust. But in fact, such emphasis is helpful especially when one considers that antitrust enforcers could be drawn into their prime enforcement objectives which make it likelier that they disregard and injure other interests held by antitrust subjects.[28] Where we address antitrust from the person-centred point of view, we could very well abhor cartels because perhaps we believe they have negative effects on different shades of antitrust subjects. Nevertheless, it is still expected that we consider other competing interests when enforcing so that we do not create a fresh deficit to the interest(s) of some other antitrust subject(s) whilst attempting to solve one.

6.4 The Potential Harm to Persons' Interests

It has been stated that it is likely that our sole focus on institutional objectives can blind us to other important antitrust concerns. Here in particular, the assertion is that institutions might fail to consider interests of some other antitrust subjects. One could take a look at regimes that are firmly focused on deterrence and efficiency. In such systems, it is likely that by focusing on end result, enforcers might dampen the regime's internal critique. In Europe for example, it is commonplace that the European Commission is empowered to initiate investigation and assess the compliance of firms. This process could be initiated either directly by the Commission

[23] Liman (1977), pp. 630–31. It was also observed that international cartelists avoid the US like a plague. The reason for this is the risk aversion of businessmen when jail is involved. See Hammond (2004).

[24] Wils (2007).

[25] Werden and Simon (2003), p. 934.

[26] France, Cyprus and Slovak Republic do provide for criminal sanction. However the enforcement seems to be limited to their statute books.

[27] See United Kingdom Office of Fair Trading press release 72/08 of 11 June 2008.

[28] From the person-centred point of view, even an infringer is an antitrust subject whose interest needs to be accommodated.

or through complaints made by a third party.[29] Where there is a complaint, the Commission is duty bound to investigate it to the extent of ascertaining whether there is enough evidence or sufficient interest to warrant a full inquiry.[30] The likelihood that the interests of antitrust subjects would be disregarded starts here. It must be noted that the problem is not that the Commission is not bound to follow up with every complaints. That could in fact be a good thing—in fact, there could be good reasons why the Commission should not be made to take up more cases than it could manage. The Commission should very well be entitled to take into consideration what it regards as public interest and can thus, target its limited resources only to those cases revealing substantial interest for the Union. It can also be claimed that such procedure could eliminate frivolous claims. The likely problem however is that where we are too focused on institutional objectives, the cases we choose to investigate and those we decide to reject may depend heavily on how clear cut or easy the complaints are, rather than on the nature of interests affected. This is more likely considering the fact that the Commission is not only allowed to refuse to investigate where a case is not serious. In fact, it has a broader discretion—it can desist from proceeding with an investigation if it considers the claim not to be worth the effort[31] perhaps even if it is potentially serious. One would expect rather that even if the Commission cannot vindicate all interests, it should decide whether to proceed on a complaint on the basis of their urgency and the nature of detriment that might be suffered by the complainant.

Once the Commission decides to proceed with a case, a fresh concern arises for another type of antitrust subject. By choosing to follow on with a case, its goal drive could go into overdrive as it would be under constant pressure to justify its decision to proceed with the case.[32] The likely impact this could have on alleged infringers is worsened by the fact that the Commission is both the prosecutor and the judge.[33] In a nutshell, the temptation to disparage the interests of alleged infringers is rife where we are too focused on procedural and/or substantive goals. Indeed, the OECD aptly stated that "combining the function of investigation and decision" may "dampen internal critique".[34] This is in no way good for the

[29] Article 6 of Commission Decision of 23 May 2001 on the Terms of Reference of Hearing Officers in Certain Competition Proceedings (notified under document number C(2001) 1461 (2001/462/EC, ECSC) states that such interested third party should submit his application to be heard in writing, together with a written statement detailing his interest in the outcome of the procedure. To determine whether or not to grant the third party's application, the hearing officer is to consult with a director.

[30] See European Commission Dealing with the Commission: notifications, complaints, inspections and fact-finding powers under Articles 85 and 86 of the EEC, 54. See generally Wils (2011), pp. 1–32.

[31] See *Automec Srl v Commission (no. 2)* Case T-24/90 [1992] 5 *CMLR* 431.

[32] See Wils (2008), p. 161.

[33] Andreangeli et al. (2009) ("GCLC Report"). See also Andreangeli (2008). See also International Chamber of Commerce (2009). Hofstetter (2009).

[34] OECD (2005), p. 62.

enforcement regime as it has been noted by the European Court of Human Right that the difficulty that arises from such structure is that impact of possible bias on outcome of a case is extremely difficult to measure.[35]

The concern also exists in the context of private enforcement. In the wake of the Commission's effort to promote private antitrust actions, Lawrence[36] called for caution. Among other specific issues he addressed, Lawrence advised that there is need for balance between claimants and defendants. He stated that procedures incorporated in order to alter the risk-return analysis that a claimant undertakes in considering whether to bring proceedings should be carefully assessed in order to prevent problems for the defendant. In sum, he contended that:

> Changes positively to incentivise litigation would not only provide a potential advantage to claimants, but also simultaneously, a real disadvantage to defendants. This could well tip the balance between claimants and defendant too far in favour of the former, unless carefully managed.[37]

It however does not appear that the Commission took the advice seriously when it came up with the White paper on Damages. This is evident when one considers the proposition made by the Commission regarding the appropriate procedure to be followed where an indirect purchaser sues an infringer in a follow-on action.

The Commission observed that in order to prove that the damage claimed was caused by the initial competition law infringement, the claimant will have to, not only reconstruct the incidence, but also bring evidence to establish harm.[38] It recognised the difficulty this could bring to both claimants and defendants where they are respectively saddled with the burden of proof. The Commission reckoned that "[b]ringing sufficient evidence of whether and if so, to what extent, the overcharge that resulted from the initial infringement has been passed on along the distribution chain is equally difficult for both the defendant and for the claimant who is not a direct purchaser. That implies that whoever bears the burden of proof risks a negative effect."[39]

In line with its drive to stamp out cartels, the Commission chose to put the burden on the defendant. This conclusion is not by itself controversial as the Commission stated clearly its reasons.[40] However, the troubling part as far as we are concerned from the person-centred point of view is that, even though it was

---

[35] Judgment of the ECtHR of 14 November 2006, *Tsfayo v United Kingdom*, App. N 60860/00 para 33.

[36] Lawrence (2007), p. 461.

[37] Lawrence (2007), p. 461.

[38] Commission Staff Working Paper accompanying the White paper on Damages Actions for Breach of the EC Antitrust Rules COM (2008) 165 final.

[39] Commission Staff Working Paper accompanying the White paper on Damages Actions for Breach of the EC Antitrust Rules COM (2008) 165 final, para 226.

[40] Commission Staff Working Paper accompanying the White paper on Damages Actions for Breach of the EC Antitrust Rules COM (2008) 165 final, para. 227.

justified on the basis of acceptable risk-allocation calculus,[41] the Commission's willingness to trade-off the interest of the infringer still raises concerns for the position of the "Other".

The Commission stated thus:

> If the claimant would bear the full burden of showing the passing-on and its extent, he risks not being compensated for the harm he suffered. In such scenario, the defendant, who may (have) successfully use(d) the passing-on shield vis-à-vis another claimant upstream, does not compensate anyone for the harm caused by the infringement. This outcome would not only be contrary to the objective of effective and full compensation of the harm caused by a competition law infringement, but it can also be qualified as an unjust enrichment of the defendant. If, conversely, the burden of proof would lie with the defendant and he cannot prove the limits of the passing-on, he risks multiple liability in case both the direct purchaser and others claim damages for the same (part of the) overcharge. In such a scenario, claimants other than the direct purchaser may receive damages for a harm they did not suffer. Such payment amounts to an unjust enrichment on their side[42]

It stated further that:

> [B]ecause the scenario according to which the defendant is unjustly enriched is more likely than the one where he would face multiple liability, it considers it appropriate to ease the claimant's burden of proving the passing-on and its extent. Indeed, for the defendant to face multiple liability, three conditions are to be fulfilled. First, he is sued for compensation of the same (part of the) overcharge by both direct and other purchasers, while only one has suffered the harm due to that given overcharge; second, the defendant cannot successfully invoke the passing-on defence; and third, the court acting in a joint, parallel or subsequent action does not offset the damages already awarded/paid to another claimant. The likelihood that these three cumulative conditions are fulfilled, and that as a consequence a defendant faces multiple liability, is considered to be much lower than the likelihood that, in a scenario where the overcharge has been passed on to the claimant, the latter is nonetheless not compensated because he could not bring sufficient evidence of the passing-on and its extent.[43]

The Commission concluded that once the victim has demonstrated that there was an infringement and an overcharge, it is considered more equitable that the one who breached the law bears the risks flowing from the infringement, rather than his victim. One would expect from a person-centred point of view that the Commission exercises some caution by stating that the decision about who holds the burden of proof in such instances would be determined in the context of the specific cases.

Proponents of the person-centred approach will be wary of the negative effects that our enforcement activities might have on other interests held by antitrust subjects. It is however conceded that it would always be difficult to get the balance right. As such, we could work around our inevitable imperfections by adopting an attitude of incremental enforcement.

---

[41] It stated that once the victim has demonstrated that there was an infringement and an overcharge, it is considered more equitable that the one who breached the law bears the risks flowing from the infringement, rather than his victim.

[42] Para 226.

[43] Para 227.

The idea of incrementalism arose from the recognition that human problems are extraordinarily complex, while our analytical capabilities are quite limited.[44] The concept of incremental enforcement derives from the incremental decision-making in general. Lindblom, one of the pioneers, argued that adjustments among competing partisans will yield more sensible policies than are likely to be achieved by centralised decision makers who rely on political analysis.[45] In other words, rather than trying to overcome complex and human limitation by brute analytical strength, we should proceed strategically. A form of strategic analysis proposed by Lindblom is disjointed incrementalism which consists of: limitation of analysis to a few somewhat familiar policy alternatives; adjustment of objectives in light of the policies potentially available, rather than considering ends in the abstract; more preoccupation with ills to be remedied than goals to be sought; a sequence of trials, errors, and revised trials; exploration of only some, not all, of the important possible consequences of a considered alternative; fragmentation of analytical work to many partisan participants in the policy making.[46]

Though it developed as a political decision-making idea, there is no reason why incrementalism should not be applicable to an enforcement regime especially where such regime seeks to take account of varied interests. However, in relating with the components of incrementalism, we are to discount the inherent differences that exist between political bodies as against judicial/administrative bodies.

Incremental enforcement is a systematic attempt at enhancing the position of antitrust subjects. It means that antitrust enforcement should take place with stronger emphasis on correcting the detrimental effect of anti-competition on antitrust subjects. This approach serves as a middle course between, on the one hand, taking excessively bold steps at correcting a perceived deficit to persons and on the other hand, taking no steps at all—It saves us from inertia and leads us towards the constructive path of dynamism. It also seeks to avoid triggering unique detriments to antitrust subjects while solving a prevalent one. It simply requires that while working our way towards achieving a big goal (for instance, to deter cartels) we should take "small steps". We should endeavour to evaluate each step in the light of broadness. Potential errors are to be corrected so that at the end of the process, we would not only have achieved our big institutional goal, but also ensure that interests held by antitrust subjects at enforcement level have been duly addressed. It means thus that the incremental approach to enforcement is progressive as we continually fine-tune the procedure. In sum, the incremental attitude is constituted by a mixture of caution and dynamism especially where we are unclear how a proposed improvement in our enforcement will affect other related parties.

An enforcement body is attuned to incremental enforcement where, for instance, it is not so blinded by its objectives by ensuring that it protects defendants' procedural guarantees such as right to fair trial, right not to be tried twice and so

[44] See generally Simon (1955), pp. 99–118 and Lindblom (1959), pp. 79–88.

[45] Lindblom (1959).

[46] Lindblom (1988), p. 239.

on. It requires that authorities reach the outer limit of their expertise so that the more far-reaching an enforcement goal is, the more cautious the authorities should be in structuring their procedures on such goal.

The idea of incremental enforcement is to be deployed whenever an antitrust institution either decides on unprecedented issues, procedures or remedies. It is also to be applied where the institution seeks to improve on existing procedures, penalties and remedies. Let us take for instance that an antitrust institution seeks to improve its procedure such that the system eases the difficulty of establishing anti-competitive practices. If the institutions are to consider introducing procedures such as disclosure, it has to take cognisance of the complexities involved. It has to be aware of the numerous interests of even a single party which may be impacted upon. By acknowledging the complexities and its inherent limitation in identifying conclusively all shades of consequences that may result, the antitrust institution might be better off with an incremental approach. In the same light, if an antitrust regime considers that antitrust fines are too weak to deter or punish anti-competitive behaviours, it might consider it appropriate to increase the level of fines. It however has to be alive to the complexities here as well—human right issues, economic impact etc. In essence, it has to proceed incrementally.

Considering the novelty of the aspect in Europe and consequently the enormous likelihood that institutions would be faced with unprecedented issues coupled with the fact that there are bound to be scopes for improvement, a full analysis of the idea of incremental enforcement will be made through the example of private antitrust enforcement. To make the example more apt, I will narrow my analysis to remedies.

Typically, the party initiating a private claim for injury suffered aims to recover damages for loss suffered. It is however undoubted that as valuable as damages awards might be, they do not necessarily serve as ideal remedy in all cases. To put it differently, there are some cases where alternative remedies would have to be sought and granted if the injured party is to be protected or restored to its pre-violation state. However, while seeking the ideal remedy in instances where damages will be inadequate, it is imperative that antitrust institutions do not forget that they cannot exhaustively analyse how the improvement should be because of the complexities of the interests at stake and because of their limited capability to appreciate every possible consequences. The *Devenish Nutrition Ltd & Ors v Sanofi-Aventis SA (France) & ors*[47] case touches on this specific issue about the adequacy of damages and more importantly, it allows us to appreciate the role of incremental enforcement. Thus, I will use this case to exhaustively explain the nature of incremental enforcement and its role in antitrust.

The argument I proffer here is that the English Court of Appeal, in line with the person-centred requirement, were incremental in addressing the claim for restitutionary remedy as sought by the claimant as against compensatory damages.

---

[47] [2008] EWCA Civ 1086; [2008] WLR (D) 317. Hereinafter referred to as Devenish.

By so doing, it is argued that the Court was able to give meaning to the interests of the antitrust subjects. It achieved this by simply asking the right questions.

6.5 Incremental Enforcement: The Example of Restitution

With restitution as the point of reference in analysing how antitrust enforcers and courts could imbibe an attitude of incremental enforcement, I start by assessing the usage of restitutionary remedies in antitrust cases. Afterwards, I detail how it has been applied in the US. Then I assess how restitution could be applied in UK competition cases. This is an important part of the analysis because there are different ways we could apply restitution and the interpretation a court chooses speaks volumes on its attitude to incremental enforcement. The English Court of Appeal had to make a choice in *Devenish* case. I start with the fact of the case and I ultimately explain the incremental aspect of the case.

6.5.1 Devenish Case

In 2007, the UK OFT suggested that courts may grant restitutionary remedies in anti-competition actions.[48] Also, some scholars have interpreted section 47A of the Competition Act 1998 (now Section 18 of the Enterprise Act 2002) to mean that restitution is an available remedy in anti-competition suits.[49] However, neither of these opinions represented the position of the law. Just a month before the OFT's recommendation, a High Court judge decided otherwise in *Devenish*. It stated that restitution was not a valid remedy in competition disputes. Though Devenish's claim was also disallowed on appeal, the court did not go as far as saying that restitution in its generic context cannot be applied in antitrust cases.

In this case, Devenish sued the respondents who, as a result of their involvement in the notorious vitamins cartel, had been fined heavily by the European Commission.[50] During the lifetime of the cartel, Devenish purchased vitamins, or products containing vitamins, from the respondents. Its practice was to mix these vitamins with other ingredients to make animal feeds which were then sold to customers. In

[48] See Private Action in Competition Law: Effective Redress for Consumers and Business: OFT's Recommendation (November 2007). It should be noted however that OFT is of the opinion that restitution should only be available in certain circumstances. See Office of Fair Trading, "Response to the European Commission's White Paper, Damages Action for Breach of the EC Antitrust Rules" published in July 2008, OFT 1006, ch 4.

[49] Beards (2005).

[50] Prior to the reduction of fines for two of the firms, the total fine imposed in 2001 was €855.22 million. See *Vitamins Cartel, Commission Decision* of 21.11.2001 (2003) OJ L611; (2003) 4 *CMLR* 22.

this follow-on action, Devenish sought for restitution instead of damages because, in its opinion, damages would have been inadequate. Moreover, Devenish argued that proving damages would have resulted in unnecessary difficulties. English law provides that restitutionary claim of unjust enrichment could be awarded either to strip a defendant of his profit or simply to cause the reversal of a benefit conferred by a claimant. In this case, Devenish's claim was to strip the defendants of the profit made from their wrongdoing which will be a sum equal to the overcharge or the amount of the respondent's wrongful net profit. Consequently, the appeal was rejected.

6.5.2 The Grant of Restitutionary Remedies in European Competition Law Cases

Member states within the European Union have procedural autonomy which implies that they can decide on the remedies that could be sought in private actions[51] (including competition-related claims). However, whatever remedy they seek to apply would have to be in compliance with the principles of effectiveness and equivalence.[52] Hence, once the use of restitutionary remedies in competition law was challenged on the basis of these EU principles, it became imperative that the court in *Devenish* addresses whether Europe allows the usage of restitution in competition law cases. The court answered in the affirmative.

In reaching its decision, the English Court of Appeal started by referring to *Courage case* wherein the Court of Justice ruled that the method for effective enforcement of private actions is to be decided by national courts subject to the principles of equivalence and effectiveness.[53] In her lead judgment, Arden LJ had to decide specifically whether the Court of Justice's statement suggested that Member States were bound to apply gain-based remedies in competition law cases. Her decision was that *Courage* did not compel national courts to grant restitutionary remedies.

Also, the court had to determine whether EU law prevented a restitutionary award in competition law. The respondents argued that an award of restitution will run counter to Article 16 of the Modernisation Regulation since such an award is aimed at deterring anti-competitive behaviours.[54] Their argument was that since the

---

[51] See generally Craig and De Burca (2007).

[52] C-94-95/95 *Bonifaci and Berto v IPNS* (1997) ECR 1-3969; C-45/76 *Comet v Produkschap* (1976) ECR 2043; C-78/98 *Shirley Preston and ors v Wolverhampton NHS Healthcare Trust and ors* (2000) ECR 1-3201; C-343/96 *Dilexport* (1999) ECR 1-579; C-410/98 *Metallgesellschaft* (2001) ECR 1-1727; C-228/96 *Aprile* (1998) ECR 1-7141; C-62/00 *Marks and Spencer Plc v Commissioners of Customs and Excise* (2002) ECR 1-6325.

[53] See C-261/95 *Palmisani* (1997) ECR 1-4025 on the principles of equivalence and effectiveness.

[54] Art 16 of Regulation 1/2003 provides that "where national courts rule on agreement ... under Art 81 ... they cannot take decisions running counter to the decision adopted by the Commission."

Commission had penalised them with high fines, another award aimed at deterrence will offend the principle of *ne bis in idem*. Devenish argued to the contrary that the award will not be punitive. To justify its contention, it referred to the opinion of Advocate General Geelhoed in *Manfredi*[55] where it was stated that public and private enforcement should co-exist, and that compensation greater than the harm suffered could be envisaged where such special form of damages can be awarded under national law.

It was held that EU law does not compel a court to refuse to grant a restitutionary award simply because a regulatory provision is capable of resulting in a fine. The Court also held that restitution is not a pre-condition for the attainment of effectiveness. Elaborating on this decision, the Court said that the principle is directed at ensuring sufficient remedies rather than the fullest possible remedies. Referring to *Manfredi,* Arden LJ ruled that purely compensatory remedies are sufficient for the purpose of safeguarding the rights of private persons under the then Article 81 EC (now Article 101).

In conclusion, it could be inferred that it is up to Member States, subject to the doctrine of equivalence and effectiveness to allow for restitutionary remedies in competition law proceedings as the case may require.

6.5.3 The Application of Restitution

Prior to the *Devenish* case, one could not particularly say how restitutionary remedy was to be applied in competition cases within domestic regimes such as England and Wales. Because restitution is multifaceted, the answer will hardly be clear cut. If one however had to imagine how it might be applied, the closest point of reference is the United States.

In 2003, the US Federal Trade Commission (FTC) issued a policy statement on monetary equitable remedies in competition cases.[56] This statement, in a nutshell, meant that the FTC was going to seek restitutionary remedies in their antitrust cases. However, the policy explains that these remedies should not be seen as routine as they will be sought only in exceptional cases. In those cases, the FTC reckoned that restitutionary remedies can play a useful role in complementing more familiar remedies.

In order to invoke restitutionary remedies, the FTC applies three vital conditions which are that: the antitrust violation must be clear; there must be a reasonable basis for calculating the amount of the remedy based on gains or injury from the violation; and that the use of the remedy would add value because other remedies will either fail or be inadequate. However, the FTC had been seeking restitutionary

[55] Art 16 of Regulation 1/2003 provides that "where national courts rule on agreement … under Art 81 … they cannot take decisions running counter to the decision adopted by the Commission."
[56] FTC 68 Fed. Reg. 45,820 (4th of August 2003).

reliefs in a number of cases[57] even before it issued the policy statement. The most recent of these cases are *Mylan*,[58] *Hearst*[59] and *Perigo*.[60]

In *Mylan*, the FTC sued Mylan Lab who manufactured two generic anti-anxiety drugs. Mylan had entered into a 10 year exclusive dealing contract with most of the producers of the active ingredients for these drugs and, in exchange, it agreed to pay the producers a percentage of its gross profits. This agreement enabled Mylan to raise its prices to consumers for the two generic drugs by 1,900 % and 3,200 %. Though the case was settled out of court, it was on the understanding that Mylan would have to disgorge the unlawful profit. $100 million was disgorged and put into a fund to be distributed to injured consumers and state agencies. This amount, according to the complaint, represented nearly all the $120 million estimated as the unlawful profits. In addition, private plaintiffs settled for $39 million.

On how it should be applied, the FTC stated that it is "important and beneficial that there be a number of flexible tools, as well as potential enforcers, available to address competitive problems in a particular case."[61] This assertion makes it necessary to give particular consideration to the third condition that has to be fulfilled in order to be able to succeed with a restitutionary remedy. The condition is that the restitutionary award must add some value to the enforcement regime.

The FTC gave instances where gain-based remedies are likely to add value to its antitrust enforcement: it would be most valuable where statutes of limitation or market disincentives to damages actions are likely to make violators escape with their ill-gotten profit; also, it will be useful where a potential claimant will either be dissuaded or lose as a result of practical and legal difficulties that may preclude the award of compensation. Putting this point into perspective, the FTC gave the example of *Hearst*. This was a case of a consummated merger that had passed through the authority's review process. If damages reliefs were sought, the plaintiffs would have faced a rather unusual burden posed by two codified laws. Another example is when significant aggregate consumer injury results from relatively small injuries not justifying the cost of a private law suit. Here, a representative body (such as the FTC) can institute a gain-based remedial action against violators.

Addressing the relationship between gain-based remedies and penalties, the FTC is of the view that civil penalties are not to be offset against restitution since the purpose of both remedies are different. While restitution is aimed at removing an unjust profit from a violation, penalties "are intended to punish the violators and

---

[57] See the Art supply cases: *In the Matter of Binney & Smith Inc*, 96 FTC 625 (Oct 1980); *In the Matter of American Art Clay Co*, 96 FTC 809 (Nov 1980); *In the Matter of the Joseph Dixon Crucible Co*, C80-700 (Ohio 1983). See also *The Matter of Commonwealth Land Title Insurance Company*, 126 FTC, 680, 688 (November 1998).

[58] *FTC v Mylan Labs*., Inc., 62 F. Supp. 2d 25, 36–7 (D.D.C. 1999).

[59] *FTC v Hearst Trust*, Civ. No. 1: 01CV00734 (D.D.C. December 14, 2001).

[60] *FTC v Perrigo Co. and Alpharma Inc.*, Civ. No 1: 04CV1397 (RMC) (D.D.C. August 12, 2004).

[61] FTC (2003) 3.

reflect a different, additional calculation of the amount that will serve society's interest in optimal deterrence, retribution and perhaps other interests."[62]

The disgorgement of gains deriving from anticompetitive practices has gained judicial support in the recent case of *US v KeySpan Corporation*[63] where in the District Court Judge ruled that disgorgement was a proper remedy under the Sherman Act.

If we view the issue from an institutional perspective, the usage of restitutionary remedy in this way is laudable. In fact, a person-centred antitrust analyst will be pleased with a regime that seeks to purge violating antitrust subjects off their ill-gotten wealth. He might however disagree with how this is to be achieved especially if it comes as a strictly private suit. This is because for such analyst, the consequence of granting restitutionary claims is more than its effect to the claimant. It could have serious repercussions for the defendant and the institution as a whole. It is thus important to appreciate the modes through which restitution can be sought. From there, we are able to assess them in the light of the person-centred requirement of incremental enforcement. After this analysis we are then able to put the US position in context and then effectively relate with the *Devenish* case.

6.5.4 Devenish Case Detailed

6.5.4.i Summary of the Court of Appeal's Decision

The decision to reject Devenish's restitutionary claim was unanimous. However, the judges gave different reasons. Of importance for this thesis is the aspect of their decision wherein they respectively showed preference for damages over restitution and substantive unjust enrichment over disgorgement. The reasoning of Arden LJ, Longmore LJ and Tuckey LJ are thus stated briefly.

Reasoning through precedents, Arden LJ refused Devenish's claim because, from the case of *Stoke-on-Trent City Council v W & J Wass Ltd*,[64] an account of profit could not be awarded in a non-proprietary tort case.[65]

Of more relevance to this thesis though is the part of her judgement whereby she considered whether disgorgement could be applied assuming her interpretation of *Wass* was wrong. Premised on the understanding that restitution could only be granted in exceptional circumstances, her Ladyship began her analysis on the basis of the conditions set out by Nicholls LJ in *Blake*. The general condition was that a

[62] FTC (2003) 3.

[63] Civil Action No.: 1:10-civ-01415-WHP.

[64] (1988) 3 All E.R. 394.

[65] In her judgment, Arden LJ said that since *Blake* and *Hendrix* did not discuss non-proprietary torts at all, it cannot be said that *Blake* had overruled *Wass*.

court should ascertain whether a claimant has a legitimate interest in preventing the defendant's profit making activity and depriving him of that illegal profit.

Applying similar conditions, Arden LJ had to decide: whether there was deliberate breach of duty which is sufficiently abusive to meet the need for restitution; whether Devenish had a legitimate interest in bringing the case; whether the respondents made any gain at the expense of Devenish; and whether the remedy was a precondition for the attainment of justice in the case.

Arden LJ stated that the "conduct of the respondents was sufficiently abusive to meet any need, as part of the overall requirement for exceptional circumstances". She based this on the Commission's abhorrence of cartels and the very substantial nature of the fine imposed on the *vitamin cartel* in particular. Further, she decided that Devenish had a legitimate interest for instituting an action because the breach had a direct effect on it. However the court noted that the determination of "legitimate interest" is subject to the passing-on defence which was not in issue in *Devenish*. To support its ruling, the court referred to the discussion paper and recommendation from both the Commission[66] and the United Kingdom.[67] Arden LJ also reasoned that Devenish's claim was justified because there had been a transfer of value to which it sought recoupment. The court substantiated this reasoning by reference to the policy initiative encouraging private actions. For restitution to be a pre-condition for justice in this case, Arden LJ stated that damages had to be inadequate. It is not for the claimant to choose which remedy it prefers. In order to determine whether damages would be inadequate, the difficulty of proof had to be insuperable. After detailed analysis, the court came to the conclusion that the claimant was in fact responsible for the evidential difficulties it encountered, hence the restitutionary claim was bound to fail.

Applying the general condition, Arden LJ held that Devenish did not have a legitimate interest in depriving the defendant of its illegal profit because proof had not been insuperable: Devenish failed to prove its loss only because it failed to maintain effective records. Secondly, the justice of the case did not warrant restitutionary relief of account of profit because it was not enough that the claimant failed to prove his loss on conventional grounds. Also, justice does not demand that a claimant should be able to seek account of profit so as to side-step the difficulties of a possible passing-on defence.

In his judgment, Longmore LJ refused Devenish's claim of account of profit as there was no obvious reason why the respondents' illegal profit should be passed on to Devenish without it being obliged to transfer the disgorged profit down the line to those who had actually suffered the loss. In general, Longmore LJ took a different approach in his reasoning. His approach goes directly to the ordering of restitution

[66] EC Commission's Green Paper on Damages Action for Breach of EC Antitrust Rules (COM 2005, 672 final).

[67] "Private Action in Competition Law: Effective Redress for Consumers and Business" (Recommendations from the OFT, 26 November 2007). See also the Department for Constitutional Affair's consultation paper "The Law of Damages" (CP/9/07) (May 2007).

and equity. He highlighted two separate claims, the first being an account of profit on the ground that the respondents had profited from their wrong while the second account of profit claim was based on Devenish's inability to prove loss of sale. Regarding the first claim, he insisted that it was a mere account of profit case because it took the form of gains that the defendants had wrongly made, which was the surplus profit remaining after the claimant had passed on the artificially high price on re-sale. In other words, he considered disgorgement claims not to be claims pertaining to restitution at all.

Longmore LJ ruled that the difficulty of proof does not necessarily mean that no damages would be awarded. Further, he stated that if no or few damages reliefs are awarded, it does not mean that such damages are inadequate since loss of a possible sale is less serious than actual out-of-pocket loss. He asserted that while it may still remain useful to consider whether damages are adequate or not in areas such as interlocutory injunction, it would be treacherous to apply the same principle for account of profit claims. He was apt in his opinion about the nature of cartels and how they could influence the remedial awards. He stated that cartel cases do not fall under the condition of exceptional circumstances envisaged by Nicholls LJ in *Blake's* case. Also, Longmore LJ stated that the Wrotham Park cases do not serve as authority as the remedy is awarded by reference to the price that the defendant would have paid to obtain a claimant's consent. In particular, he stated that it was not possible to apply Wrotham Park because "it may be said that the defendant should be content with a proportion of the defendants' profit rather than all of it". He stated further that "it is not possible to see a principled way in which that could be done since there is no obvious way in which the claimant's loss can be related to the defendants' gain."

According to Tuckey LJ, Devenish sought to obtain the overcharge arising from the cartel activities as if that overcharge were the defendant's net profit. By doing so, Devenish tried to prevent the court from taking into account that it passed on the whole of the overcharge to its customers. Thus, in his decision, Tuckey LJ agreed with Arden LJ that *Wass* prevented restitution in non-proprietary torts and also agreed with both Arden LJ and Longmore LJ that there were no exceptional circumstances warranting such remedy.

6.5.4.ii Relevant Aspects of the Reasoning

There are two vital aspects in the decision that deserve to be exhaustively addressed in the light of incremental enforcement. First is whether the applicable remedy should be damages or restitution while the second question is whether restitutionary remedy should be granted on the basis of either substantive unjust enrichment or disgorgement. While Arden LJ and Tuckey LJ addressed only the first one, Longmore LJ addressed both questions.

Pertaining to the first question, the court's attitude would be considered incremental if it seeks to balance the interests of both claimant and defendant. Where a claimant suffers damages and the court grants compensatory reliefs, the claimant's interest is protected. The interest of the defendant is considered because the court would seek to ensure that the award is not excessive. A claim may however be made in specific cases where the award of damages would not serve the claimant's interest and as such, restitutionary remedy should be applied. The court in *Devenish* was faced with similar issue. In assessing whether it was possible in principle that restitution be applied instead of damages in competition law cases, Arden LJ answered in the affirmative. She however stated that the remedy would only be applied on fulfilment of certain conditions. By affirming this possibility, Arden LJ takes into account the interest of the defendant (as against excessive awards) but also that of the claimant as there could be instances where damages would not be enough. Though she justifiably refused the restitutionary remedy, of more importance here is that she took little steps before she came to the ultimate conclusion. All the way, she was weighing the interests of both parties in line with incremental enforcement.

Longmore LJ addressed the second question. He identified correctly that the task before the court was to determine whether it should grant restitution on the basis of either substantive unjust enrichment or disgorgement of profit.[68] In a manner which shows that he took into consideration the interest of the defendant, Longmore LJ refused Devenish's claim because there was no obvious reason why the defendants' profit should be passed on without Devenish being obliged to transfer the profit to those who had actually suffered the loss. The judge appreciated the need to deter cartels, but it did not blind itself to the institutional goal. In fact, he stated that though cartels are evil which we should seek to expunge, it is not in the place of the courts to provide remedies solely to deter. Disgorgement has a deterrence tone so it could be suspect—while the court should be determined to rid the defendant of his illegal gains, it should equally take time to solve the puzzle as to why the claimant had resorted to a disgorgement remedy. It may simply be that the "claimant has no other remedy because the claimant deserves none."[69]

There is no doubting the fact that Longmore LJ considered the interest of the defendants: surely the defendants will be interested in knowing why Devenish should benefit when it (the defendants) might still have to face claims from the final consumers who actually suffered the loss. Hence, it could be argued that he imbibed the attitude of incremental enforcement while deciding whether to grant restitutionary remedy in competition law on the basis of either substantive unjust enrichment or disgorgement.

[68] He saw substantive unjust enrichment claims as restitution while disgorgement sought as not restitution but mere account of profit.

[69] Hedley (2001), p. 106.

6.6 Incremental Enforcement: *Effective Leniency programme v Right*

The need to be incremental in enforcement could come up when for instance a regime is attempting to improve its enforcement. Earlier on, examples have been given on how Europe has steadily strengthened the effectiveness of its enforcement drive through the continuous refinement of existing enforcement tools and the introduction of new ones. The gradual pace over the years is clearly incremental and thus is in line with the proposition herein made. There is however another aspect to incremental enforcement which was explained above through the *Devenish case*. That aspect of incrementalism dealt with how a regime should proceed where an enforcement body is caught between its desires to achieve two conflicting enforcement objectives. A third aspect to incremental enforcement can be observed from the *Pfleiderer AG v Bundeskarllamt* case.[70] Here, it is to be argued that there is need to be incremental where institutions are caught between two plausible and settled but conflicting principles.

This part details the third aspect by analysing the *Pfleiderer case* which showcases the severity of the dilemma institutions could face where high level principles conflict and how such problems could be by-passed through incremental enforcement.

6.6.1 Pfleiderer Case

In 2008, the German Competition Authority (the Bundeskartellamt) imposed fines amounting in total to EUR 62 million on three European manufacturers of decor paper and on five individuals who were personally liable for agreements on prices and capacity closure. This decision has since become final. The cartel was uncovered through the use of the Leniency programme.

Subsequently, Pfleiderer submitted an application to the Bundeskartellamt seeking full access to the file relating to the imposition of fines in the decor paper sector, with a view to preparing civil actions for damages as it had purchased goods with a value in excess of EUR 60 million over the previous 3 years from the penalised cartel members. In response, the Bundeskartellamt sent three decisions imposing fines, from which identifying information had been removed, and a list of the evidence recorded as having been obtained during the search. Dissatisfied, Pfleiderer expressly requested access to all the material in the file, including the documents relating to the leniency applications which had been voluntarily submitted by the applicants for leniency and the evidence seized. The Bundeskartellamt partly rejected that application and restricted access to the file to a version from

[70] Case C-360/09; [2011] WLR (D) 196.

which certain information such as confidential business information, internal documents had been removed, and again refused access to the evidence which had been seized.

This refusal led Pfleiderer to initiate an action before the Amtsgericht (Local Court) Bonn challenging that decision of partial rejection. The Local Court delivered a decision by which it ordered the Bundeskartellamt to grant Pfleiderer access to the file, through its lawyer, in accordance with German laws. In the view of the Court, Pfleiderer was an "aggrieved party" within the meaning of application legal provisions given that it may be assumed that it paid excessive prices, as a result of the cartel, for the goods which it purchased from the cartel members. Further, the Court held that Pfleiderer had a "legitimate interest" in obtaining access to the documents, since those were to be used for the preparation of civil proceedings for damages. It therefore ordered access information relating to the notice on leniency and to the incriminating material and evidence collected. It however limited access to confidential business information and internal documents such as notes on legal discussions of the Bundeskartellamt and correspondence within the framework of the European Competition Network ("the ECN").

According to the Local Court, various interests had to be weighed in order to determine the extent of the right of access, which is restricted to documents required for the purpose of substantiating a claim for damages. However, following objections to that order, the Court, without intending to change its view on the law, reversed the state of the proceedings to that which existed before the contested order was made. Thus, in order prevent violating European laws and to avoid undermining the ECN Model Leniency Programme, the Court stayed proceedings and referred the case to the Court of Justice for Preliminary Ruling. The question formulated goes thus:

> Are the provisions of the Community competition Law – in particular Articles 11 and 12 of Regulation 1/2003 and the second paragraph of Article 10 EC, in conjunction with Article 3 (1)(g) EC – to be interpreted as meaning that parties adversely affected by a cartel may not, for the purpose of bringing civil-law claims, be given access to leniency applications or to information and documents voluntarily provided in that connection by applicants for leniency which the national competition authority of a Member State has received, pursuant to a national leniency programme, within the framework of proceedings for the imposition of fines which are (also) intended to enforce Article 81 EC

6.6.2 Court of Justice's Ruling

The Court of Justice started by affirming the role of the Competition authorities of Member states and their courts and tribunals in ensuring the effective application of Article 101 and 102 TFEU. More specifically on the right of access to documents, the Court stated that the provisions of the EC Treaty nor Regulation 1/2003 did not lay down common rules on leniency and access to documents relating to leniency procedure. It also emphasised the non-binding nature of the Model Leniency

Programme as well as notices on cooperation within the ECN. More importantly, it asserted that "it is, in the absence of binding regulation under EU law on the subject, for the Member States to establish and apply national rules on the right to access, by person adversely affected by the cartel, to documents relating to the leniency procedure".[71]

Hence, though noting that the effectiveness of the cooperation and leniency programmes could be jeopardised if documents relating to leniency procedures were disclosed to persons wishing to bring an action for damages, it nevertheless concluded that EU law does not preclude any person who has been adversely affected by an infringement of EU competition law and is seeking to obtain damages from being granted access to documents relating to a leniency procedure involving the perpetrators of that infringement. The Court however added that it is for national courts and tribunals to determine on the basis of their national law, the conditions under which such access must be permitted or refused by weighing the interests protected by EU law.

6.6.3 Implication of the Decision and Potential for Incremental Enforcement

Due to the fact that it was a preliminary ruling and that the Court of Justice was not obliged to state issues of procedure, it appears as though the Court succeeded in dodging the main issue and effectively deflected the problem to Member States. If however one addresses the Court's reasoning from the person-centred point of view, especially when one considers the strength behind each of the incommensurable principles underlying the conflicting claims, one would note a potential for incremental enforcement especially in very hard cases of this nature.

The Court of Justice recognised the value of both ideals. In the spirit of incremental enforcement, it leaves open the room for Member States to seek to respect the right of antitrust victims as well as maintain the effectiveness of the leniency programme. The careful step to enforcement taken by the Court should even be more appreciated when one consider that the Advocate General had given a categorical opinion which would have effectively institutionalised the quest for effective leniency programme and would have thus relegated individual rights in antitrust cases.

Advocate General Mazak had identified the tension between the need to keep public enforcement effective and the right of individuals in private enforcement. He however argued that the tension is more apparent than real. He contended that in addition to being effective in meeting public interest, leniency programmes are also beneficial to private parties injured by cartels. He supported this position with two arguments. First, he stated that in the absence of effective leniency programmes,

[71] Para 23.

many cartels may never come to light and their negative effect on competition in general and on particular private parties could therefore persist unchecked. Second, he contended that final decisions reached by competition authorities could at least be treated as corroborative evidence and hence softens the evidential burden on private parties.[72]

In this case, both the claim to vindicate individual right as well as the need to maintain the attractiveness of the leniency programme are perfectly justifiable reasons to support the claim for improving or maintaining the level of antitrust enforcement. Though the path it chose is rather uneasy and perhaps might have some other practical consequences,[73] the Court of Justice rose above finding reasons for picking one of the enforcement ideals and rightly recognised the need to be incremental by allowing for the balancing of these interests in individual cases.

6.7 Conclusion

It has been argued so far that antitrust institutions and courts should imbibe the attitude of incremental enforcement in order for them to be able to take account of plural interests. It has been shown that there is a high tendency that institutions will fail the requirement of plurality and broadness if they are strictly focused on institutional enforcement goals. Thus incremental enforcement requires us to take little steps which should be continually reviewed in the light of the person-centred requirement of broadness.

Illustrations of how we could achieve broadness have been given. It was stated for instance that in order to balance the interest of different antitrust subjects who all make different allegations against different alleged violators, the antitrust enforcer should choose objectively between these interests. It is also argued that in between victims of cartel infringement and (alleged) infringers, public enforcers should balance the interest of both parties. Thus, institutions should not only be motivated by the urge to detect and punish violators. Rather, they should, for instance, be equally interested in respecting the procedural guarantees of the (alleged) infringer.

In greater detail, I illustrated with private remedies. The main point discernible here is that in the context of a claim against an infringer, we should seek to achieve deterrence. However we should equally be cautious of the interest of the (alleged) infringer. On the flip side, while there is great need for caution in order to protect

[72] See para 41 of Opinion of Advocate General Mazak on Case C-360/09 *Pfleiderer AG v Bundeskartellamt* delivered on 16.12.2010.

[73] For instance, it is possible that the decision might lead to the emergence of different standards for the disclosure of different leniency documents from various Member States. This could lead to a breakdown of co-operation and information exchange between Member States.

the interest of defendants, we should also be wary of simply switching from the "mantra" of deterrence to the "mantra" of excessive caution. This will amount to mere reversal with the likely effect that we might trivialise or inadequately address the interests of claimants.

The value of incremental enforcement could however be compromised if it is shown to diminish the effectiveness of antitrust enforcement. Regarding cartel enforcement, enforcers seek to utilise relevant tools in order to deter anti-competition. Fines, for instance, are often aimed at deterring future violations. If enforcers and courts have only in their mind, the need to compensate the society for deadweight loss and ultimately to discourage anti-competitive practices, they might be disposed to setting the fine to such an amount that it would have the requisite deterrence effect. Such fine would be effective where it creates a credible threat of penalty which weighs sufficiently in the balance of expected costs and benefits in order to deter calculating firms from committing antitrust violations. In the words of Calvino, such fines would be optimal "if and only if, from the perspective of the company contemplating whether or not to commit a violation the expected fine exceeds the expected gain from the violation".[74]

On the other hand, where we adopt an attitude of incremental enforcement, we would, for instance, have to put into account the interest of the infringer by seeking a balance between a relatively high fine and the need to ensure that the punishment is proportional.

The way we value fines would thus depend on our enforcement attitude. Where we have a strict deterrence attitude, the value of the expected fine will depend on the effect it has on violators while for a regime with the attitude of incremental enforcement, the value of its fines is not limited to the deterrence effect but also the "fairness" of the fine. It could be plausibly argued that while the latter might be more effective in ensuring an acceptable state of competition, the effectiveness of the latter could be relatively weakened as a result of the compromise involved. We must however be cautious not to overstate this possibility. Aside the fact that interest of one antitrust subject is as important as those held by others who desire an effective enforcement regime, one must not lose sight of the fact that we need to take a holistic view of the enforcement regime in order to assess its effectiveness rather than addressing enforcement tools in isolation. Thus, by combining different enforcement tools, antitrust enforcers might be able to achieve the requisite effectiveness while at the same time give considerable attention to the interests of other antitrust subjects. Hence, even with relatively reduced fines, the fact that there are other tools such as leniency and criminalisation means that the effectiveness of the antitrust regime will not be necessarily weakened.

In sum, we stand a greater chance of achieving broadness as inclusiveness as required by the person-centred approach where antitrust institutions imbibe an attitude of incremental enforcement. Antitrust enforcers and courts are more likely to be incremental in their enforcement where they are alive to the interests of all

[74] Calvino (2007), p. 320.

parties and continuously strive to balance those interests rather than concentrating on one at the expense of another.

References

Andreangeli A (2008) EU competition enforcement and human rights. Edward Elgar, Cheltenham
Andreangeli A et al (2009) Enforcement by the commission – the decisional and enforcement structure in antitrust cases and the commission's fining system. Report presented at the fifth annual conference of the Global Competition Law Centre, 11–12 June 2009
Baker J (2003) The case for antitrust enforcement. J Econ Perspect 17:27
Beards D (2005) Damages in competition law litigation in the United Kingdom. In: Ward T, Smith K (eds) Competition litigation in the UK. Sweet and Maxwell, London (Chapter 7)
Calvino N (2007) Deterrent effect and proportionality of fines. In: Ehlermann CD, Atanasiu I (eds) European competition law annual (2006): Enforcement of prohibition of Cartels. Hart, Oxford, p 320
Coffee J (1981) No soul to damn: no body to kick: an unscandalised inquiry into the problem of corporate punishment. Mich Law Rev 79:408
Connor J (2006) The global vitamins conspiracy: sanction and deterrence. American Antitrust Institute Working Paper No. 06-02, 22 February 2006
Connor J (2001) Global price fixing: our customers are the enemy. Kluwer, London
Craig P, De Burca G (2007) EU law: text, cases and materials, 4th edn. Oxford University Press, Oxford
Grout P, Sonderegger S (2007) Structural approaches to Cartel detection. In: Ehlermann CD, Atanasiu I (eds) European competition law annual 2006: enforcement of prohibition of Cartels. Hart, Oxford, p 83
Hammond S (2004) Cornerstone of the effective leniency program. ICN Workshop on Leniency Programs, Sydney
Harrington J (2007) Behavioural screening and the detection of Cartels. In: Ehlermann CD, Atanasiu I (eds) European competition law annual 2006: enforcement of prohibition of Cartels. Hart, Oxford, p 51
Hedley S (2001) Restitution: its division and ordering. Sweet and Maxwell, London, p 106
Hofstetter K (2009) EU Cartel fining law and policies in urgent need of reform. Antitrust Chron 2
International Chamber of Commerce (2009) The fining policy of the European Commission in competition cases. ICC Document No. 225/659, 2 July 2009
Kovacic W (2007) Bounties as inducement to identify Cartels. In: Ehlermann CD, Atanasius I (eds) European competition law annual 2006: enforcement of prohibition of Cartels. Hart, Oxford, p 578
Lawrence J (2007) Seeking the perfect balance: some reflections on the Commission Green Paper on Damages Actions for Breach of the EC Antitrust Rules. In: Ehlermann CD, Atanasiu I (eds) European competition law annual 2006: enforcement of prohibition of Cartels. Hart, Oxford, p 461
Liman A (1977) The paper label sentences: critique. Yale Law J 86:630–631
Lindblom C (1959) The science of 'muddling through'. Public Adm Rev 19:79–88
Lindblom C (1988) Democracy and market system. Norwegian University Press, Oslo, p 239
Monti M (2000) Fighting Cartels- why and how? Why should we be concerned with Cartels and collusive behaviours? Speech 00/295 (11/09/2000)
Motta M (2008) On Cartel deterrence and fines in the European Union. Eur Competition Law Rev 29:211
Motta M, Polo M (2003) Leniency programs and Cartel prosecution. Int J Ind Organ 21:347
OECD (2000) Hard core Cartels. In: Meeting of the OECD Council at Ministerial Level

OECD (2005) European commission – peer review of competition law and policy, competition law & policy in the European Union, p 62
Rey P (2007) On the use of economic analysis in Cartel detection. In: Ehlermann CD, Atanasiu I (eds) European competition law annual 2006: enforcement of prohibition of Cartels. Hart, Oxford, p 69
Simon H (1955) A behavioral model of rational choice. Q J Econ 69:99–118
Werden G, Simon M (2003) Why price fixers should go to prison. Antitrust Bull 32:934
Wils W (2007) Is criminalization of EU competition law the answer? In: Ehlermann CD, Atanasiu I (eds) European competition law annual 2006: enforcement of prohibition of Cartels. Hart, Oxford
Wils W (2008) Efficiency and justice in European antitrust enforcement. Hart, Oxford
Wils W (2011) Discretion and prioritisation in public antitrust enforcement: in particular EU antitrust enforcement. World Competition 34:1–32

Chapter 7
Conclusion

Addressing antitrust from the deconstructionist position, this thesis identified that the traditional modes of antitrust analyses are incomplete. This incompleteness, it has been shown, has the tendency of unjustly denying some interested parties from being considered in antitrust deliberations. Concerned about the tendency of injustice resulting from the traditional approaches, I sought to fashion an account of antitrust which is particularly modelled on the idea of *justice as inclusiveness*. The thesis justifies the pursuit of inclusiveness by alluding to the intrinsic urge of an average person to be included in decisions that affect them. The idea of inclusiveness is also justified from an extrinsic perspective as it legitimises the decision-making process.

Conscious of the need to avoid the problems of incompleteness identified with the traditional approaches, this thesis sought a purely procedural approach. Hence, it was shown that the pursuit of pure procedural justice is the means through which we can achieve *justice as inclusiveness*. It was also considered important that the alternative approach puts the "person" at the centre of antitrust analysis.

In order to proceed accordingly with the exercise, two options were considered—Habermas' discourse ethics and the person-centred approach. After a thorough analysis, it was shown that the discourse ethics does not effectively solve the problem identified in the thesis. Focus was thus placed on the person-centred approach.

The person-centred approach has been shown to be closely linked with broad-based procedural accounts such as Coleman's account of right and Sen's capability approach. The approach emphasises the bottom-up perspective to antitrust analysis. A large part of the thesis was devoted to developing this approach by clarifying its content and scope and by differentiating it from other accounts. Ultimately, just as Habermas' account was evaluated in light of the theme of the thesis, the person-centred approach was also assessed and unfortunately, was also found to fall short of the "utopian" height of justice as inclusiveness.

Based on this revelation, it is conceded that even though the overall idea of inclusiveness in antitrust is laudable, there are some aspects (particularly the substantive aspects) where inclusiveness remains a "yearning" which cannot be

A. Al-Ameen, *Antitrust: The Person-centred Approach*,

DOI 10.1007/978-3-319-01724-2_7,

attained in practice. The impossibility of maintaining the interests of all parties till the very end and at the same time making concrete decisions between competing normative accounts is fatal to the exercise as its very operational core is easily deconstructible. The exercise appears to be an all or nothing affair as, for instance, one cannot be partly objective. It means thus that the problem is not merely about the "yearnings" that are insatiable but rather about unrealistic "yearnings".

We are thus left with a rather damning revelation which is that any account of antitrust will be ultimately deconstructible. In effect, if antitrust is to make any practical sense, relevant institutions must identify the normative standard upon which such regime stands. However, this thesis does not go as far as suggesting the goals and objectives that are "ideal". Indeed, any argument that a goal is better than another is a mere contestable assertion and should, as such, not be treated as an analytical truth.

Even though we cannot possibly pursue *justice as inclusiveness* in our decisional exercise, there are aspects of this thesis which I believe will aid in the holistic understanding of antitrust policy and also enrich antitrust regimes. First, an understanding that all traditional approaches could potentially be too narrow helps to reinforce the argument that antitrust provisions should be implemented in a broader fashion. Secondly, the thesis demystifies the idea of "right" and "wrong" in antitrust by stressing that any such claim as to the rightness or wrongness of a theory is merely a contestable normative assertion. Thirdly, this thesis will help antitrust pedagogy by opening students to various perspectives and thus disabusing stereotyped ideas of antitrust. Fourth, it will help practitioners think outside the box when assessing facts and also help them to anticipate counter-arguments. Fifth, it is believed that this thesis will facilitate independent thinking and consequently regime-specific approaches. This is very important for transition economies and countries yet to firmly establish their path in competition policy. Further, the person-centred approach is valuable as it provides a personalised perspective to antitrust. The approach in itself could help policy makers to think not just as policy engineers but also as antitrust subjects. Perhaps, with the revelations from the person-centred approach, antitrust subjects could be considered not merely as means to an end.

For the purpose of emphasis, I will focus on two aspects that reflect the value of the person-centred approach. First, I explain the assertion that there is no universally right way of understanding and addressing antitrust by illustrating through the question of international competition law. Secondly, I expatiate on the way the approach helps to avoid treating persons as means to an end through an illustration of antitrust enforcement.

7.1 International Antitrust Law

As revealed in this thesis, the person-centred approach allows us to assess "welfare" at an atomistic level. It is thus argued that regardless of the shortcomings of the approach, antitrust scholars and institutions could potentially find plausible conceptual basis for assessing the extent to which their national law should be influenced by outside forces. Since the turn of the century, the spate of globalisation has increased the clamour for some form of harmonisation of antitrust systems. It has thus been contended at some quarters that globalisation has rendered the position of difference rather unhealthy.[1]

To justify the need to internationalise antitrust rules, references have been made to transnational cartels and international mergers. The argument is that such transactions and activities, if not addressed in a harmonised fashion, might undermine antitrust enforcement in general.[2] Proponents often flag up the problems associated with the divergent practices in the treatment of anti-competitive behaviour especially where such behaviour is capable of preventing foreign firms from penetrating domestic markets.[3] They have considered internationalisation to be the best solution as other alternatives such as the extraterritorial application of one country's law to another could be counterproductive.[4] Different variations of the internationalisation agenda have emerged. While some seek to merge plurality with the internationalisation agenda,[5] others advocate a uniform law.

Broadly speaking, the person-centred approach does not kick against the internationalisation agenda. In fact, it recognises the legitimate concerns that may arise from the divergence of practices. However, by addressing antitrust issues from the perspective of persons, perhaps, proponents of internationalisation may avoid the temptation of developing an inflexible international antitrust code and instead explore the possibility of respecting the diverse national perspectives whilst they proceed with the internationalisation project.

The role of the person-centred approach in building a broader conceptual base for antitrust can be brought to light by analysing Taylor's internationalisation proposal. Proposing a largely inflexible international antitrust code, Taylor justifies his call for countries to look beyond their national interest in formulating their antitrust policies and laws on the grounds that such nation-centric practice increases the potential for under- and over-regulation which could consequently impact on collective global welfare. He contends that this would occur either where the coverage of domestic competition law is incomplete so that anti-competitive

[1] See Dabbah (2003), pp. 12–14.

[2] See Dabbah (2003), pp. 12–14.

[3] See Dabbah (2003), pp. 12–14.; Taylor (2007).

[4] E.g. Boeing/McDonnell Douglas merger 1997; MCI/Honeywell merger 1999; GE/Honeywell merger 2001; Dabbah, ch 7.

[5] E.g. Boeing/McDonnell Douglas merger 1997; MCI/Honeywell merger 1999; GE/Honeywell merger 2001; Dabbah, ch 7.

conduct is not regulated at all or where the relevant anti-competitive conduct is regulated by national competition laws but the level of regulation is below the globally optimal level.[6] He also argued that absence of harmonised competition code may lead to over-regulation which might impact negatively on collective global welfare. Citing the example of cross-border mergers, Taylor contends that a country, acting in its national self-interest may prevent conducts that would have adversely affected its national markets, regardless of whether or not the same conduct would significantly benefit other nations. He feels collective global welfare would be unduly diminished when the benefit to one country is outweighed by the loss to other nations vice versa.[7]

Where the person-centred reasoning is applied, the danger inherent in Taylor's conception of "welfare" becomes apparent. The person-centred approach reveals the potential for disconnection between policy makers and antitrust subjects where welfare is assessed on a global scale. From a person-centred point of view, one might therefore be more likely to appreciate the need to protect interests at the atomistic stage by, for example, fashioning a person-specific understanding of common competition terms such as economic freedom, free competition, and efficiency.[8] Where, for instance, we think of efficiency, the person-centred approach will emphasise the need for countries to adopt a definition that suits the need of their people. For example, it could be disastrous for a least-developed country to follow a Schumpeterian definition of competition. To this effect, Bhaduri states that where low income market economies adhere to the idea of dynamic efficiency, there is a tendency that:

> [t]the poorest section of the population becomes economically marginalised mostly through their lack of access to productive assets, education and acquisition of skill through employment in a market economy. The Schumpeterian process of destruction operates by denying them access to reasonable livelihood, training and skills through the usual mechanism of price rationing in the market economy.

In the same light, arguments that have been made in favour of plurality include that of Ratnakar and Knight-John who identified the need for developing countries to formulate for themselves unique competition law and policy that will align with their developmental needs. Otherwise, they contend, the law will fail to serve national development objectives and improve on respective consumers' welfare.[9]

Short of endorsing any particular definition of terms for any kind of economy, the illustration here simply reinforces the need for a bottom-up, person-centred approach to antitrust. For instance, a regime with a large informal economy should be able to explore broad range of possibilities within the limit of economic competition that it might find most suitable in addressing the interest of its people.

---

[6] Taylor (2007), p. 45.

[7] Taylor (2007), p. 46.

[8] See e.g. Bakhoum (2012), pp. 408–440.

[9] Knight-John and Adhikari (2004), pp. 1–25.

The person-centred approach could be applied in formulating a conceptual basis for the internationalisation agenda. It can also be used as the basis for engaging in a thorough comparative and empirical analysis of the present internationalisation schemes such as those undertaken by United National Centre for Trade and Development (UNCTAD), OECD, World Bank, the International Competition Network (ICN), Commonwealth Organisation etc. Such analysis will invariably extend to the model laws that have been proposed by these organisations.

The person-centred approach also helps us to better appreciate the need for flexibility in a dynamic world. With this in mind, technocrats and policy maker can move beyond populist and political pandering by identifying the true value of competition policy in light of their level of socio-economic development. In Japan for instance, between 1950 and 1973 when the country was undergoing industrialisation, the government prioritised the generation of high rates of profit and reinvestment for industry. To achieve this aim, some "anti-competitive" practices such as cartels, coordination of investment by rival firms, and state intervention in firm exit and entry had to be encouraged. At this point, the aim is not to decide the propriety or otherwise of any such competition regime. It is merely to show how, within a single jurisdiction, the idea of welfare could change over time. More importantly, the person-centred approach can serve as the conceptual basis for the evaluation of an antitrust regime's policies in specific periods.

7.2 Person-Centred Enforcement

As stated at the beginning of this chapter, it is conceded that the laudable idea of the person-centred approach cannot be applied to its logical conclusion as it falls short at the point of application. It has however been contended that the idea behind the approach can still be of value to antitrust. Example of its potential value to international competition law in general and development in particular have been shown above. Here, the value of the person-centred approach to antitrust enforcement is emphasised. As shown in Chap. 6, the person-centred approach strengthens our urge to strike a balance between maintaining an effective enforcement regime and the need to respect the rights and interests of parties. Thus, by seeking an incremental enforcement approach, we are more likely to seek effectiveness without compromising the interests of parties.

Conclusively, the person-centred approach should be seen as an avenue to foster a more correct and thorough understanding of antitrust. Given that this thesis addresses antitrust concerns in general terms, there is scope for further research on specific antitrust issues. At this point however, the hope is that the thesis successfully stirs up healthy curiosity on how antitrust can be better conceived, articulated, and applied.

References

Bakhoum M (2012) Reflections on the concepts of 'economic freedom, free competition, and efficiency. In: Zimmer D (ed) The goals of competition law. Edward Elgar, Cheltenham, pp 408–440

Dabbah M (2003) The internationalisation of antitrust policy. Cambridge University Press, Cambridge, pp 12–14

Knight-John M, Adhikari R (2004) What type of competition policy and law should a developing country have? South Asia Econ J 5:1–25

Taylor M (2007) International competition law: a new dimension for the WTO? Cambridge University Press, Cambridge

Bibliography

Books

Birks P (1989) An introduction to the law of restitution, revised edn. Clarendon, Oxford, p 41
de Búrca G, Weiler J (eds) (2001) European Court of Justice. Oxford University Press, Oxford
Cameron J, Demaret P, Geradin D (1994) Trade & the environment: the search for balance, vol 1. Cameron May, London, pp 245–246
Chapman B (2001) Public reason, social choice, and co-operation. In: van Benthem J (ed) Rationality and knowledge. Morgan Kaufman, San Francisco, pp 319, 328
Edelman J (2002) Gain-based damages: contract, tort, equity and intellectual property. Hart, Oxford
Goff R, Jones G (2002) The law of restitution, 6th edn. Sweet and Maxwell, London
Gyselen L (1994) The emerging interface between competition policy and environmental policy in the EC. In: Cameron J, Demaret P, Geradin D (eds) Trade and the environment: the search for balance. Williams Gaunt & Sons, London, pp 245–246
Kilpatrick C (2001) Turning remedies around: a sectoral analysis of the court of justice. In: de Búrca G, Weiler JHH (eds) The European Court of Justice. Oxford University Press, Oxford, p 143
Morse H (1909) The guilds of China. Longmans Green and Co, London, p 12
Neven D (1998) Legitimate goals and objectives of competition policy. In: Ehlermann and Laudati (eds), European Competition Law Annual 1997: the objectives of competition policy. Hart, Oxford, pp 111–118
Ng YK (1979) Welfare economics. Macmillan, London, pp 111–146
Rawls J (2005) Political liberalism. Columbia University Press, New York

Articles

Alexy R (2003) Constitutional right, balancing and rationality. Ratio Juris 131:136
Birks P (1982) Restitution and wrongs. Curr Legal Probl 35:53
Blair R, Harrison J (1989) Rethinking antitrust injury. Vanderbilt Law Rev 42:1559
Macgowan D (1886) Chinese guild or chambers of commerce and trade union. J North China Branch Royal Asiatic Soc 21:141 at 182–183
Menéndez AJ (2003) The sinews of peace: right to solidarity in the charter of fundamental rights of the European Union. Ratio Juris 16:380

A. Al-Ameen, *Antitrust: The Person-centred Approach*,

DOI 10.1007/978-3-319-01724-2, © Springer International Publishing Switzerland 2014

Robertson E (2009) Does antitrust regulation violate the rule of law? Loyola Consum Law Rev 22:108
Ross E (1916) Organisation of will. Am J Sociol 22:145, 149
Shelanski H, Klein P (1995) Empirical research in transaction cost economics: a review and assessment. J Law Econ Organ 11:335–361
Townley C (2010) The goals of chapter 1 of the UK Competition Act 1998 (the UK Equivalent of Article 81 EC Treaty, now Article 101 TFEU). Yearbook Eur Law 29:308
Weinrib E (2002) Deterrence and corrective justice. UCLA Law Rev 50:621

Papers

Kaplow L (2010) Keynote speech at the 5th ASCOLA conference at Bonn 27–29 May 2010

Reports

ABA Antitrust Section, Monograph No. 13, Treble-Damages Remedy 16-21. (1986)
Andreangeli, Ariana et al "Enforcement by the Commission – The decisional and enforcement structure in antitrust cases and the Commission's fining system", draft report presented at the Fifth Annual Conference of the Global Competition Law Centre, 11–12 June 2009
Charles River Associates, "Innovation and Competition Policy, Part1 – Conceptual Issues" Economic Discussion Paper 3, March 2002, report prepared for the Office of Fair Trading
Copenhagen Economics, *Practical Methods to Assess Efficiency Gains in the Context of Article 81 (3) of the EC Treaty Final Report* by Copenhagen Economics published on 21 April 2006 2208 DG Enterprise and Industry, 56
International Competition Network, *Report on the Objective of Unilateral Conduct Laws* (2007) 21
International Chamber of Commerce, 'The Fining Policy of the European Commission in competition cases', ICC Document No. 225/659 of 2 July 2009
OECD Policy Roundtables: Competition on the Merit 23 (2005)
UK House of Lords, *The Lisbon Treaty: An Impact Assessment* (vol 1, London, Stationary House Limited, 2008)
World Bank, World Development Report: Building Institutions for Markets (2002)
Commission RCP 1979 – Commission Sixth Report on Competition Policy 1979
Commission RCP 1983 – Commission XIIIth Report on Competition Policy 1983
Commission RCP 1985 – Commission XVth Report on Competition Policy 1985
Commission RCP 1993 – Commission XXIIIrd Report on Competition Policy 1993
OECD (2010) – Competition Committee Policy Roundtables on Information Exchanges between Competitors under Competition Law 2010
OECD (2011) – Competition Committee Policy Roundtable on Emission Permits and Competition 2011
OECD (2005) European Commission – Peer Review of Competition Law and Policy, Competition Law & Policy in the European Union, 2005, 62

Legislations

European Union
Treaty on the Functioning of the European Union
Commission Regulation (EU) No 1217/2010 on the Application of Article 101(3) of the Treaty on the Functioning of the European Union to certain categories of Research and Development Agreements
Council Regulation (EC) No 1/2003 of 16 December 2002 on the Implementation of the Rules on Competition laid Down in Articles 81 and 82 of the Treaty

United Kingdom

Enterprise Act 2002
Communications Act 1998
Communications Act 2003 (CA 2003)

United States

Sherman Act 1890

Communication and Official Documents

European Union
(COM 2005) 672 – EC Commission's Green Paper on Damages Action for Breach of EC Antitrust Rules COM (2005) 672 final
OJ C11 (2011) – Guidelines on the applicability of Article 101 of the Treaty on the Functioning of the European Union to Horizontal co-operation Agreements
OJ C 101 (2004) – Commission notice: Guidelines on the application of Article 81(3) of the Treaty
OJ C 3 (2001) – Guidelines on the applicability of Article 81 of the EC Treaty to Horizontal Cooperation agreements
OJ C 298/11 (2006) – Commission Notice on Immunity from Fines and Reduction of Fines in Cartel Cases
(2001/462/EC, ECSC) Commission Decision of 23 May 2001 on the Terms of Reference of Hearing Officers in Certain Competition Proceedings (notified under document number C (2001) 1461(2001/462/EC, ECSC)
OJ C 210 (2006) - Guidelines on the Method of setting Fines imposed pursuant to Article 23(2) (a) of Regulation No 1/2003
OJ C167/1 (2008) – Commission Notice on the Conduct of Settlement Procedures in Cartel Cases
COM (2000/C 291/01) Guidelines on Vertical Restraints, OJ C 291, 13.10.2000
(COM 2008) 165 – Commission staff working paper accompanying the White paper on damages actions for breach of the EC antitrust rules
COM (2008) 165 – European Commission, "White Paper on Damages Actions for Breach of the EC Antitrust Rules" COM(2008) 165 final
IP/01/1035 (2001-07-19) – European Commission Press Release

United Kingdom

149/06 – OFT press release, dated 19 October 2006
49/07 – OFT press release dated 22 March 2007
72/08 – OFT press release of 11 June 2008
Cartel cases (2006/C 298/11)
CP/9/07 – Department for Constitutional Affair's consultation paper "The Law of Damages" (May 2007)
OFT 1006 – "Response to the European Commission's White Paper, Damages action for breach of the EC antitrust rules" published in July 2008
Private action in competition law: effective redress for consumers and business (Recommendations from the OFT, 26 November 2007)

United States

FTC 68 Fed. Reg. 45,820 (4th of August 2003)

International

UNCTAD document TD/B/COM.2.EM/10/Rev 14

Cases

European Cases
Case 106/77: *Amministrazione delle Finanze dello Stato v Simmenthal* [1978] ECR 629
C-228/96 *Aprile* (1998) ECR 1-7141
Case C-238/05, *Asnef-Equifax v Asociation de. Usuarios de Servicios Bancarios (Ausbanc),* (2006) ECR I-11125
Case T-24/90 *Automec Srl v Commission (no. 2)* [1992] 5 CMLR 431
Case C-94-95/95 *Bonifaci and Berto v IPNS* (1997) ECR 1-3969
Commission decision *in CECED* OJ 2000 L187/47
Commission decision Cewal, Cowac and Ukwal [1993] L34/20
Commission decision of 23 May 2001 on the Terms of Reference of Hearing Officers in Certain Competition Proceedings (notified under document number C(2001) 1461 (2001/462/EC, ECSC)
Case C-194/94 *CIA Security International SA v. Signalson SA and Securitel Sprl* [1996] ECR I-2201
C-45/76 *Comet v Produkschap* (1976) ECR 2043
Joined Cases 56/64 and 58/66, *Consten and Grundig,* [1966] ECR 429
Case 6/72 *Continental Can v Commission* [1973] ECR 215
C-453/99 *Courage v Crehan* [2001] ECR 1-6297
Joined Cases C-178/94, and others *Dillenkofer and Ors v Germany* [1996] ECR I-4845
C-343/96 *Dilexport* (1999) ECR 1- 579
Commission decision 88/138/EEC *Eurofix-Bauco v. Hilti* 88/138/EEC, [1988] OJ L 65

Joined Cases T-374/94 and others, *European Night Services v Commission* [1998] ECR II-3141
Case C-63/93 *Fintan Duff v Ministry of Agriculture and Food and Attorney General,* [1996] ECR I-569
Case T-340/03 *France Télécom* [2007] *ECR* II-107
C-202/07 P *France Télécom* [2009] 4 *CMLR* 25
C-679/90 *Francovich & Bonifaci v Italy* (1991) ECR 1-5357
Case C-8/08 *T-Mobile Netherlands BV and Others Raad van bestuur van de Nederlandse Mededingingsautoriteit*
Case T-168/01 *GlaxoSmithKline Services v. Commission* [2006] ECR II-2969
Case C-501/06. *GlaxoSmithKline v Commission* [2010] 4 *CMLR*. 2
Case C-250/92 *Gøttrup-Klim v Dansk Landbrugs,* para 5654
OJ L118/24 *Commission decision IBM Undertaking* [1984]
(COMP/C-3 /37.990 - Intel), D(2009) Commission Decision of 13 May 2009, relating to a Proceeding under Article 82 of the EC Treaty and Article 54 of the EEA Agreement (COMP/C-3 /37.990 - Intel), D(2009)3726 final
C-295/04 to C-298/04 *Manfredi v Lloyd Adriatico Assuricazione*
C-62/00 *Marks and Spencer plc v Commissioners of Customs and Excise* (2002) ECR 1-6325
C-410/98 *Metallgesellschaft* (2001) ECR 1-1727
T-112/99 *Metropole Television (M6) v Commission* [2001] ECR II-2459
COMP/E-2/36.041 – PO/Michelin. *Michelin II*
Case C-19/77 *Miller International Schallplatten GmbH v Commission* [1978] ECR 131
Case T-201/04 Microsoft v Commission [2007] ECR II-3601
Case C-253/00 *Muños and Superior Fruiticola* [2002] ECR I-7289
Case 258/78, *L.C. Nungesser KG and Kurt Eisele v Commission* [1982] ECR 2015. T-213/01 and T-214/01, *Österreichische Postsparkasse AG v. Commission* and *Bank für Arbeit und Wirtschaft AG v. Commission* [2006] ECR II-1601
Case C-261/95 *Palmisani* (1997) ECR 1-4025
Case C-360/09 *Pfleiderer AG v Bundeskarllamt*; [2011] WLR (D) 196
Case C-36/92 *PSEP v Commission* [1994] ECR 1-1911
Case C-354/95 *The Queen v Minister for Agriculture, Fisheries and Food, ex p National Farmers' Union and Other*
Case C-213/89: *R v Secretary of State for Transport ex p Factortame Ltd* [1990] ECR I-2433
C-37/98 *Savas* [2000] ECR I-2927
Case 56-65 *Société Technique Minière v Maschinenbau Ulm GmbH* [1966] ECR 337
Case C-78/98 *Shirley Preston and ors v Wolverhampton NHS Healthcare Trust and ors* (2000) ECR 1-3201
Case 29/69 *Stauder v City of Ulm* [1969] ECR 419
Cases 1/58 *Stork v High Authority* [1959] ECR 17
Case No COMP/M.2416 – *Tetra Laval/Sidel*
Case T-51/89 *Tetra Pak Rausing SA v Commission* (Tetra Pak II) [1990] ECR II-3092
Judgment of the ECtHR of 14 November 2006, *Tsfayo v United Kingdom*, App. N 60860/00
COMP/38.233 – *Wanadoo Interactive*
Case 26/62 *Van Gend en Loos* [1963] ECR 1
OJ L318/17 (2002) *Visa International-Multilateral Interchange Fee* [2003] 4 *CMLR* 283
OJ L611 (2003) – *Vitamins Cartel, Commission Decision* of 21.11.2001 (2003) OJ L611; (2003) 4 *CMLR* 22
OJ 1992 L37/16 – Commission decision, Assurpol
OJ 1993 L20/14 – Commission decision, Ford/Volkswagen
OJ 1994 L144/20 – Commission decision, Exxon/Shell

United Kingdom Cases

A.G v Blake (2001) 1 *AC* 268
A.G v Guardian Newspapers ltd (No 2) (1990) 1 *AC* 109
Carr-Saunders v Dick McNeil Associates (1986) 2 *All E. R.* 888
1 *WLR* 798
Chief Constable of Leicestershire v M (1989) 1 *WLR* 20
Devenish v *Sanofi-Aventis SA (France) & ors* (2008) EWCA Civ 1086; (2008) WLR 317
Fibrosa Spolka Akcyjna v Fairbairn Lawson Combe Barbour Ltd (1943) *AC* 32
Fyffes Group Ltd v Templeman (2000) 2 *Lloyd's Rep* 643
EWHC 52
Halifax Building Society v Thomas (1996) 1 *AC* 109
Livingstone v Raywards Coal Company (1880) 5 *App Cas* 25
Macmillan Inc v Bishopsgate Investment Trust Plc (No 3) (1995) 1 *WLR* 978
1 AC 109, 286
Penarth Doc Engineering Co Ltd v Pounds (1963) 1 *Lloyd's Rep* 358
Phipps v Boardman (1967) 2 *A.C* 46
Reading v A.G (1951) *A.C* 507
Strand Electric and Engineering Co Ltd v Brisford Entertainment Ltd (1952) 2 *Q.B.* 246
Stoke-on-Trent City Council v W & J Wass Ltd (1988) 3 *All E.R.* 394
Whitwham v Westminster Brymbo Coal and Coke Co. (1896) 2 *Ch* 538

United State

Associated Gen. Contractors of Cal., Inc. v.California State Council of Carpenters, 459 U.S. 519 (1983)
Atlantic Richfield v. USA Petroleum, 495 U.S. 328 (1990)
Atlantic Thermoplastics Co Inc. v. Faytex Corp, 23 USPQ 2d 1481 (Fed. Cir. 1992) rehearing denied, 24 USPQ2d 1138
Columbia University v. Roche Diagnostics GmbH, 57 USPQ2d 1825 (D. Mass. 2000)
Continental T.V., Inc. v. GTE Sylvania Inc 433 U.S. 36, 38–39, 59 (1977)
Eastman Kodak Co. V Image Tech. Service, 504 U.S 1 451 (1992)
Florida Seed Company and Anor v Monsanto 915 F.Supp. 1167 (1995)
FTC v Hearst Trust, Civ. No. 1: 01CV00734 (D.D.C. Dec. 14, 2001)
FTC v Mylan Labs., Inc., 62 F. Supp. 2d 25, 36-7 (D.D.C. 1999)
FTC v Perrigo Co. and Alpharma Inc., Civ. No 1: 04CV1397 (RMC) (D.D.C. Aug 12, 2004)
Queen City Pizza v Domino's Pizza, 124 F.3d 430, 433 & 438 (3rd Cir. Pa. 1997)
Re/Max Int'l Inc., 173 F.3d
Illinois Brick Co. v. Illinois, 431 U.S. 737 (1977)
Illinois ex rel. Hartigan v. *Panhandle Eastern Pipe Line Co.,* 852 F. 2d 891, 894 (CA7 1988)
In re Stephens, 345 F.2d 1020, 145 USPQ 656 (CCPA 1965)
In the Matter of American Art Clay Co, 96 FTC 809 (Nov 1980)
In the Matter of Binney & Smith Inc, 96 FTC 625 (Oct 1980)
In the Matter of the Joseph Dixon Crucible Co, C80-700 (Ohio 1983)
Jack Walters & Sons Corp v Morton Building Inc 737 F.2d 698. 711 (7th Cir.), cert, denied 469 US 1018 (1984)
Law v. NCAA, 134 F.3d 1010, 1019 (10th Cir. 1998)
NCAA v. Board of Regents of the University of Oklahoma, 468 U.S. 85 (1984)
The Matter of Commonwealth Land Title Insurance Company, 126 FTC, 680, 688 (Nov 1998)
Scripps Clinic & Research Foundation v. Genentech Inc., 18 USPQ 2d 1001
USA Petroleum Co v Atlantic Richfield Co 859 F.2d. 687 (1988)
Weyerhaeuser Co v Ross-Simmons Hardwood Lumber Co., 549 US 312 (2007)

The manufacturer's authorised representative in the EU is Springer Nature Customer Service Centre GmbH, Europaplatz 3, 69115 Heidelberg, Germany. If you have any concerns regarding our products, please contact ProductSafety@springernature.com

Printed and bound by CPI Group (UK) Ltd, Croydon, CR0 4YY

30/09/2026

02225566-0009